Charon

Mark Edgar

chipmunkapublishing
the mental health publisher

Mark Edgar

Published by
Chipmunkapublishing
United Kingdom

http://www.chipmunkapublishing.com

Cover Design by Beka Smith

ISBN   978-1-78382-023-8

Chipmunkapublishing gratefully acknowledge the support of Arts Council England.

For Emma Harding, a woman who inspired me to greater heights in mental health, showed me that there is life beyond recovery, and whose humility puts me to shame. I am proud to call her my colleague, collaborator, and friend.

Mark Edgar

Biography of Mark Edgar

Mark Edgar was born in Surrey in 1969. Educated as a chorister at King's College Cambridge and a music scholar at Lancing College he returned to Cambridge in 1988 as a choral exhibitioner at Selwyn College to study History. He gained a BA Honours in 1991 despite experiencing an undiagnosed and untreated psychotic condition. In 1995 he was awarded MA (Cantab).

Following many years on benefits Mark went back to Cambridge in 1999 to undertake a Post Graduate Certificate of Education and was awarded Qualified Teacher Status in 2000. Yet teaching did not work out so he became a mental health practitioner by accident working for South Kent College, Kent Social Services, and Rethink.

In 2007 Mark was appointed the very first Mental Wellbeing Advisor at the University of Hertfordshire. The role encompasses a range of areas including supporting students and staff with mental health difficulties, advising on policy, public speaking at conferences as well as teaching on a number of mental health related courses at both undergraduate and postgraduate level. He was elected to the Council of Governors of Hertfordshire Partnership Foundation Trust in 2013.

Starting writing in 1997 his poem The Archbishop's Palace won the Rethink Pringles Award in 2002 and was exhibited in the Art Works in Mental Health Exhibition in 2003. He co-wrote Voicing Psychotic Experiences, a Reconsideration of Recovery and Diversity along with other services users and carers edited by Mark Hayward and Ruth Chandler in 2009. His autobiographical work A Pillar of Impotence was published in paperback in 2011.

Mark has an interest in sport, music, and is a keen amateur chef. He played American Football, coxed a boat in rowing, and played rugby in Cambridge as well as coaching for a number of years in Kent. Singing appearances are rare now but do occur from time to time.

Mark Edgar

Special thanks go to the following people who played a significant role in either the writing of the book or in my story:
Jason Pegler and Will Kettle at Chipmunkapublishing. My readers Marie Forbes and Katie O'Brien. Jacqueline Seager for not only convincing me I had another book to write but also affirmed to me that it was a worthwhile undertaking. Beka Smith for her eternal friendship and the provocative and haunting artwork on the cover. Katherine Howes and Colin Egan who helped me to edit the manuscript-any errors now are down to me. My friends in Cambridge, Christopher Kelly, David Smith, Michael Tilby, and Christine Counsell who all continue to support me years after I left. Heather Murray my long time friend and mentor. Emma Harding to whom this book is dedicated. Beth Hart who was helpful to me over the years of searching for success. Ian Morrison, Christine Cason, David James, David Ball, and, Marcella Wright all of who saw fit to look beyond my weaknesses and employ me when no one else would. Jacek Kolsut, Kym Winter, Allan Smith, Geraldine Ward, and Kay Robertson who kept me going with friendship when I uprooted my life and gave up so much to go to Hertfordshire. And finally to Dr Heather McAlister whose insightful intervention saved my life and made this story possible.

Mark Edgar

Prologue

Have you ever thought about becoming the complete opposite of who you are? I guess we have all thought of it and to an extent in life we do that. But what of a radical change from having an identity then morphing into something that you have always detested and feared? The pupil to the teacher; the criminal to the law enforcer; the carer to the cared for; the poacher turned gamekeeper?

Charon's Ferry is intended as a sequel to my first book A Pillar of Impotence. It is of course quite possible that you as a reader have neither heard of nor read the first book. I am after all an unknown, a no one other than in my own little world. If that is the case I will try briefly to elaborate on my previous work.

A Pillar of Impotence is the story of a journey undertaken during the 1990s. It is my story. It is the story of a highflyer whose life came crashing down in a mental breakdown. A tale of mental illness, despair, decay, breakdown, suicide, incarceration, misdiagnosis, and psychosis. Of power gone wrong, of condemnation, judgement, poverty, unemployment, shame, and stigma. But there is a very strange and unexpected twist that brought about my recovery and a return to a more normal life, accepted by society. It was not a return to the old life but to a radically new one. Had my life been as stable and sorted as I thought, I might never have got ill.

People who have read it tell me that it reads as if they were on the journey with me. It takes the reader from the arrogant decadence of Cambridge to the decay of a Victorian Asylum; the great cathedrals of Europe to the hopelessness of a Social Security Office; the splendours of the Middle East to the caged roof of a "modern" psychiatric clinic in Central London; the wonders of Van Gogh to the ghettoes of South London; the hedonism of Brighton to the moribund stuckness of a Day Hospital; the coffee shops of Amsterdam to the grinding boredom of a small, quaint but run down town on the Kent coast; the mysticism of the abode of a Buddhist healer to the judgement of a DSS tribunal. And finally back to Cambridge.

That was supposed to have been the end of my story. But fate once again intervened and threw me back into the System that had so utterly failed me throughout that decade. This time the outcome was different. For it was then that I met a psychiatrist who was different. She asked me what I thought, she listened, she dismissed the bullshit, she offered me choices, and most importantly she came up with a simple solution.

A Pillar of Impotence ends the day I first took the atypical antipsychotic Risperidone. It was a miracle. I had found my Holy Grail.

There are of course many good books out there about people's recovery journeys. As I started to write it in 2002 I wanted to try to do something a little different. At heart I am a historian; it was my great passion as a child and indeed what I studied at Cambridge. I wanted to include some of that too. It is not just my journey but also a limited historical record of the 1990s. So it is set against the backdrop of the First Gulf War, Bosnia, Rwanda, and Kosovo. The rise of Tony Blair and New Labour, the death of Princess Diana and arguably more importantly of Mother Teresa of Calcutta. Of OJ Simpson, Fred West, and Michael Stone. The Good Friday agreement and David Copeland's outrageous bigoted bomb attacks on London. The world changed so much during that decade.

But as some have asked me, what happened next? Well Charon's Ferry is the story of the next decade, from 2001 until 2011. It is how I became someone completely different.

Chapter 1
Terra, Terra Tremuit

It was a slightly abnormal Tuesday. I got up unusually early to a bright and beautiful morning. Summer was hanging on as autumn should have begun. Rare was an occasion when I rose before I needed to, sleep was so precious to me. Often I struggled with sleep and today was one of those days.

I left the house long before I needed to. But why? What drove me that morning was the mental dilemma I was facing. The previous day I had had a job interview for a part time teaching post. Ordinarily I would be happy for a phone call to come that might bring good news. But I was trying to avoid that call. Not because I feared being rejected but more to keep my options open. For the very next day I had another interview for a full time post in a school.

Knowing what my head of department was like he would have wanted an answer straight away rather than allowing me the choice. That is if there would be a choice; maybe I would be rejected by both.

So who was I on that bright Tuesday morning?

Mark Edgar, just turned 32, holder of eleven O Levels, four A Levels? Cambridge graduate with MA (Cantab) and PGCE to his name? Recently given Qualified Teacher Status? Holder of three grade 8s in music, the ex King's chorister and Cambridge choral exhibitioner, former president of American Football Club, Cambridge University, as well as rugby player and cox?

Or was I someone else?

Mark Edgar, just turned 32, the man who had battled mental illness for eleven years? Survivor of suicide and two psychiatric admissions? The victim of the Department of Work and Pensions (DWP) persecution, the judged, the lied to, the one seen as a fraud? The man who no longer did music or sport and earned £6 an hour doing a part time job he was overqualified for? Reject of so many schools with few if any prospects to get work? The man who still lived at home with his parents in a quiet and forgotten seaside town in Kent?

In truth I was probably a combination of all those things. But how did that help in a ruthless world where one spent much of one's life trying to justify one's existence? On paper I looked brilliant; in reality I was nothing.

My life had been a catastrophe for the best part of a decade. Throughout the 1990s, in reality the whole of my twenties, my life had been disastrous. With the dawn of a new millennium I was trying hard to change that.

Terra, terra tremuit, the earth, the earth trembled. When one has a breakdown it is like being consumed by an earthquake, as if the very nature of one's being, the whole edifice comes crumbling down; and then the rejection starts.

Yet, on that Tuesday morning my life had changed. The previous week I had discovered the Holy Grail of mental health. It was what we all sought but few achieved. After eleven years of illness and about ten years of what I would loosely call "treatment" I had found a simple solution.

Risperidone, an atypical antipsychotic on the market since 1995 saved my life. Terra, terra tremuit et quievit, the earth, the earth trembled and was still. For a week now a curious calm had descended on my chaotic and troubled mind. I was well again.

Well or not though I still had to face a world that was at times hostile and intolerant. The standing of the mentally ill was not very high in British society at the beginning of the 21st century. I may have had out of body experiences but I was now firmly in that world. And that world expected - get a job!

As I wandered the streets of Folkestone and Cheriton I mused on my different outlook on life. It was indeed looking up after all those years. I mused also on how futile it was in the early 21st century trying to avoid contact from the world. I had escaped the landline but there was always my mobile.

I was certainly well qualified for the job, perhaps more so than others. It was to teach on the course on which I had been a pioneer. Open Door had been a ground breaking initiative in Kent to get those with severe and enduring mental health problems back into education. I had been amongst the first students in 1997. It had led me to another A Level and ultimately back to Cambridge.

When I returned to the quiet seaside town in the summer of 2000 I was no longer just a psychiatric patient, a label that had defined my life for a decade. I was now a teacher, albeit one looking for a job.

But fate had intervened late in 2000 when once again the actions of others threw me into mental meltdown and I was back in the System that had let me down so badly. This time though it was different. Early in the summer that was now beginning to pass I had met a softly spoken Scottish psychiatrist who finally got it right. Theoretically once I found Risperidone the rest should have been history. But life is more complex than that.

Standing in the way of my prospects were two people I knew well. They had both been doing the same job already; time would tell.

Late that morning time ran out. I switched my mobile on and within minutes the inevitable call came through. Another rejection. Foolish perhaps to think I could take a job from others. There was always tomorrow, perhaps that would bring more joy.

I got to work at lunch time. It was just another day. I ate in the refectory as usual then did the afternoon session supporting my students.

When the day was over I got in my car and headed back to the small seaside town I viewed as a temporary home. A tape played quietly as I drove but I can't remember what I listened to. By then most people had CD players in their cars. But my car was older and only played tapes.

At precisely 5 o'clock the tape ended. The system took me straight back to the radio just in time for the news. It was then that I knew. Terra, terra tremuit. This time the whole world shook.

That day was 11th September 2001.

Mark Edgar

Chapter 2
A Most Ingenious Paradox

Back in the heady, arrogant, and decadent days of Cambridge we had witnessed the fall of the Berlin Wall and the end of the Cold War that had dominated all of our lives. President George Bush subsequently heralded a new world order of peace. World War III had been averted in a manner that we had not expected; Reagan had seen the policy of containment through to the end by outspending the Soviet Union. The other super-power had been mired for ten years in Afghanistan; Gorbachev pulled them out in that very same year.

1989; I had turned 20 a couple of months before the Wall fell. I was heading into my second year at Cambridge and life looked good. We were too busy playing rugby and getting pissed to really notice the end of the Cold War. It would be another six months before I met Rachel. Rachel, the girl from my past who had triggered my madness and haunted me through my voices for the next decade.

But from those who did notice the end of the Cold War another warning came. The intellectuals at Cambridge all agreed that the next war would be Islam. What we didn't know was how it would start.

In my very middle class, public school educated way, my view is that World War III started on 11th September 2001. Of course others, the bombers included had a different view. To some of them it had started the day the West moved forces into Saudi Arabia to confront Saddam Hussein in Kuwait in 1990/91. Bush's new world order got off to a very bumpy start.

By the end of 2000 Bush's son George W Bush had won a controversial election and was about to become president. The West's response to the bombing began in October 2001 and by December the targets of that retribution, the Taliban and Al Qaeda were in full retreat and holed up in the Tora Bora mountains being bombarded by B52s with satellite guided weapons. But that would not be the end of it.

The intervention was hotly debated in the West, some wondering why we were there. But there was one thing I knew, and that was that the bombers would one day come to Britain.

Back in the small corner of Kent my life became a surreal paradox. After fighting my madness for eleven years I had finally found a solution. Risperidone had given me my life back. It was not the same life as before. But Rachel no longer haunted my life and suicide, my faithful companion for a decade now, seemed absurd to me. My mood was utterly buoyant and I was full of hope.

But as always seemed to happen in my life good was followed by bad. That very week I had my follow up appointment with the softly spoken Scottish Doctor.

"How are you?"

"I feel better than I've felt in years." A truly honest way to describe the utter miracle that had just transpired in my world.

She checked for side effects; I had none. We talked on for a while. She gave me a new prescription and was reading between the lines as surprised as I was at the astonishing impact of my new medication. She had actually had a great deal of success with Risperidone but I think even she was shocked at how rapidly it had impacted on my life.

We arranged a follow up appointment and as I left the room she made a parting comment:

"It will be interesting trying to give you a specific diagnosis."

Those words haunt me to this day for just before my next appointment I received a short, terse letter from the Trust saying that she no longer worked for them. It would be nearly another year before I realised how disastrous that would be.

Losing the Scottish Doctor was not the only problem I faced that autumn. My job as a Learning Support Assistant at the local college was only ever supposed to have been a temporary arrangement until I secured a teaching job. The interview on 12th September had brought me no joy either.

I was actually doing my job under the Therapeutic Earnings scheme whereby sick and disabled people could work up to sixteen hours a week to gain a small income and aid their recovery. I was limited to only earning an extra £20 per week. The rest would be topped up with benefits.

The DWP and its previous guises seemed to have been fighting a personal crusade against me for ten years. I had fought for five years to get Disability Living Allowance (DLA). That ran out in August 2000 and as at the time I was doing well they refused to renew it. Three months later I had my epic relapse.

So my income was very low anyway. Then the next act of persecution occurred. I was only paid for the hours I worked and even then only two months in arrears. That meant that for two months in the autumn I would only have my benefits to live on. At precisely that moment, the DWP swung the axe. I was left with £40 a week to live on for two months. My basic outgoings were £32 per week. To put it mildly, I was fucked!

But they didn't stop there. They claimed that they had never approved my therapeutic earnings and so effectively I had been working illegally since January. Not only that, they had failed to tell me that there was an upper weekly limit of £66 which would negate any benefit claim. The weeks I worked I earned more than that; on the weeks I didn't I earned nothing. But the System would not allow for that.

Eventually I got to see a senior benefits officer who acknowledged that I was doing everything I could to get a job but there was nothing they could legally do to help me.

All I could do was keep trying to get a teaching job. The world of teaching is cyclical in both its operational incarnation of three terms but also in the availability of jobs. Early in the autumn there was not much around but things got better as winter approached. Then there would be a lull at New Year before another crescendo of activity in the spring. By July it would be all over.

Throughout the autumn and winter, as war raged in Afghanistan I applied, sometimes went and was then rejected. In my quest I was greatly assisted by my friend Beth who was living in Hackney for a year and allowed me to use her flat as a stopping off point on my travels. Beth, the quiet, rejected, and angry girl whom I'd met when she was 15. She had a penchant for piercings and had by then done a remarkable job in reinventing herself from school refuser to budding university artist. She helped a great deal. But still the rejection went on.

My life took on a curious duality. My illness was under control and my mood was elated but the constant lack of money and rejection brought on an insidious creeping depression that lay underneath. When I first sought help for my illness they told me I was depressed because I didn't have a job. That was nowhere near the truth.

Depression is not my illness but I began to learn what depression was as I desperately tried to get a job.

Early in the New Year I took a radical step that I had wanted to take for years. Ever since I had been thrown into the place I called the Archbishop's Palace, the Victorian Asylum I found myself in in the summer of 1991, I had sworn that one day I would write a book about it all to expose the truth. That February I started writing what I would eventually call A Pillar of Impotence. And that was a very good if painful thing to do.

Winter turned to spring and still I applied. There were some memorable moments at interviews where I came so close but fell at the last hurdle. I loved a school in Somerset that I visited. I even had an interview at Eton early in the summer when I had only applied for a joke. Other experiences were shameful and discriminatory. But what could I do?

As expected with the coming of summer the well ran dry. Jobs were scarce and I faced yet more barren times ahead. Almost a year after finding my salvation in Risperidone my life had descended into limbo; a paradox of being mentally well but utterly depressed. And I had no idea how to get out of it.

Chapter 3
A Slow Train to Nowhere

The station concourse was virtually deserted. God I hate early mornings went my internal thinking voice. That voice, the one I now had under control. Not the separate ones of the last few years, the ones that fractured off from my whirlwind thoughts and became separate entities. Who in their right mind would be at Victoria station at 6 o'clock on a mildly warm summer morning?

I had a bit of a wait for my train so I thought I'd head for the Iron Duke for a coffee. Yes, the Iron Duke was open at that time. Pretty unusual for the days before twenty four hour opening, but on this day it was open.

As I made my way through the station, the noise level slowly rose. So someone else was up at this God forsaken time. As I got to the entrance it was clear that it was packed. The reason? England was playing Nigeria in the World Cup needing only to avoid defeat to qualify for the next round. It was so busy I couldn't even get in the door. Dispirited I walked off and sat down. As I sat in the early morning I contemplated the last three years and what would transpire in the coming hours. It would be a defining day.

Shortly afterwards I boarded the slow train to Hampshire. As the train meandered slowly through the Surrey and Sussex countryside I continued to muse on those three years. For it was three years before that I had gambled everything on becoming a teacher. Financially it had been a catastrophe sending me into spiralling debt and costing me every penny I had. But it seemed a good gamble to take. A chance to get out of the world I knew only too well; the world of mental illness.

During those three years I had applied for about a hundred and fifty jobs. Today would be my eighteenth interview, this time at a small privately run 11-16 school in the Hampshire countryside. For the first eighteen months no one had even bothered to invite to me to interview. Who after all would want to take the risk on someone with my psychiatric history? That changed after I got my job at the college. But for all that no one had wanted to employ me.

I had spoken to the Headmaster of this school a few days before and he seemed most enthusiastic to meet me. I was told that I had to be there at 9 o'clock-that was a tall order given how far I had to travel. And now here I was on the train.

When the train hit the coast I saw a familiar sight. My old school, the huge chapel jutting imposingly out of the hill. I had first been there in 1982, twenty years before. So much had happened since then and my illness had taken more than half of that time.

The train snaked ever onwards until I got to a small Hampshire station whose name I can no longer recall.

Getting into a taxi that morning I gave the driver the name of the school. He didn't seem to know where it was so he had to look it up. I got there just before the prescribed time of 9 o'clock. I made my way to reception and was greeted by a woman with a slightly bemused look.

"My name is Mark Edgar, I'm here for the interview."
"Oh," she said, "you're very early, you didn't have to be here until 11 o'clock. Don't worry I'll get you a cup of coffee and you can wait in the staff room."

It had not been a good start. Thoroughly un-amused by the misinformation I had been given I sat alone and ignored for the next two hours. The coffee arrived and it was white; I hate white coffee. Then I spilled it and had to do the best I could to clear it up. Perhaps it was an omen.

When things finally got underway it was the usual round of fairly informal meetings and being interviewed by various teachers. I met the outgoing history teacher as well as the remaining one. I met the other candidates too; they were all older and more experienced than me. A pleasant lunch ensued and the school had a warm, friendly, and family feel to it.

In mid afternoon I had the more formal interview with the Headmaster, his deputy, and the outgoing history teacher. All seemed to be going well and I was feeling more positive than earlier in the day. But then came the killer question.

"You do realise that if you get the post you will be the only qualified history teacher in the school? Would you still be interested?"

"Of course I would." But my internal voice said something different; but you'd be mad to employ a newly qualified teacher for this post. I knew the game was up. There was no chance of getting the job.

As I caught the slow train back home I felt betrayed and used. Why would they invite me all that way when they knew there was no way they would give me the job?

I had a deflated demeanour as I got off the train at Folkestone and walked slowly to my car. I knew at that point it was over. There really was no way back from here. I was now viewed as out of date as well as a damaged commodity.

Perhaps I was not a good teacher. Maybe I had been deluding myself that I could ever make it work. That after all had been a linchpin of my allegedly disordered personality. Now I almost began to believe they were right.

That was the day I gave up on teaching; or perhaps teaching gave up on me. I've never really been sure which of those two options was closest to the truth. Nevertheless, I turned my back on teaching.

Did the rest of the country care? Probably not. They were just celebrating England's progression to the next round following a 0-0 draw with Nigeria. But it would as ever all end in tears, knocked out by Brazil.

In my little world I faced a very uncertain future.

Mark Edgar

Chapter 4
The Enemy Knocks at the Door

Once one had entered the Mental Health System in the 1990s it was very hard to leave. Professionals talked about getting better then moving on. They also used words like institutionalised, dependent, and independent. The second of those words was like a dirty word. In fact few people I knew ever did move on and mental illness defined their lives. It became their identity as so little in their lives did not revolve around mental illness.

I was as guilty as anyone as for so many years I was Mark who was mad or mentally ill. I couldn't do anything as I was mentally ill. Most of us dreamed about being well but very few of us actually knew what that would look like. I had no idea what to do if by some miracle I got well. Others talked a great deal about becoming a nurse, an occupational therapist, and a few in those days to become social workers.

My experience of the System was so shit that I swore I would never do that. In the late 1990s I had fought my way through illness and gone back to Cambridge. In retrospect I was desperately trying to reinvent myself. And the new identity was to be a teacher, a much more worthy occupation in the eyes of the world than as a nutter. But now that dream was gone. So what next?

Something quite significant had happened in my life shortly before that last fateful train journey to an obscure school somewhere miles from home.

Heather was my old friend, mentor, advocate, and confidante. She had guided me through the System and out the other side. She gave so much to us all. Without her I would never have returned to education or got through my many battles with the DWP. It was she who had helped me through the maze of paperwork when I started my new job whilst struggling with despair and psychosis. I owed her a lot.

I visited quite often for tea that summer. During my last visit she had posed me a very interesting question.

"Would you like to work in mental health?"

"I'd love to but I would never work for the enemy." The question was how on earth would I make that career move without selling out the enemy? And beside I had no qualifications.

"What would you want to do in mental health?"
"I want to be a consultant." A lofty ambition.
"But you have to start at the bottom."
I guess that was sound if unpalatable advice. As I left that afternoon I didn't really think anything of it. But my life was about to change.

It was late in the morning of a warm July day. I was at home as the college holidays were well underway. My mum was starting to prepare lunch and the front door was wide open as she was wont to do at that time of year.

"Hello? It's Carol" came what seemed a disembodied voice. Carol was the partner of my neighbour. She shot in the door clutching a few sheaves of paper. Carol worked for Community Support, a small offshoot of Social Services that supported people with mental illness. I'd never known how and why anyone was given Community Support but it had helped some of my friends. They were only really partly in the System. "We've got a job coming up. It's only fifteen hours a week but I think you would have a really good chance of getting it. The closing date is today."

She came in, sat down, and gave me the job description. I wasn't quite sure how to respond. It was both a solution and a problem. How on earth would I get the paperwork in on time? Did I really want to work for the enemy even if they weren't fully integrated? But maybe, just maybe I could get into work and away from the clutches of the DWP.

Carol couldn't stay long but I looked through the papers and thought it was worth a go.

Most of the afternoon was taken up with downloading the application form and filling it in as best I could. Somehow, despite my technical limitations on computers I managed to get it done and faxed it off from my dad's office. Then all I could do was wait.

The wait was mercifully short. Within days a letter had arrived inviting me to attend an interview the following week. I didn't know the building that I had to go to but I knew it was near Tesco. It may seem strange that someone as familiar with the System as I was would not know all the buildings. But this was in the days before Partnership Trusts and Social Services were distinctly separate from health.

As I drove past Tesco that afternoon I felt quite confident. Carol had advised me that her manager who was on the interview panel talked a great deal about empowerment and using words related to that would go in my favour.

When I got there it was terribly formal. I had to sign in and was asked to sit in the waiting room. Not long after a shortish woman in her 50s with a northern accent came to collect me. She was Chris the woman who was into empowerment.

There were four of them on the panel including Chris. They all had pads of paper. The opening comment was rather took me aback.

"So you have come for the twenty hours a week post then?" said the smartly dressed chair of the meeting.

"No for the fifteen hour a week post but I would be quite happy to do twenty hours."

Apparently that was not possible but we went ahead anyway. Nothing threw me for the rest of the session; each question answered quickly and precisely using many of the words Carol suggested.

In what seemed no time at all it was all over. I left the room, signed out then climbed into my car for the journey home. I felt I had done what I could. Now it was time to wait. I certainly knew that feeling well; my life had so often been in the hands of others it was just as familiar as many times before.

Mark Edgar

Chapter 5
If It's Not Written Down It Never Happened

By mid summer 2002 I had been taking Risperidone for nearly a year. I'd heard no voices nor felt suicidal during that spell of time. Despite being well I continued to see a psychiatrist every three months or so. Or so I thought. It was not until later that I became aware that the Doctors treating me were not psychiatrists. In fact they were not even fully qualified. They were trainee GPs doing a psychiatric placement.

I should have realised something was amiss when I went to an appointment and the new Doctor asked me "why are you on Risperidone?" Slightly baffled I merely said that it was to stabilise my mood and was working extremely well. By that stage I had gone back on the blue and white capsules that I had taken for years and another part of the puzzle was complete; I had good sleep.

As far as I was concerned all I really needed now was a job and some money. The two month college pay gap was looming so once again I faced a difficult few weeks ahead. My experience with all the interviews I had been on was that if one was successful one would normally be told that day. If unsuccessful a letter would come within a few days.

But two weeks after the Community Support interview I had still heard nothing. It was only when I had a phone call from my GP asking me to come and see him that a glimmer of hope appeared.

He was a new GP although I had known him for a while as his daughter Lucy was a friend of mine. When I went to see him he said that he had been asked to write a letter to Occupational Health to confirm I was fit to work. I couldn't see any problem with doing that but I did ask to exercise my right to see any letter before it was sent.

A few days later I got a call from the surgery to tell me that the letter was ready and I could come and read it before it was sent. There was no need to see the Doctor but rather just go to reception and ask for it.

When I got there I curiously scanned the letter. But I was in for a shock. In the section that said diagnosis were three separate comments, "traits of a borderline personality disorder, moderate depression, and dysthymia". I had no idea what the latter was but I knew of the first two. I had spent a year apparently clear of the diagnosis of personality disorder but there it was in black and white. There was no mention of the mood disorder that I was very treated for. The traits comment was absurd because the whole world has traits of BPD. But here things were being passed off as a definitive diagnosis.

It was only later that I became aware that these comments were differential diagnoses made by an unqualified Doctor at a time when I was chronically depressed, utterly suicidal, and psychotic.

I was so shocked that I merely handed the letter back to the receptionist and said it was okay. Over the next couple of hours I realised the folly of that decision which prompted me to return to the surgery and block the letter being sent. I was told that was fine but I would have to make another appointment with the Doctor to talk about what I would accept.

That of course would take more time and summer was marching on. When I did go and see him he was quite angry with me as he felt I had been messing his staff about. But I got him to remove the reference to PD although he said he would only do that if he added a paragraph stating that I had asked for the letter to be changed. That was the only way I could do it so I agreed.

So it was back to waiting. Unofficially news came from Carol that the job was mine but only if I could get through Occupational Health. I had been there before whilst waiting for clearance to do my PGCE. My life in the hand of Doctors I didn't know. It had an awful familiarity to it.

As the weeks of August slipped away I heard nothing. It was not an idle time as I continued to work on the book. By that stage I had completed the first of three parts. Sometimes progress was slow, at other times much faster. It was not always easy to write as I was recreating and by extension reliving some of the darkest and most dangerous times of my life. I recalled breakdown and suicide as if I was there again. Some asked if it was therapeutic, it was anything but. My determination to do it was undiminished; I would one day have my vengeance on those who had got it so wrong and utterly failed me.

In times away from the book I battled with the idea of what had gone wrong with the diagnosis. I resolved that I would try and get some clarity and get someone to give me a specific diagnosis other than PD. The facts completely contradicted that. The man I had known as god had once told me that "you will never find a medication that works for you". That translated to "you are not mentally ill". How wrong he had been.

It would be another four years before I realised that the quiet Scottish Doctor had been a brilliant shrink but her capacity to write good notes was sadly lacking. If only she had stayed longer.

I was in the run up to 33rd birthday at the end of the month when the phone rang. It was Chris. She told me that I had got through Occupational Health and she wanted to offer me the job. It was only later that I found out it had taken so long they had almost re-advertised the post.

I said I could start the following Monday but she wanted a little more time than that. We settled on Monday 9th September.

I celebrated my birthday with more vigour that August. I had reason to celebrate. With the exception of the year I did my PGCE I had been on continuous benefits since July 1991. Even during my year away in Cambridge I was still receiving DLA. Now finally after eleven years I was about to come off benefits.

Mark Edgar

Chapter 6
The Mysteries of the Other Side

Autumn was a good time for me as it heralded the coming of the new NFL season. My beloved St Louis Rams had at the time one of the most dominating teams in NFL history. They had won their first Super Bowl after the 1999 season and had narrowly been defeated in the Super Bowl the previous February in one of the greatest upsets of all time. I've never really been able to explain my passion for this American sport that many people regard as too confusing and too stop/start to follow.

I had seen my first action on the TV in early 1980 when the World of Sport had shown highlights of the Super Bowl XIV. The then Los Angeles Rams had lost to the famed Pittsburgh Steelers. But I decided I liked the Rams and followed them as best I could. A couple of years later Channel 4 started showing it and I was hooked. Being only 5' 6" and nine stone I never thought I would ever get to play. But then Cambridge intervened and I played for three years including captaining the university team in 1990/91. In fact during that madness driven final year, playing football had been the only good thing in my life.

After my complete breakdown in the summer of 1991 I found a junior team near me in Kent and I proceeded to coach for the next five years. But that was long ago now so I contented myself with reading and watching when I could. Watching was hard as I didn't have satellite TV. But it provided a good background even in my madness. That year the fates did not smile on the Rams and they lost their first five games as autumn unfolded. They never recovered.

This autumn would be different of course; I finally had work. The world of mental health had always been a story of them and us. A fraught relationship at times the two camps only intermingled in certain ways. Now I was about to have their secrets revealed to me. It proved quite an eye opener.

I had been around mental health for so long that I knew many of the people who used Community Support. Many were my friends, some had been students with me, and most of them attended the Mind Centre which I still visited every Wednesday and Sunday. It never crossed my mind that I couldn't work with any of them so I was somewhat surprised when in the first week Chris asked me "are there any clients you can't work with?" What a strange question. There was only one really, my friend Steve who I used to visit most Wednesday evenings. That was not because I didn't feel I could do it but more that Steve wouldn't want me to.

This was my first introduction to what professionals called "boundaries". It would occur to me very quickly that this was one of main barriers to recovery and helped to reinforce the stigma that we all felt. At that stage I was blissfully unaware that for some on the new "side" it was somewhat disconcerting that I was working there.

Next I learned about "lone working policies". I was given a mobile phone and told that I had to phone in at the end of my day to let them know that I was safe. Again that seemed very odd, why would I feel unsafe? I had spent eleven years surrounded by the mentally ill but I had never been harmed and rarely threatened. There were those I had learned to be wary of but we all had a sense of belonging to each other so why would we harm one another? Apparently if I didn't phone in they would call the police. Details were taken of my car, my description, and my plans of exactly where I would be at any given time. What sort of a message did that send out? You are the mad and we're frightened of you? There was a further caveat to lone working in that if I got in trouble I had to use the code words "purple file". This would bring the police to my aid within minutes. I was not really sure I liked these new mysteries but I had to play by the rules. In retrospect maybe they were trying to get me to switch sides even from day one.

The other thing that struck me as odd was the utterly rigid way in which they worked. A task was set and had to be followed. That might be to take people shopping, or to the launderette, or just for a coffee. There was no way but that one. It was backed by a very prescriptive system they called Service Delivery Orders (SDOs). My day was planned to the minute not by me but by Chris or Ian the other Senior Support Worker. There was no other real purpose to the job except to talk to people. And that was something it transpired I was very good at. I did after all speak the language of the mad.

Whilst we all talked about empowerment and independence that System in reality was holding people in their lonely stuckness. But that was the way it was to be.

I was also told that I had to have supervision once a month. That involved meeting and talking about our clients and to an extent about how we were feeling. I guess in a small way that was how they kept the professionals sane.

Throughout the autumn I did three hours in the morning for Social Services and a few hours four days a week at the college. In all I was working about thirty hours a week, not quite full time but nearly. I did find it tiring though and at times it was a struggle getting up. Now that I was free from the DWP I increased my hours at the college and took on more work. For the first time I started working with students who were not mentally ill. That was ironically much tougher. I found myself once a week working with a group of disaffected young men who wanted to become builders. In the main they had done poorly at school and really had no interest in academic work. But the government of the day felt it was vital that all students be taught "key skills". Some fool in timetabling thought it was a good idea to give them a whole day of it. The result? Something akin to feeding time at the zoo. They were climbing the walls. This was when it started to occur to me that I had been wrong in my belief that people were at college because they wanted to learn. It was a nightmare which I dreaded on a weekly basis.

Away from the college it did not take long before I earned a name for myself and accidently ruffled some feathers further up the Social Services food chain.

By the time I started working there the Care Programme Approach (CPA) was well entrenched as the backbone of mental health. It should have been in place in 1991 when I first went into the System but did not become a reality until several years later. I had worked under the auspices of Mind on a committee to implement it in the mid 1990s. It was essentially a two tier system with Enhanced Care and Standard Care. The reality of that was almost a Premier League of mad people and the rest. I was not at that stage deemed mad enough to be on Enhanced and hence had no care co-ordinator or a written care plan. But the clients I now worked with were on all on Enhanced and every six months or so they had a

CPA review with the consultant and anyone else involved in his or her care. And that meant sometimes I had to attend.

I had known Sarah the consultant since she came into post at the age of 37 although I had only once seen her professionally when my own consultant had been on paternity leave. We had however crossed swords on a few occasions. That said as I went for the first CPA review I attended I had no real belief that Sarah would remember who I was.

The client in question was a highly intelligent man with bipolar. By that stage the term bipolar was beginning to be used rather than manic depression. He lived a rather chaotic life and I had been told that he was hard to get on board. But we had hit it off straight away and had some most interesting discussions. He was not taking medication out of choice and seemed to me to be reasonably well. He was however due in court for something he had done whilst unwell and we thought he would go to prison.

The day of the meeting his care co-ordinator asked me to pick him up as she thought he was "more likely to attend then". When we got there this woman kept repeatedly trying to convince Sarah that he was very unwell and needed medication. In fact she was trying to shut the stable door after the horse had bolted to cover up for her lack of care when the offence took place.

Much to my surprise Sarah asked my opinion.

"So what do you think Mark?"
"I have seen no deterioration in his mental state since I met him and under the circumstances he seems to be holding together very well."

I didn't think anything of that really. We concluded the review and he remained off medication. The two of us got in the car and headed back to his flat. Just as we got there the phone rang. It was Chris. Unable to speak with the client still there I said I'd call her back.

When we did speak it transpired that the social worker had been extremely angry that the review had not come up with outcome she wanted. She had apparently accused me of colluding with Sarah against her and that I had intimidated her. She had also asked that I be immediately removed from supporting the client.

I was stunned. I had done nothing but what was asked of me. Chris was rather vague and did not want to take sides so to speak but it all made me feel most unsupported and angry. I had in fact been right all along and several years later Chris admitted to me that the social worker had been the one in the wrong.

Fortunately that particular woman was the exception rather than the rule. Most of my colleagues worked extremely hard and were really supportive of their clients. This was not something that was always appreciated by those on my side of the fence. In fact it came as a bit of a surprise for me. It was only then that I learned there were many angles to each story and the mad usually talked only from their perspective.

As autumn turned to winter and the days got colder I reflected on the dramatic changes in my life in the previous few months. I now had an identity beyond being mad, I had a purpose, and I was writing the book I swore I would always write. From what I recall that was a good Christmas and New Year as 2003 dawned. I was better.

Away for the small world in which I lived war still seemed to go on in a quiet way in Afghanistan. The Taliban were gone but there was no sign of Bin Laden. He had simply vanished. Al Qaeda had had its revenge in the Bali bombings. Some high profile people had been captured but we were still not prepared for what would transpire there a couple of years later.

Nearer to home the storm clouds were gathering once again in the Middle East. Iraq was to be the next target of retribution with George W Bush seemingly hell bent on finishing what his father had started a decade before. The link to Al Qaeda appeared very tenuous but many feared and believed that he had Weapons of Mass Destruction. They apparently would trigger the war that was soon to be unleashed.

But in my world peace reigned.

Mark Edgar

Chapter 7
The Registry Office

In the world of the mentally ill sudden death was a stark reality. There is of course the obvious reason of suicide but that only accounts for a small part of the premature death count. Over the previous twelve years I had seen far too many of my friends die young. As far as I was aware then seven had been victims of suicide. In fact the figure was actually eight; an old school friend had apparently drowned herself but I would not pick up that news for a few years. Others had died through natural causes, side effects, and misdiagnosis. There was always a fear that a physical problem would be put down to mental health by mistake. One friend died of cancer only a week after being diagnosed; she had been saying she felt ill for months. And then there was the medication; although not really well known at the time atypical antipsychotics such as I took were life shortening treatments.

So death was normal to me. Far less common in my life were marriages and births. I had missed all my Cambridge friends getting married. It was one of the few regrets I had about my illness. In fact only two of our crowd were unmarried, my former housemate John and me.

Only one friend had had a child back in 2000. All that changed as 2003 got underway. It heralded the start of five years of births, marriages, and deaths amongst my friends. The first two were great; the third alarmingly frequent. I went to an average of five funerals a year during that period; far too many for a 33 year old. With all that, my circle kept the Registry Office exceedingly busy.

Away from the big events both happy and sad my new life continued in the normal way. In the main I enjoyed work. In fact I never took a single day off in all the time I worked for those organisations. As ever with me though there was a but.

Working almost full time I was still on an incredibly low income. Had I worked for Community Support full time I would only have had a salary of around £12,000 per annum. Back in the days of Cambridge before the recession struck few of us would have even considered getting out of bed for less than £18,000 a year. So I was earning more than two thirds less than I would have hoped for eleven years before. But my life had changed all that. However, it was more than I had had whilst only at the college. When I finally got a pay cheque from both employers the first thing I did was go out and buy a video recorder; I had loads of videos but was too poor to buy a machine before.

Despite the change in circumstances I still tried to find full time employment.

I had had a stroke of luck though when I had started work. My old nemesis the DWP seemed to be running a scheme called a Back to Work Bonus. After all my part time work this had accrued to some £900. It took some time to come through but as I waited I decided that rather than fritter it away in the pub at the bottom of the hill I would go on holiday.

I had been to Seville twice before. We had sung there in 1988, the last choir trip before I left school. I had returned with the same choir in 1993 although that day we were not singing just visiting. I had very fond memories and decided that when the money came through that is where I would go.

As winter began to wane and there was a slight improvement in the temperature the money finally came through. Quickly I booked a flight and accommodation over the internet. Then late in February I flew out.

Seville was as glorious as I had remembered it. I took in museums, churches, and the Alcazar Palace with its astonishing gardens. Each day I wandered about looking for new things and new bars. I was somewhat hampered by the only real legacy left from my illness; I had lost all sense of direction when I got ill. So there was an underlying anxiety of getting lost which meant I was more restricted than I might have been.

Spring came to Seville during those few days and by the end it was like a summer's day in the UK. But all good things come to an end and I had a certain sadness as I left to go home. Set against that though were the memories of many cervezas, much Zoco, and countless soft packets of Fortunas. In fact as I got home I still had many Fortunas to consume in the following weeks.

Back in the real world the hunt for full time employment continued. That would be the only way in which I could increase my meagre financial resources. Living at home with my parents still meant that my outgoings were lower than for many people but what I really wanted to do was move out. And to do that I would need to get a full time job.

For months there had been very little about on the job front. That all changed during my supervision with Ian in March 2003. At the end of our session he took me by surprise.

"I wanted to draw your attention to this." He handed me piece of paper. "Community Support in Maidstone is looking for a Senior Support Worker and I thought you might be interested."
"That sounds most interesting, I'll look into it." And with that the static of the winter months was broken.

Over the coming days I acquired an application form, hurriedly filled it in and sent it off before the deadline. I actually felt quite confident but all I could do now was wait. Waiting, that old familiar game. Unknown to me something else was about to crop up.

Most Fridays I went to the pub at the bottom of the hill to meet with friends. So it was that on a Friday in April I got there, bought a pint and sat down out the back. No one else had arrived by that stage. To fill the time I picked up the local paper and started to read it. When I got to the job section I turned a few pages and was then struck by something remarkable. There like a shining light was an advert for a Community Mental Health Worker for the charity Rethink. I was very familiar with Rethink and its previous incarnation of the National Schizophrenia Fellowship. Heather had worked tirelessly for them over the years and had been one of the driving forces locally in work that had helped so many. They had helped me many times.

Reading on it seemed like a dream, supporting people in the community. Nothing new in that but this time it was full time. Willow Lodge Rethink's flagship supported housing project had been Heather's baby. The job was to be based there initially but then moving out into the community. They were also looking for a manager but I ruled myself out as it required experience of managing budgets. That was something I knew not nor really cared about.

Having read through it all, one thought popped into my head; that's my job. I called Heather there and then. She agreed that I had to go for it.

The night was memorable as I could finally sense movement. Early the following week I obtained the application form and sent it off.

It was still time to wait but I had a great sense that things were about to move in a good way.

Chapter 8
Party in Pall Mall

Back in the dark days of 1994 I had been sent to a special hospital unit in London along with all the other un-treatables. That effectively made us the elite of nutters. I named it the Hotel California. It was deemed the last chance saloon. Like everything else that had been tried in the early years of my madness it had failed. But there were some things that remained with me all those years later. The man I came to know simply as god once asked me "have you lost all your friends?" To a great extent I had. He had deemed that "inevitable".

In the intervening years I had re-established links with people from Cambridge and to an extent down in Sussex. But I had always shied away from the people I knew when I sang as a child in Cambridge. I was simply too ashamed to face them. In my mind they were probably all wildly successful and would have no time for a madman like me.

All that had changed in 2002 when a chance phone call to one of the few friends I had left from those days led me reluctantly to a reunion in a London hotel. Much to my surprise it was great night. Contrary to what I thought there were many other casualties as well as me and many had most interesting tales to tell.

In May 2003 I was invited to another of these events in the Royal Automobile Club in Pall Mall. Highly exalted company. I had replied eagerly and was all set to go.

In what passed for normality in my world I received an invitation to an interview with Rethink. By chance it was the same day that I planned to go to Pall Mall. The interview was to be at Willow Lodge and I was somewhat surprised to be informed that one of the tenants would be on the interview panel. That sounded like a most enlightened and interesting idea.

Time passed very quickly in the run up to the interview. I arranged to stay with Beth in the evening; she had now moved on to Colliers Wood and Wimbledon School of Art. I arrived at the interview with my bag over my shoulder and planned to get the train straight to London afterwards. As I walked up the path a familiar face came out of the door.

Once inside I dumped my bag in the downstairs office and was then led to an upstairs office and asked to write a formal letter as if I was writing to a Doctor. That struck me as slightly odd but I got on with it anyway.

Before I had time to finish it I was led into another room where four people sat. I knew none of them. That was unusual for me as I was so well known in the mental health community.

Then the questions. Nothing too difficult. I spoke confidently and concisely. After each answer the panel all looked down at the collections of paper they held. It never occurred to me that they had possible answers written down before asking the questions. I was used to Cambridge interviews which were much more fluid.

At the end the chair asked if I would be prepared to work at Willow Lodge instead of the community. That didn't really appeal to me so I declined. As I walked away at the end it vaguely crossed mind that my incompletion of the writing task and declining the other option would work against me. But I was still pretty confident.

Boarding the train to London I took out my book and tried to focus on what lay ahead rather than what had just transpired. There was after all a party to go to. I took lunch in China Town as was my habit then I had a bit of wander about before heading for Beth's.

Having showered and changed I headed back up to the West End in eager anticipation of what was to come. I was standing in Trafalgar Square trying to find my way when the mobile rang. It was Rethink. Without any bullshit the man immediately offered me the job. Ecstatic I accepted on the spot and made the arrangement for a start date in June.

With that, my mood flying I headed to the party. In a decadence that arguably surpassed that of Cambridge we drank long and hard. It had once seemed very important to me to be a member of a Gentlemen's Club but no longer. It was just a passing night. I saw many old friends and swapped stories of the old days. There were new faces I'd not seen the year before and my reintegration continued.

When the drinks ran out we adjourned to a roof top bar overlooking Nelson's Column and on we went. It almost smelt of money in there and was way beyond what I could afford but for one night only I was there. My mood continued to fly into almost mania. I had waited so long to get on with normal things in life and finally it was happening.

I left before the others as I wasn't sure I could drink anymore. Catching a black cab I headed back down south of the river and passed out in a haze of brilliance on Beth's sofa.

The next day complete with cigarette burn, thunderous hangover, and a bad hip that to this day has not been explained I caught the train back home. Straight to work with my challenging young men, I didn't care much how badly I felt; I was on my way to full time employment. At nearly 34 it was an unusually late time to start my first full time job but my life had been anything but normal in the preceding thirteen years.

Away from my life, Iraq was proving rather harder than the West had anticipated. The invasion was completed fairly quickly but what we saw as liberation was to many Iraqis turning into an occupation. Saddam had not been found and the insurgency was just beginning. Soon we would all know the name of Fallujah. Further east things continued in Afghanistan although it seemed far away and quiet to us. Both would get worse and cost so many lives; not the easy victories some had predicted.

Mark Edgar

Chapter 9
The Recovery Model

We very rarely heard the word recovery during my time in the System. There was a simple reason for that in that hardly anyone did recover and move on. Most of my friends from those days were still as stuck as they ever were. There were a few exceptions most notably my friend Graeme who had actually managed to get sufficiently well to go back to work. My friend John whom I had met on the very first day at the Day Hospital had made a recovery of sorts and certainly enjoyed much better health than he had before. But he was still quite restricted in what he did. He like me had been greatly helped by Risperidone. James who had played such a part in my story too had, to an extent moved on. And then of course there was me.

In my case my recovery had been as spectacular as it had been miraculous. In the early summer of 2003 I had been on it nearly two years and had had barely a symptom since. That said I was only just about to start full time work and I still lived with my parents. Perhaps changing that was the next step in my evolution from psychiatric patient to "normal" member of society.

Around the time I was due to start with Rethink I began to hear the term Recovery Model. Initially it seemed a most attractive idea that really encapsulated my recent transformation. In my naivety I began to believe that if I could recover to that extent then maybe through my agency I could help to bring about that change in other people's lives. The new job would present just such an opportunity. I was in a way ready to unfurl my colours and that seemed to fit into the philosophy of my forthcoming employer.

There was but one thing that troubled me about thinking in these terms. Amazing though my change had been following the advent of Risperidone it was by no means over. I still had to take the medication; in reality that meant for life. But it was not a cure. The word recovery has connotations of a cure rather than of management. In subsequent years I would learn that many psychiatrists wrestled a great deal with this concept. Was it really possible to cure schizophrenia? People talked about a third of people recovering from schizophrenia. In my way of thinking they did not have schizophrenia. I knew to my cost that it was perfectly possible to have a psychotic condition without it being schizophrenia. As far as I could tell those people must have been misdiagnosed in the first place. Just as I had been.

The term that seemed more pertinent to my life was being in recovery in the same fashion that an alcoholic can be in recovery. That was a better way of looking at my situation. What I didn't learn until I joined Rethink was that the organisation had taken on a blanket belief that the recovery model was for them. Any of us could recover however serious one's condition was.

Whilst working my notice at Social Services Chris told me that she thought I was making a mistake moving. But what chance did I have of getting full time employment other than where I was going? I also sensed that they were uneasy about what Rethink was offering. It later transpired that they feared losing their clients. That month of June passed more or less uneventfully apart from a belated call from Maidstone inviting me to interview for the Senior Support Worker post. They had taken so long to get back to me that it was too late.

There was an event that was truly remarkable in my life during that period of time. I was invited to hear a woman called Emma talk about her experience of schizophrenia and working for the NHS in mental health. Emma was one of the best known service users in the country as she had done a great deal of media work to challenge stigma. I met her in Canterbury two days after I was offered the job. She was utterly inspirational in her talk and I took the chance to speak to her after. I had hoped to ask advice on getting a job but by then it was superfluous. We exchanged email addresses and stayed in touch. She would play a part in my story.

It was a blazing hot week in June when I started my new venture. I went through a fairly hasty induction which involved trawling through a variety of rather boring policies. I met my new colleagues. Some like me were just starting out. Others such as my immediate colleague Lisa had been there some time. The new managers had not at that stage been appointed so we had to wait to see how that would pan out.

I was struck by the enthusiasm of them all, really committed to helping. Initially we were based in Willow Lodge and had their rather impressive manager who had interviewed me until the new one was appointed. Outreach work had been going on through Lisa and others for some time for those tenants who had previously moved on from Willow Lodge so it was all very familiar to her. The new Floating Support service in Folkestone got underway and we thought it was going to be straightforward; no real change from the past. What both Lisa and I were completely unaware of was the power of the new funders; we would learn that in time to our cost.

Many of the new tenants or service users were not so new to me. Some like Marie had been amongst my students at the college. Others such as Matt had been long term friends from the Day Hospital, and others like Richard I had known from Mind. It did not take long before I started to hear that infernal word boundaries. But what was I supposed to do, disown those who had played a part in my journey?

They were a most eclectic and disparate group, those known and those unknown. What they all had in common was that they were very needy and had housing issues which it transpired was where the funding had come from in the first place. There did not seem to be rhyme or reason why this group had been chosen. Nor why there were only fourteen of them.

Did we have clear vision of what we were doing? In our minds and in those of the organisation we were effectively trying to sort out their lives and get them into recovery. But it soon became clear that many would need help for the rest of their lives. It was vaguely promised that support to them was to become on-going even though theoretically we could only work with them for two years.

I threw myself into the work like a dervish. My mood was extraordinarily elevated and I was full of energy. It mattered not to me that Lisa went off long term sick within two weeks of me starting. I knew I had more than enough to work with all of them and thrive in the environment. Burnout had not crossed my mind.

What made things more difficult was that one of the new people, an old friend and former student had had a major relapse in his psychosis and was really struggling. Work that was only supposed to be for two hours a week went up to daily contact of astonishing intensity. I was determined that we had at all costs to keep him out of hospital after his previous experience. I worked each and every day with him not noticing the toll it was taking on me. Daily there were more reports of his strange behaviour and expressions of concern.

Of course whilst that went on I still had another thirteen needy people to look after. But still I managed.

It was not all contact though. I went on a series of courses that were quite interesting and I seemed to be getting noticed within the organisation. What appeared to have lapsed though was the promised induction course up in Birmingham. For some reason they had forgotten about that with us.

As the summer moved on we got our new manager. I wasn't really sure what to make of this small and rather chaotic Welsh woman. She had worked for Rethink before. I was unaware at that stage that she had been the only person to apply for the post and her former colleagues had very grave doubts about her ability to do the job. But we would learn that in time.

Away from work I made a momentous decision. Now that I was working full time albeit on a still fairly low income I decided I would move out and find my own place. My old friend JB whom I met as a doorman in a bar in the small seaside town at the height of the epic summer of 1995 rented out rooms in his large house. It was full when I started my new job but he promised that I could have the next room that was available.

Barely three weeks before my 34th birthday a room became available. In a short space of time I packed up what I needed and with the help of my dad finally moved out. Another step in the normalisation of my life.

Moving out was certainly an eye opener. I had a large room with a giant bed and a wash basin. The bathrooms and kitchen were communal although there was nothing new in that after boarding school and hospital. The plumbing was very noisy and the seagulls worse. This did not do my sleep patterns much good but I did get used to it.

It was of course much more expensive than living at home. In fact it cost more than treble what I had been paying before and that was before food. It is one of those strange ironies of moving on that as one goes to better places so one's disposable income actually goes down. That was new to me. And I had had to start paying back my student loan from the PGCE as well as tax and national insurance. There were so many financial barriers to moving on. But I managed as best I could. I didn't learn until much later that I would have been entitled to tax credits in that period of time as my income was so low but I was ignorant of that. I would also have been entitled to housing benefit but JB like most other landlords in the area wouldn't accept it so I had to make do.

The other tenants were a friendly if at times strange bunch. We all had one thing in common and that was that we all worked. JB refused to have people who didn't work. The house gave me my first extended chance to practise my love of cooking and it was not long before the smells of Far Eastern food appeared in the house. Most enjoyed it and I shared what I could.

There was but one problem in the house. My neighbour directly above had a habit of blasting out Eminem at 6 o'clock in the morning before he went to work. He was utterly oblivious to the effect it had on others and he was truly mortified when JB asked him to turn it down. On the whole though I settled quickly.

Away from work life looked great. I was very busy exploring new places in my new town. I started frequenting a subterranean bar I had been to a few times before. Twice a week I went down to the quiet seaside town that had once been my home with JB. He took his karate class and I went to the pub, Tuesday for the quiz, and Thursday just for a drink. After each session he taught we adjourned to the fashionable bar on the beach between the two towns. It was the place to be seen.

I chose it for my birthday at the end of August and we had a great night that went on long after closing time. On many evenings JB and I had Chinese food and drank red wine into the small hours. For that I am eternally grateful to him and others whose generosity allowed me to live a wonderful life despite my meagre resources.

Then each morning I got up, went to work, and did all I could to help my many charges. Lisa had returned to work by then although her attendance was rather sporadic. In my eagerness I was disappointed to have to give up some of my charges to her. But in retrospect I needed to do that.

Throughout this period I kept my friend out of hospital and lived on the boundless energy that my recovery had bestowed on me.

I took two weeks off for my birthday to recharge the batteries. Some of my new colleagues came out for my birthday and I went to a rather good BBQ during that time. But I decided I needed to get away for a few days.

I chose to visit my old friend Beka, the eccentric artist who lived in Bristol. So it was that I spent a warm and blissful few days back in the West Country where I had lived for five years before we moved to Kent.

On my return I was ready to go again. Sadly the battle to keep my friend out of hospital had been lost during my absence. It had been a baptism of fire that had tested me to the limit. Now we had had to bow to the inevitable. That did not sit easily with me as summer gave way to autumn.

Chapter 10
It's Not a Competition

As I settled into my new home Monday night became writing night. By the autumn of 2003 I had been writing for eighteen months. When I had started I had tried to write every day. But that had been too much. It was a most odd experience writing a book about my life. The process was one of immense highs and lows. Each chapter I relived all the pain of my life. People asked if it was therapeutic; my answer was an emphatic no because it was as if each time I was reliving the psychosis as if I was still in it. Whilst still at my parents' house my sister came to visit when I had just written the chapter about my incarceration in the old Victorian Asylum. She sat in total silence before she was able to speak. "That's really powerful" was all she could muster. A few days later she phoned me and apologised for her lack of response, "I couldn't speak, you had taken me back there."

As each chapter was written the ebb and flow of emotion followed a regular pattern. The first challenge was finding a chapter title. Once that was done, the first sentence of each chapter was crucial. When I had done that I was away. With the completion of each chapter my mood soared for a few days; then came the doubts. It went from being great to shit in seventy two hours. I had however devised a system to back it up and maintain my at times fragile ego. I had three readers, my old friend Jayne in Cambridge, my colleague from the college Jan, and another Kent friend Jody who was now living in Nottingham.

Once I had done three or so chapters on my old fashioned word processor I took them to my dad's computer on discs then laboriously converted them to MS-Word. When that was done I would email those chapters to my three readers and await their comments. They provided the reinforcement that I needed.

Ego restored my mood would lift again before sinking once more. Got to make progress went my internal voice. I was battling myself as well as the content. After a period of beating myself up I would launch forth with the same process.

Eighteen months in I was now in the heart of the second part. It seemed just endless. I couldn't see the beginning nor visualise the end. That was the hardest part. But I had to keep going; in my eyes the story was too important not to tell. Perhaps that was one of my much vaunted delusions.

One thing I did have on my side was time. I was not working to a deadline but to my own agenda. It was not a competition.

It's a shame the same could not be said of work. On my return from my break the pace was just as frenetic as ever. But two things were about to happen that would darken my experience and make me begin to doubt what I was doing.

One of the first tasks allocated to the two new managers of the Floating Support teams was to find office space away from Willow Lodge. That autumn the small disorganised Welsh woman set about finding that space. She found it above a shop in the Old High Street in Folkestone. For reasons I didn't understand she was in an enormous hurry to make the move. What I didn't realise was that she was competing in an ego race with the other manager to get there first.

When we did move that autumn we had no phones, no desks, no computers, and no chairs. How on earth were we going to keep working without a viable office space? It then got worse when she told us that to save money we had to step back from supporting our people to paint the new office. Given little choice we merely went about it for a few days until we realised we would really had to leave it to the professionals. After a few days' interruption I returned to what I was good at unaware of what would follow.

Competition seemed to underpin the thinking of Rethink. Yes people were very enthusiastic and hard-working but did that really make us better than all the other providers? We seemed to look down with disdain at other organisations both statutory and voluntary. It was a collective ego we were expected to embrace. To me it didn't matter as long as people got a good service. I hoped they got that from me.

The office interruption was swiftly followed by the news that our funders Supporting People would be auditing the service in November. We had been working extremely hard to support our people and what went by the wayside was the paperwork. Often we were weeks behind in our notes as so many of them went into crisis. We didn't realise just how important that was until Supporting People came knocking.

I don't really recall when risk assessments came into widespread use. As far as I was aware during my time in the System nobody had assessed anything about risks I might pose to myself or even others. Following a tragic incident at Willow Lodge in the recent past the Welsh woman's manager had completely rewritten Rethink's risk assessment process. It was extremely detailed if rather too intrusive. The problem was that in our desperate efforts to get out and support the extremely vulnerable clients we had, no one had had time to write risk assessments.

So it was in the run up to audit that I sat down with three managers and wrote risk assessments for our people. This produced a very vocal response from one of the staff at Willow Lodge who contended that risk assessments should be done in conjunction with the clients rather than separately. Whilst in principle I would have liked to have done that there were some questions that I would feel exceedingly wary of asking.

What was true though was that many of our people were at risk, most to themselves but a small number were potentially a risk to others. I worked out pretty quickly that any risk assessment was flawed in that it relied on what people chose to tell us; they were useful only in a limited way. As my life progressed through mental health I became both wary and irritated by the whole process. Some had risk assessments that were way out of date mentioning things that might have been one off incidents fifteen to twenty years before. Others did not tell the whole truth. It is still a live and contentious issue for me now that I am long removed from that organisation.

With the risk assessments completed I went back to what I was good at. News filtered through that Supporting People would be visiting in November. It also transpired that my long delayed induction course in Birmingham would take place at the same time. I was actually quite pleased with that as I didn't want to have to justify myself to a load of bureaucrats.

As the weeks drew closer to the audit it became clear that there was no way we could get the paperwork done as well as support out people. So it was that I was withdrawn from the real work to spend nearly two weeks catching up on bureaucracy. This did not sit well with me though - I had never got into the business to fill in forms. Yes they were a necessary evil but should not in my view have detracted from what we all wanted to do. Sadly I didn't realise until it was too late that Supporting People had a different view.

The first major crack in my relationship with Rethink occurred just after I had completed the herculean task. I was out visiting just before the audit took place when I had a call from the Welsh woman.

"You haven't completed all your paperwork."
"Yes I have down to each last contact."
"I'm missing a contact for R and you must complete it"
"I'll have to check the dates when I get back to the office." With that I hung up and got on with the rest of the day.

When I got back the following day I checked the dates for the alleged missed contact sheet. It transpired it was during the week in which I was made to paint the new office. I went into her office to tell her.

"I didn't have an appointment with him that week as you had me painting the office."
"You still need to fill in a contact to say you cancelled the appointment that week."
"But I didn't make an appointment that week because you asked me not to."
"You still have to write it."

Fury erupted in my mind as the enormity of the order filtered into my conscious mind. Effectively I was being asked to fake paperwork. I don't recall much of what happened next. My colleague told me afterwards that I squared up to her and he thought I was going to hit her. The one bit that I do remember was that I walked out for a couple of hours rather than have that argument. The incident was never mentioned again but it brought to light in my eyes the credibility of the organisation as well as what we were really doing. That was the day the first major crack appeared.

As October turned to November and the weather got colder and wetter, I was still flying in mood. My energy had not yet been sapped and I had lost touch with the need to stay well. I worked hard and partied harder. The evenings of beer in the fashionable seaside bar became an almost nightly occurrence. And with them more Chinese food and red wine until the early hours. Then each morning I walked the few hundred yards from my house to the office. Relapse seemed so unlikely now. Had I forgotten just how awful is was to be ill? In truth yes I had except on my Monday nights of writing. Then it all came back. But even then I realised it was extremely hard to recall the depths of despair which had once been my norm when I was well. And God was I well.

I travelled by train to Birmingham and caught a cab to the hotel where the induction took place. The next two days were a massive ego trip for me as I used all my experience to wow those around me. That night we drank long and hard. A report got back to the Welsh woman that I was last seen at 2 o'clock in the morning surrounded by women in the bar.

By the following afternoon after intensive propaganda about how good Rethink was and that there we no hopeless cases I headed to the station. It was almost as if they had set themselves up as the Oxbridge of mental health. Did I believe it? To an extent yes but more important I believed in myself in my flawed arrogance. At the station the Welsh woman called my mobile and told me the news that we had got through the audit. Life looked good.

It was not until I got back that I realised there a caveat to that. Having assessed everything they had decreed that we were not doing enough contact time and could therefore take on many more clients. But of course there would be no more resources.

The months of crisis management seemed to have passed them by. I wondered how on earth we could take on more. But the funders had spoken so we had to obey.

That was when I began to doubt the whole thing. Was Supporting People, a flagship policy of New Labour and the arrogant chancellor Gordon Brown really about helping the vulnerable? Or was it about political control and capital?

But these were questions for people more important than me. I just got back to what I was good at.

There was of course more to life than work and something very special happened that November. I had long been an ardent supporter of the England rugby team. Exactly forty years to the day after the assassination of JFK England won the World Cup. The "angry old men" as the Australian press had dubbed them had conquered the world. The party went on long and hard that day.

November turned to December and I prepared myself for my first Christmas living away from my parents. We worked a half day on Christmas Eve and went over to the Black Bull pub opposite Willow Lodge for drinks. After that I went down to see my parents for a few days before returning to the house to feast on rabbit with JB and drink the rest of the holidays away.

It had been a good year.

Chapter 11
Et Tu, Brute?

How many of us in our teens can imagine being over 20? Many of us aspired to be 16 when we could legally smoke and have sex. Likewise 18 held a certain resonance, drinking and voting. When one hits one's twenties it seems down hill all the way; next stop 30. One of the things I had learned since Risperidone was that life is on the whole is very long. When I hit 30 just before my return to Cambridge I was aware that there were probably many decades to go. But it had not been an attractive prospect at the height of my illness in my twenties.

Then it had seemed that nothing apart from the people I had met had come out of mental illness. After my dramatic recovery my view changed; I now had so much to give and my career was going well even if I was a mere bottom feeder in the grand scheme of mental health. But even then how many of us could really imagine being retired? That was a particularly weird thought when for nearly a decade I had doubted I would ever make 30.

When I started out on my new and unexpected career I began to think about retirement. I had to start somewhere and despite my very low income it seemed wise to begin a pension when I joined Social Services. It ate up precious resources but that was the price I had to pay.

Moving on the Rethink in 2003 I was confronted with a dilemma. For reasons that were never explained to me the organisation had a rather strange policy which prevented employees from joining the pension scheme until after a six month probation period had been completed.

Six months or so after I joined I sailed through my probation period with flying colours. Having done that I immediately contacted head office and requested the information about joining the pension scheme. What I didn't realise was that I was in for a wait.

As 2004 got underway the world was still a strange and confusing place. Bush's so called "War on Terror" had been going on for nearly two and a half years. The second front opened in Iraq had not gone as the West had expected. There were no Weapons of Mass Destruction to be found although Blair was exonerated in the

Hutton report of deliberately misleading the people at the end of January. Rather than making the world a safer place every would-be Jihadist was flocking to Iraq to fight and casualties were mounting. We heard perhaps less about the Afghanistan but that too would come. Some young Muslims were becoming radicalised by the war and turning to more extreme views. Four men were quietly lurking apparently missed by the security services in the UK.

The great New Labour resurgence was now in its second term following two landslide victories; for me 1997 was a lifetime away. But more and more we heard of clashing egos, Blair the man who had taken us to war and his arrogant Chancellor Brown were at times almost at war with themselves. I mused on why on earth New Labour would ever want Brown to be leader and Prime Minister. But I was just a small nobody.

In what was more significant in my quiet and largely irrelevant life my beloved Rams crashed out of the NFL playoffs in double overtime. We didn't know it at the time but the days of the vaunted "Greatest Show on Turf", arguably the greatest offensive machine in NFL history, were waning; the ring master Kurt Warner would never again play for them.

But my life was still good that winter. Back at work, my great passion, the pace quickened. We took on more and more clients at the behest of our funders. Some were people I knew, others randomly selected on very dubious grounds to receive the service. It was beginning to dawn on me that this was getting out of control.

We still had no clear vision of what we were supposed to be doing. More and more people went into crisis as our numbers grew. Hugely overstretched we continued to be friend, supporter, social worker, confidante, psychiatrist, and pretty much everything else to our growing band. We had not yet worked out what would happen when the two years were up for our needy people.

There was some good news though that January. My friend who had been admitted the previous September was discharged in the New Year. He was to an extent a changed man but still very needy. That added to my growing workload.

One of the more challenging aspects of the work was in our dealings with other services, most noticeably with the statutory ones. Relations with the Community Mental Health Team (CMHT) were at times strained. Many of our charges were not deemed ill enough to qualify to for Enhanced CPA and so received very little support from mental health services. Not until later when I moved on did I really come to appreciate that CMHTs try and bat off as many referrals as they can citing how overstretched they are. This remained a serious bone of contention as more and more of ours crashed and needed more help.

The arrogance of Rethink and its superior collective belief did not always go down well with other voluntary sector organisations either. And of course we were vying for funding from the same body and felt a perpetual sword of Damocles hanging over our heads.

But worst of the lot were the Children and Families Team of Social Services. A small number of women on our books had or had had dealings with them. One of mine had her children on the at risk register. This meant on occasions having to sit in Child Protection meetings to watch them tear her life apart. The needs of the child were deemed so important that the needs of the parents were seen as totally irrelevant. Children and Families were most suspicious about us. Other clients had faired worse and had had their children taken into care. They were the ones full of rage and in danger of receiving the dreaded personality disorder label.

Throughout the late winter and early spring life became more frenetic. Increasingly I found myself working much longer hours than I was contracted to do and rarely having the time to claim that back. It was also an expensive business and I used considerable amounts of my own money on coffees and meals. Yes we got it repaid but this usually took far too long.

By that spring I had been attending the Mind Centre every Wednesday for as long as I could remember. That was my time, the time in which my mental health was looked after. But more and more I was expected to support clients in that time; Rethink and by extension Supporting People pushed ever harder.

Away from work I continued to party. At other times I religiously went over to France to buy cheap cigarettes and tobacco - there were certain advantages to living by the Channel ports.

It was on one such day that I planned to take the afternoon off to go to France that the first of the dramatic events of the spring took place. One of my charges was an old friend with bipolar. I'd known her since I started going to Mind in the early 1990s. I got a call from her that morning. There was but one word - "help." Knowing how reluctant she was to take up people's time and ask for help I knew she was in trouble.

I cancelled what I was doing and rushed down to the Mind Centre to see her. Nothing could prepare me for what I saw. Shaking and crying she sat there barely able to speak, a shadow of the strong woman I had known for years. I had never seen her so low nor seen a collapse so rapid. There was little I could do but what I did seemed to help.

That afternoon I called Heather from the harbour in Calais to warn her of the calamity that had struck our friend. We knew we had to go into overdrive. Neither of us knew then that it would take another two years for her mood to lift. Another one I was trying to keep out of hospital. It became almost a mission for me.

But she was not the only one who was struggling that spring. At about the same time I went on one of my regular visits to one of my most needy people. She had been on a real roller coaster not helped by her contact with Children and Families who seemed to be doing what they could to destroy what little she had left in her life. On that day she looked tired, low, and angry.

"The social worker has been asking me strange questions about you. I wish they would just leave me alone."
"Do you want me to go and speak to her?"
"If you would that would be great."

It didn't seem a big deal, just another example of the suspicion with which we were viewed. When I got back to the office I mentioned it to the Welsh woman. Much to my surprise she told me that she would go and speak to them. This rather annoyed me but I had long since come to stay out of things where other people's egos were involved.

The next day she told me she had been to see Children and Families. Rather than get the complete backing I would expect from my manager she too started asking strange questions. She seemed to be implying that I was doing more than my job with this woman. She asked if I had been round to see her outside of work time. I had of course never done that. As the questions continued I realised she was questioning my integrity. For the second time in my relationship with my manager my mind erupted in fury. Raging I got to end of the day and went home.

Back at the house my mind was aflame. She had stabbed me in the back. How could I work for someone who didn't trust me? Et tu, Brute. Later she would ask me what the most important role of a manager is - my terse response was simple - "to look after your staff."

It was on that day the earth fractured in my relationship with Rethink. I had still not heard back from the Head Office about my pension. Now I realised that I couldn't go on working for them. More importantly I knew I had to get away from Supporting People. Rethink had sold their soul to the devil and so I realised I had to get out. But how?

With my mood yo-yoing on my next visit to the shrink he increased my Risperidone to 2 mg.

I had a rather uneasy feeling as Easter came and summer beckoned. I started casting my eye around at jobs but there was nothing there. I had been betrayed. What I didn't know was that I was about to face a more personal crisis.

Mark Edgar

Chapter 12
Icarus Burning

As a young child I had always been fascinated by stories. Heroes, Kings, battles, myths, legends, and Biblical stories were all deeply rooted in my early years. My love of history came very early and later I would prove to have a real talent for it. Ultimately my talent for history took me to Cambridge in 1988. My favourite book was one my parents bought in a jumble sale about Greeks Myths. Beautifully illustrated I marvelled at the pictures and loved to hear it read to me. My paternal grandmother severely disapproved of this book - young boys should only hear nice stories!

The first of two stories I remember most is the story of Icarus who built wings of feathers and wax and learned to fly. But he flew too close to the sun, the wax melted, the wings collapsed, and he plummeted into the sea and to his death. The second story I remember is that of Echo and Narcissus. Narcissus the man who fell in love with his own reflection and Echo the nymph who fell in love with him and could only echo his words. All that was left was the narcissus flower and the echo by the pool.

I wryly smile at that now nearly forty years later; what irony for someone with a mood disorder who was misdiagnosed as a Narcissist? During my madness when I spent a spell in hospital in London I used to go to look at the book shops on Charing Cross Road and I would always stop at the print shop there that had a large sized print in the window of John Waterhouse's Echo and Narcissus. It became one of my mad obsessions.

There was but one problem in my childhood stories; they were all too hard for a beginner reader to read. My sister Miriam learned to read at the age of 2. When I had failed to do that by 6 I had my first brush with the shrinks. They thought I had dyslexia but tests showed I was very bright and very bored. I did not learn to read until I was 8.

One of the other passions of my life that I discovered young was for sport. I discovered West Ham when I saw them beat Fulham 2-0 in the FA Cup Final in 1975 on a small black and white TV. For my sins I have followed them ever since. Football though was a lesser of my passions but by 2004 I tried to watch all the England games that I could. I had a greater passion for cricket and a love affair with American Football.

With Easter over and the weather warming the summer had the prospect of two major sporting events. From May England would be playing two test series, one against New Zealand and the other against the West Indies. These were the final home dress rehearsals for the much anticipated Ashes series the following summer. In the football world, England would be competing in the 2004 European Championships. Spirits were high with the prospect of a young man called Wayne Rooney about to hit a greater stage.

But sport was just something that kept me going through the various parts of the year. In the real world I had a job to do. And that job was getting more difficult.

Alongside the eternal crises and suicide watches we provided, the pile of bureaucracy grew higher and higher and threatened to overwhelm us. If there was one thing that I knew everyone hated it was filling in forms. This was not just for the mortal enemy the DWP but also the perpetually changing and long risk assessments we were expected to update with people. In crisis this was the last thing people needed. But it did not stop there. We were required by Supporting People to use a form of recovery action plan. This consisted of targets that we were supposed to cross off as they were achieved then set yet more targets. What we didn't know was the ultimate end to this.

We did undoubtedly have successes. Many of them went to college, often through my connections with Open Door. People got into flats and with a great deal of help most managed to maintain them. Some got voluntary work. These were all good things but few of them ever got near what we were supposed to do which was to live without support and contribute to society. That of course meant paying taxes. For most that was all they could achieve.

For me it was a mission. I had been thriving for so long and had so much energy. Even the long hours were managed with ease.

As the summer drew on the European Championship came on and we cheered England on all the way. I liked to watch it in the underground bar that I now regarded as my local.

Nothing was out of the ordinary the day England faced Croatia. I came back from work, cooked, tidied up, then headed for the bar. There were a lot of people there but crowds were no longer a problem for me. It was just another night.

Then it happened. As England led the psychosis switch in my mind suddenly shifted and my mood collapsed. Time to die, time to die screamed the man's voice. Rachel, that echoing nemesis of so much of my life came back with a vengeance. Two voices, one murmuring, one shouting took over my mind. My mood slumped to the floor and like an old friend suicide came back; he had so long been my partner.

I stared at the screen as all around me the crowd cheered England onto a 4-2 victory. But I was as oblivious to that as they were to me.

Finishing my drink I slowly headed back to the house with the lumbering gait of my madness. My eyes were hooded and almost closed. I prayed that no one would see me on the street or at the house. No one did. As soon as I got to my room I quickly poured a glass of water and swallowed three Risperidone tablets. Slowly the voices subsided, suicide left me, and my mood inched higher. I was exhausted as always happened when my psychosis returned. I was but a shell of who I had been. Icarus had flown too close to the sun.

The next day I called in sick for the first time in my life. Since I started work in 2001 I had never missed a day however ill I was. I was ashamed. Having lost so much of my life to my madness I had sworn never to let it get me again. But of course it did.

As the hours ticked by I reflected. I had been driven to this by work. They were driving me into the ground. It was a lonely place. From that day on I realised that my health was more important than the collective superiority complex of my employer. I was already resigned to leaving but I knew now that I would only do what I had to do for my people but I would no longer go the extra mile for Rethink. And if I got ill with anything, I would take time off like everyone else.

The following day I returned to the chaos as if nothing had happened. In retrospect I should have taken longer but I was too proud for that. I would learn the folly of that sooner than I thought.

I recovered quickly and got on with the rest of the summer. England went from victory to victory in the test series. By August they had won all seven tests of the summer. The football team as ever had done less well.

Before the end of the test series I had an interesting diversion from my normal chaotic life. Sometime earlier I had heard on the mental health grapevine that the local branch of the charity Home Start was looking for someone to provide them with mental health training. I got their number from Heather and called them. They accepted my offer for a small fee and we set a date. I decided that my story had to be the central part of my training as it was so important they heard the reality. I put something together on paper and on a bright sunny day I sat before a group of women to do what I could. I had no idea how it would go but I knew I could teach and knew what they needed. The day was a mighty triumph and set the scene for further sessions in the future. Years later I still had people coming up to me in the supermarket and on the street to tell me how much they remembered my session. It was a buzz I looked forward to. But I kept it from the Welsh woman; this was my project not Rethink's.

We partied hard on my 35th birthday. The fashionable bar on the beach was now like a second home. We reserved a couple of tables and many people came. For all the troubles that had just happened I was still me, partying and having fun. There was nothing on the job horizon but I knew something would come up at some stage. The autumn would once again bring the NFL back to my life. I did know that in a little less than a month I would be headed to Spain again. What I didn't know was that the impact of overwork was about to come back in a very different form. As I partied though, my mind was oblivious to that.

Chapter 13
The Viral See Saw

Looking back on my life to the tragic summer of 1991 I sometimes muse on whether it was the loneliness and isolation which awaited me in Kent that finally drove me to suicide and breakdown. I had led such a nomadic life. At 9 I had gone away to school in Cambridge. But it was no ordinary school. Part of the price one pays for being part of a famous choir was that there was hardly any time off. I came home from school on Christmas afternoon. Later in the year I would not return until Easter Day. In the summer we kept singing through that strangely Cambridge institution of the long vacation. Then there were the tours; they took up maybe a month of the summer each year.

At 14 I went away to Sussex. Life was easier and freer than in Cambridge. I did get the long holidays in the summer and came home before Christmas. There was usually a tour at Easter. Most of my friends lived locally and saw each other in the holidays. I lived too far away to go home at weekends and I didn't really want to go back.

After A Levels at the age of 19 I went back to Cambridge for another three years. We had long and lonely holidays that I endured rather than enjoyed. Of course it was there that my life took a dramatic turn and psychosis suddenly took over my life.

The consequence of that was that although theoretically I lived in Kent, in reality I knew no one. Leaving Cambridge I simply had no other place to go. The next four years were spent in almost complete isolation except for my mad friends. I understood them but I didn't understand the world of others, that of being well. In fact I greatly feared the wider world, my own little paranoia.

Viewing from a different angle after I got well I always put the turning point as being when I met the mysterious Buddhist Healer Caroline. She gave me the hope that I could recover. Later though, as I think now, my recovery journey predated that. On a quiet night in December 1994 I had gone to the pub at the bottom of the hill with my old friend James. He introduced me to two women who lived in the real world; the fun loving and open Laura, and the guarded beauty of Jayne.

As 1994 waned my isolation decreased rapidly. The following summer will forever be known to us as "that summer". It was only then that my life changed and I had a foot, or perhaps it was merely a toe in the world beyond my madness.

Of all the many people I met during that epic summer, the one I understood least was the enigmatic Anders. I met him in the pub at the bottom of the hill. He was quiet and brooding with a penchant for Stella Artois - we called it "wife beater" in Kent. He only really opened up when he had had a few of those. Even then he said little. I knew he rented a room from a woman called Sue. Other than the fact that she had previously been married to his dad he spoke very little of home. Women noticed him for his striking looks but struggled with his silence. It would be several years before I met his adopted family; ironically that was through Beth not Anders.

By 2004 we had been friends for nearly ten years. I had met both Sue and her son James and daughter George. Life had been good to Bohemian Sue with her tarot and clairvoyance business thriving. They no longer lived in the small seaside town but had a large house in the more upmarket village at the top of the hill. She had done a tarot reading on me when I first met her and she knew nothing about me. It was around the time I started writing A Pillar of Impotence. The last card she pulled was the ten of swords. Her first comment was "you have lived a lot of shit." It was an ironic, eerie, and apt card to get. Most of the reading was uncannily accurate.

Business had in fact been so good in 2004 that she had bought an apartment in that playground of the rich Puerto Banus earlier that year. There was one thing that played on my mind a little about Anders during my madness and that was that he shared a birthday with Rachel, 26th September, a time at which I had invariably seen a huge dip in my mood. But that was behind me now and we had a plan for Sue, her son James, Anders, another friend Rob and me to go on holiday to Puerto Banus to celebrate Anders' birthday.

With that all set up for a few weeks time I returned to the ever spiralling chaos of work. It was on my first week back that the Welsh woman called me and said she was unwell and would not be in. It sounded like flu which elicited much sympathy from me as I had been ravaged by flu a few years before. The strange thing was, two days later she came back looking healthy, fit, and feeling well.

A couple of days after that she phoned in sick again. Within a week I too had caught it.

For the next two weeks I vacillated between feeling like I was going to die to feeling on top of the world. The bad days were wracked with fever and hallucination, the good days just like normal. As soon as I felt okay I would reappear at work. But it always came back. I don't think we used the sexist term of "man flu" in those days but this certainly wasn't that; the Welsh woman continued to struggle as I did.

The drive for work at Rethink translated into a pressure to get back as soon as possible. My devotion to my people also drove that along the way in which I perceived things. Each time though, the virus took its revenge.

With each passing day I feared the worst for my forthcoming holiday. And then it broke. Just in time and I got on with my life.

The night before we went to Spain I stayed at Sue's. We had a really early flight and I figured that was easier than driving over in the morning. One of the few restrictions my illness placed on my life now was that the sedation of the pills made it impossible as well as dangerous to drive early in the morning. None of us enjoyed getting up so early except Sue; she always seemed to rise at an unearthly hour. Anders drove us to Gatwick and by lunch time we had got to Puerto Banus in time for al fresco dining accompanied by white Rioja which I had not tried before. Then the party began.

I never worked out whether it was by accident or design, but only Sue could buy an apartment above a lap dancing club. James and Anders seemed to relish the prospect of that in the evening. Before then though we trawled the bars, enjoyed the sun, and ate. I struggled to find anywhere Spanish to eat so on the first night I settled for Chinese which was surprisingly good. Later we took in the fashionable and expensive Sinatra's bar before the infamous club.

Most of the night I sat there drinking. I had no desire to witness a private dance but the others soon found themselves doing it all night. With credit cards whirring we stumbled on through the night. In the early hours the lack of sleep caught up with me and I left them to it and headed back to the apartment. After some trouble getting my key in the door - it had been a long night - Sue let me in and I settled down for a night of broken sleep.

I have no idea what time the others came in but they slept long after Sue and I got up. When they finally emerged we all headed off for lunch. Anders stopped at a cash point and tried to draw out some money on his new credit card. He failed. Moving onto another machine, it failed once again. A third yielded no monetary response.

In desperation he called the credit card company. The response caused a great deal of laughter and is remembered long afterwards.

"I can't get any money out on my card". They checked the details and then responded.

"There were a large number of irregular payments in a lap dancing club in Marbella. We thought it was stolen so we have cancelled that card."

"No" said Anders, "that was me." What a splendid response! Only he could come up with something as deadpan as that.

Fortunately he was able to secure funds to continue the party for the duration of a memorable trip. And with that the party went on.

The days took on a surreal feel as they passed by. Much of my time was spent in small bars drinking café solo before moving to the beach bar where the Swedish massage table was to drink ice cold cerveza and chain smoke Fortunas. Anders was once told off by the masseuse for inappropriate behaviour. James and Anders quickly got together with two of the girls from the club and were nightly visitors. Rob, with the gift of the gab often did his own thing and seemed to come back each night with more money than he went out with and tales of girls he had slept with. Sue did what she did best, lie in the sun and go shopping. For someone with her means Puerto Banus was a retail heaven.

Most nights we ate together but it was hard to find much else that was affordable other than Italian and I had never been much of a fan. So a couple of times I went back to the Chinese over the road.

Some days it was far too hot so we adjourned indoors with cheap cerveza and Rioja from the incredible hypermarket. As a foodie it was a rare sight to see although I didn't do any cooking.

There was very little to do in Puerto Banus other than that. But on the Monday by way of something different, Sue, James, and I took a taxi over to Malaga to see the Picasso gallery. Unfortunately we had chosen the one day of the week that it was shut so that didn't work. We did have a glorious lunch of tapas in a quiet square in the old town; finally real Spain. Malaga surprised me as I had always thought it was just a place where tourists flew to before moving on. But the narrow alleys and fine bars of the old town changed my view in a really good way. Anders and Rob just carried on oblivious.

But of course the blissful days inevitably passed quickly and it was time to return to the chaos of my mad life. On the final night everyone was sat around the outside bar of Lineker's drinking bottled beer and talking to the very attractive Eastern European bar girl. With each bottle she gave us a free B52. I had long since given up spirits but I was still partial to the odd cocktail every now and again. But I was not used to large quantities. Within a few hours I had drunk myself into oblivion and somehow made it back to the apartment. The others as ever carried on.

The next day I woke with the mother of all hangovers. I went down to a nearby bar for very strong café solo and tried to eat a croissant. I managed about half of it. Most of the rest of that day was spent indoors suffering. Our flight was at 10 o'clock in the evening and when we got to the airport I tried to eat some more; not a good plan. But I did survive.

Anders drove us back from Gatwick in the early hours. When we got to the house I drove back to JB's via Tesco. It was strange to see it so empty. I got home at about 4 o'clock to find JB still up and having his after work wine. Feeling much better than I had I consumed a couple of glasses before retiring. What a week it had been. A time that would live on long in my memory.

With my holiday over I returned to work. Nothing had changed but a least I was well, refreshed, and looking very tanned. It was not long afterwards that I started to hear rumours of a new model of work for Community Support. That was the first time I heard of the heralded

Support, Time, and Recovery workers. So recovery had finally come to statutory services.

Intrigued, one afternoon I went back to my old office to speak to Chris about it. This, as was my way now, was kept from the Welsh woman. Chris explained that it was new form of targeted short term interventions with more purpose and more responsibility than the old model. Now that sounded like what I wanted to do. Chris was not too specific but she anticipated that they might be recruiting in the New Year. Going away, it seemed there might be some hope of moving on. And with that my mood rose.

It was but a few weeks before I was once again felled by a virus. Early in November I woke feeling dreadful and called in sick. Different but just as debilitating as the last one it would in the end keep me off work for four and a half weeks. The landlord of the pub at the bottom of the hill later told me I looked like a ghost. JB as it he did with all his tenants looked after me and was once so alarmed he called the Doctor. When I had moved I was not given a choice of surgeries but allocated to a small one man practice run by an Asian Doctor. He had always seemed quite nice.

As the weeks passed and I got no better I visited weekly for a sick note. This time I refused to go back before I got completely well. After a couple of weeks he kept telling me it would do me good to go back. But I held out even at the cost of my trust in him.

I did return in the run up to Christmas. My colleague ventured the opinion that perhaps it was being worked into the ground that had led me to fall prey to such awful viruses. Perhaps he was right.

But I did get well and partied hard at Christmas. I was blissfully unaware that this would be my final Christmas at JB's. My world was about to change once again as the see saw of life took me upwards.

Chapter 14
The Tides of War

As 2005 dawned the world trundled on in its usual chaotic way. Life was still very uncertain. It was nearly three and half years since the unleashing of a war that threatened so many. As ever in war, civilians bore the brunt of the casualties. The "War on Terror" did not appear to be going well. Al Qaeda had struck in the heart of Europe the previous year; Madrid had been the target this time. In Iraq, thousands were dying each month in waves of bombings and fighting. Bush had famously flown onto the deck of USS Eisenhower and declared major combat operations over shortly after the fall of Baghdad in April 2003. How wrong he was. Iraq was on the brink of sectarian civil war. In the Shia south where the British forces were based the insurgency had been even less expected but had just as much vigour. Along with countless civilians, Western military casualties were rising and that was the one thing the West couldn't tolerate. Rumour had it that Afghanistan was getting worse too although we heard less about that part of the world.

Back at home we knew there was an election coming up. New Labour had descended into a less bloody sectarian struggle between Blairites and Brownites. I don't think anyone seriously thought they would be defeated but the political world was changing. I still couldn't figure out why on earth they would accept Brown as leader. He was demanding that and this dominated our airwaves.

Away from there though, there was the coming selection of a host country for the 2012 Olympics. Britain had put in a bid although they were not favourites. The announcement would come on 6th July.

In my small and insignificant part of the world I was coming to the end of the epic journey of writing A Pillar of Impotence. It had been a long and hard road that had taken the best part of three years. The emotional roller coaster continued but having completed the second part the previous year progress became easier. The end was in sight. I didn't know how long it would take but I knew that I would get there.

My world was also in a state of flux. I knew sometime in the early part of that year it was likely that I would get a call from Chris to tip me off about the new job. It was anyone's guess how long I would have to wait. I knew that I was in with a very good chance but there was always my old nemesis called chance. When I had worked there before other people had expected to get that job. I had appeared out of nowhere and apparently blown them away. I was confident but maybe there was someone better than me out there. That would have left me high and dry working for an organisation I was thoroughly disillusioned with.

The grind of Rethink went on. One of the hardest parts was the staggering length of time it took in meetings and supervision. Team meetings often took four hours. My supervision usually took just as long. After the act of betrayal the previous spring I had stopped even responding to the section in my supervision that was supposed to be devoted to my wellbeing. Enquiries were inevitably met with a reply of "I'm fine."

When this was coupled with the distances we sometimes had to cover it was impossible to meet the perpetual demands of Supporting People to have more contact time with the clients. I would have loved to have spent all day every day doing what I did best but it simply wasn't possible.

But my wait for news did not last long. 2005 was but a few weeks old when Chris called to say the job would soon be advertised and interviews set for early March. It would be a temporary contract in the old community support model with a view to reapplying when the change was made to Support, Time, and, Recovery (STR) later in the year. So it would be a gamble; keep a permanent full time job or go for broke and take the risk?

The news of STR had reached Rethink some time before. The Welsh woman had dismissed it as "workers on the cheap". But they were asking less of workers for potentially a fair amount more money. I decided quickly that I would take the risk and filled in the form. Time would tick by quickly until March. Life continued in the meantime.

On a Monday night in late February I finally did it. The book was complete. I stared at the screen and wondered what on earth to do next. There was an eerie absence of triumph. In my confusion tears rolled down my face. This was not what I had expected nor did I anticipate the chronic feeling of emptiness. It was only later when I talked to artists, writers, and composers that I realised that is what all creative people feel when they complete a mighty work.

Deep down I knew that would be the easy part, much harder would be for a nobody like me to get published. I had put out some tentative feelers already but had had no luck. In fact as far back as my first week at Rethink I had found a niche publisher whom I felt would certainly publish it. But as one of my readers had said "it's too good for that." Whether that was true or not only time would tell. But I did decide on one thing, I would have a party.

Time moved quickly in February. As chance would have it I had booked the week of the interviews off as I was going to a friend's wedding. Emma, one of the many I had met during the epic summer of '95 had finally found the right man. We were all so pleased for her and she was set for the fairy-tale wedding she had always wanted.

In an equal chance the interview date came through for the day before. There had probably been little doubt that I would get an interview but I had learned years before never to believe anything until it actually happened.

By then, even statutory services had taken on the excellent idea of having service users on the panel. One of the strange things about my side of the fence was that there were a group of self-appointed activists who had really made careers out of shouting at the services. They were usually hard line and spent most of their time slating professionals as being clueless. I had learned to stop "ranting" as a now deceased Cambridge academic had suggested very early on in my illness. Sadly that advice had not been heeded by so many of the activists. Privately I called them the ranters. They of course had sewn up the positions on the panel. It was useful to stay on the right side of them. The one who was on my panel was not known to me but I was confident my background would help.

I told the Welsh woman nothing about the interview even though she was down as a referee. But I had ticked the box requesting that referees be contacted only after any interview. The other one was Heather and I knew I could rely on her.

The interview took place in the same building that I had first stepped into in the summer of 2002. In between times I had paid several visits there for meetings as the Children and Families Team was based there. I was my usual calm self during the process. All the faces were familiar except that of the service user. The questions were straightforward and I managed to speak with my usual eloquence. It seemed that the service user took quite a shine to me although it was clear that she detested Social Services and came across as if she was the only one with any knowledge in the room full of fools.

With the questioning over I retired to JB's house for tea and some reading. As the day waned I sat reading Hugh Fearnley-Whittingstall's brilliant book Meat. My phone rang just before 5 o'clock. It was Chris. She rapidly explained that I had got the job but it had been a very close run race. As had happened before with me a candidate came out of nowhere and had really impressed them. Apparently after some juggling they had managed to secure funding to employ both of us. His name was Dan.

As the conversation went on it got better. Chris had persuaded the panel that as I was so experienced they should pay me at the highest rate possible prior to gaining further qualifications. There was an expectation that at some stage that I would have to undertake an NVQ but even without that she was offering £3,000 more than I was earning at Rethink. I accepted on the spot. Finally I would be getting away from Supporting People.

There was a further caveat in our conversation. One of the social workers I knew from the past was moving on to another job. There was a plan for a leaving party at another fashionable bar not far from the one on the beach. Chris invited both Dan and me. It would give us a chance to meet each other.

Feeling most triumphant I headed out in the evening with JB. It was time to celebrate. It was a long and very good night but much to my surprise I woke with a clear head.

Later that day I drove up for the wedding in West Kent. I had arranged to stay in the pub where the reception was to be held. I showered and changed then called Lisa to tell her the news. She was delighted but clearly wished she could do the same.

The wedding was the fairy-tale Emma had always wanted. With the service over we went on to the reception and drank long into the night. We smuggled other guests in who stayed too as we drank ourselves into oblivion. We got some strange looks at breakfast but so be it. It had been a memorable couple of days. My mood was at its highest.

I returned to work the following week and told the Welsh woman the news. She didn't really let on how she felt but she did seem pleased for me. I'm not sure she appreciated the slightly devious way by which I had done things but I owed her nothing. Rethink was just my employer and as such a means to an end. I wasn't sure what that end would be but it was time to move on to the next part of the journey; I had given them everything I could at great cost to myself. The area manager jokingly said he would not accept my resignation so I guess there was some gratitude for my efforts. It was just a shame that had rarely been expressed during my time there.

On Maundy Thursday I joined the now combined Shepway Community Mental Health Team to party the night away. Many faces were familiar. Some were new but they all seemed to accept me and look forward to working with me. It appeared my reputation had preceded me and my works at Rethink were well known and respected. Sadly Dan could not make it.

I had doubts. Was I really being asked to join the enemy? That was a course of action I had long resisted. But deep down I still harboured the delusion that I could change the System from within. I did learn one thing that night: they liked to party long and hard and that suited me perfectly. In fact we were so outrageous we forgot to pay on the way out. It was the first of many great nights out. JB picked me up afterwards as he drove back home with Laura and another old friend Helen. Laura told me afterwards that I was slumped against a wall and it was the most drunk she had ever seen me.

It proved to be great Easter. Life was looking up and my mood was soaring. The energy that had been sapped by the driven expectations of Rethink returned in abundance. The tide of my life had turned and I was on my way. And first stop was the forthcoming book party.

Mark Edgar

Chapter 15
April Fools' Day

Technology has always baffled me. In fact I would take it one stage further, it frightens me. When I went back into education in the spring of 1997 I had to confront one of those fears. I battled for two and half years to master the art of using a computer; there was always much swearing involved. Ian remembers my battles even now all these years later.

When I went back to Cambridge in 1999 my dad bought me my first mobile phone, long after much of the rest of the world had them. I simply couldn't afford one before. He was also forced to buy me a word processor to do my work because of the chronic lack of necessary equipment at the college. It was on that very same machine, having progressed on from one finger to two that I had written A Pillar of Impotence. It was a nightmare converting it to computer legible files, every time I did anything it went wrong; more swearing. But I had got it done in the end.

Like most people with little money I only had a pay as you go phone; a contract was simply too expensive. That was still my situation as I started to invite people to the forthcoming book party. This was all going on at the same time as I was getting the new job. I had so many trips into the shop for top ups that the woman behind the counter told me I might be much better off getting a contract.

My plan was simple, set a date then text everyone I knew and ask them to come along. I decided on Friday 1st April 2005 at the fashionable bar on the beach. I really didn't know how many if anyone would come. The staff asked me how many tables I wanted to reserve. Expecting no more than ten people I suggested two tables and hoped that one or two other people would drop by as they went about their normal Friday night business.

On that Friday I left work slightly early to pick up one of my PGCE friends from London. Katherine, unlike me had managed to get a teaching job but hated it and got out. She didn't drink but wanted to join the celebration and planned to stay at my house in a vacant room. We got home, I showered - I always seem to do things in a topsy-turvy way – we got a take away and then headed down to the bar with JB fairly early. We got some drinks and sat down at one of the reserved tables.

I had been adamant that some friends who had received services from Rethink had to come. But I knew for some of my colleagues from Willow Lodge that fraternising with the tenants would be frowned upon. My bipolar friend who was still desperately depressed and Matt had been my friends for years. With Marie I was forced to merely say that if she happened to go to that bar by chance on that given night she would be most welcome.

Slowly a few people came by, collected drinks and sat down at our reserved tables. But then it snowballed. They came in their droves from miles around. We quickly filled the part of the bar where we were sat. Then it spilled over onto the terrace and finally with about sixty people there we practically filled the bar. I was in disbelief. I simply couldn't imagine so many people wanting to come and celebrate with me. But they were there to party and salute what they all seemed to think was the monumental achievement in writing the book.

Those who entered the bar were most intrigued by this bizarre gathering. We went on oblivious to others. I'm not sure if I bought more than one drink all night. Sadly in the pre twenty four hour drinking regimen of those days the party had to come to an end when the bar closed at midnight. Fortunately a friend offered his house and a number of us then went back there. Last I remember I was drinking from a wine glass so big it held half a bottle. Somehow I completed it. A memorable night was followed by a deep and comparatively dreamless sleep.

The following morning, Katherine had to go back early to London so I took her to the station then returned home. Considering the decadence of the night before I felt remarkably well. I was basking the glory of the achievement, the quality of the night, and the sheer turn out. My mood was flying. When JB got up he suggested we go for brunch at the cliff top café at Capel between Folkestone and Dover. On a glorious spring day we dined in splendour overlooking the English Channel. Every few minutes my phone bleeped with yet another message about the night before. Outrageous stories of people waking up in ditches, strange houses, and utter confusion. It appeared that had been a night that would long be remembered by so many.

But all good things come to an end and of course on Monday I was back in the office working out my notice at Rethink.

The last couple of weeks were utterly surreal. There was a strange paradox of being relieved to be going but also a sadness at leaving behind my people. My people, my nutters. Most wanted to come with me but of course someone as lowly as me could not make that happen. Saying those goodbyes was very hard.

The Welsh woman was very cordial in those few weeks. I wanted my people to come to any leaving event that was planned. That was a highly irregular request but that was what I wanted. In the end we had a team lunch in a very nice restaurant and then had a party in a Chinese buffet restaurant. They gave me a wonderful card signed by all of them. There were so many words from those I had tried to help in the previous two years. They all wished me well but each really wanted me to stay. It was their comments that mattered. They were after all what I was in the business for.

As I left Rethink I was thoroughly disillusioned with the whole organisation. Originally set up as the National Schizophrenia Fellowship it had sought to support the carers of those afflicted by that most complex of mental illnesses. Later it had branched out to support people with schizophrenia and after that to others with severe mental illness. But the Rethink I left in 2005 was not the Rethink or NSF that Heather had worked tirelessly for for years. It was one that had got into bed with a funder with a different agenda. As far as I could see selling out to Supporting People had marked the death knell of the organisation.

It was populated by enthusiastic, caring, and hard-working people, but the management structure was flawed and patchy. The Welsh woman was not a bad person. In fact she did it all for the right reasons. But she was hopelessly out of her depth and unsupported by those above her. The man who interviewed me was a rare exception of a good manager.

When I had my induction I had been told that the aim was to double its turnover in a couple of years. Was that really the mark of a charity?

It was time to move on. But with my next move, was I selling out to the enemy too? Only time would tell. What I did know was that I was infinitely better at my craft than I had been when I started. And I had gained an inkling of the complex relationship between the System, the people who ran it, and those who paid for it. Those would prove useful things to know as I walked into a brave new world.

In a bizarre parting shot the Welsh woman told me that I wasn't allowed to contact any of my friends for at least two years. This combined with the equally bizarre policy Rethink had that staff could only have a sexual relationship with a client one year after they had left the service was a strange idea; as I wryly pointed out afterwards to my friends at Mind, I could have sex with them in a year's time but I was not allowed to speak to them until another year after that. I ignored her on the talking front.

Chapter 16
Are They Dangerous?

The election was barely three weeks away when I re-joined the enemy. The country was gripped with election fever although we heard continual comments about voter apathy. Blair, the once of obscure figure of politics was seeking a historic third term for his Labour party; no Labour leader had ever achieved that. Up against him was my own MP Michael Howard. He was a man whose politics I cared little for but he was an excellent constituency MP. Few if any political heavyweights visited their constituencies during the weekend. Howard was the exception never to be found in London when the weekend arrived. He had helped me all those years ago when having fought for nearly five years to get the benefits to which I was entitled yet the DWP still refused to pay me.

New Labour, whilst not exactly in trouble, was beset by infighting. Blair's arrogant chancellor still coveted the prized job. Few thought Labour would lose but it was anticipated that the massive majority of one hundred and sixty in the last parliament would be dramatically reduced. All would be revealed on Thursday 6th May.

Back in Howard's constituency, the world of mental health was changing rapidly. Health and Social Care had now joined forces to form a Partnership Trust. Finally, joined up thinking. Kent was still divided into East and West but a new entity would soon be born. Kent and Medway Partnership Trust would come into existence in the next year or so.

What was newly named the Shepway Community Mental Health Team was now combined although it was split over two sites. I returned to my old office but would in time move to a new office based at the hospital in the future. The hospital where they had "treated" me for all those years. A sense of déjà vu perhaps?

I had some mixed views. Yes I was moving on in the world even if I was still around the lowest end of the food chain. But with the combining of services I became quite uneasy at being drawn further into a System that had nearly destroyed me. Community Support had always been like a halfway house, not too close and not too far out of the System. The theory was that the STR roles would be further in and with more responsibility. The latter was good, but the former unnerved me. I had sworn I would never work for the enemy but I was now finding myself more drawn into such a flawed place.

What hadn't changed that April was the way in which the old Community Support was working. The new working model was a few months away and there was some disquiet in the ranks. Those who had worked in one way for years were putting up some resistance to change. But that change was inevitable. The clients were all the same ones I had known two years before. Predominantly middle aged women they were utterly dependent and completely stuck. None apparently could shop on their own, nor clean, nor indeed use the buses. The new role took on a familiar route just doing what had been planned through the Service Delivery Order and completely controlled by the centre. I had no control over my diary but was merely told to go to a particular place, at a given time, and undertake a specific task.

Dan who I finally met the day I started was a great and enthusiastic man. Much younger than me, he too had a degree, which was rare in those days for Community Support. He had studied photography at Newcastle and had plans to train as a CPN. I didn't find the latter out until some time later though. As he was new to the business he was helped out somewhat and given a fairly thorough induction. I was on the road that very first day. Some of the people I saw were well known to me. Others were new.

The routine came very quickly back to me. As before there were queries about boundaries but there was never really a problem. In something of coup my bipolar friend who had battled depression for more than a year came along with me. They let me work with her acknowledging that without me she would have been in hospital long ago.

My travels took me rather further this time extending down to Romney Marsh. But that was familiar from my Rethink days. This trip took in many pleasant walks along the beach early in the day before the hot sun did its utmost.

Within a couple of weeks I was back up to speed on the job. I certainly made my presence felt in the team. Community Support Workers were rarely listened to but I was not going to let that happen. I had too much to give. In the main I was very open about my illness and history to those who hadn't known me before. Some felt slightly threatened by this but others, such as Andrew who had been my CPN back in the 1990s spent a lot of time extolling my virtues. It was useful to have allies like that. Chris was also a great supporter although she quickly reminded me that she thought it had been a mistake going to Rethink. But what was done was done.

What was different this time was the amount of training I was expected to do. Much of it was not particularly interesting but one course riled me considerably. Quite early on Dan and I attended a health and safety course. It was to be run by the Head of Health and Safety at the Trust. One of our OT colleagues attended that day too. What unfolded was an affront to mental health service users and an absolute disgrace to the profession. All the man went on about was how dangerous these people were and how one could never drop one's guard. Had mental health not moved on? When I challenged him on his utterly archaic view he responded by saying "as far as I'm concerned you're a threat to me sitting in that chair now." I simply couldn't believe it. I left furious but said and did nothing. Some dinosaurs could not be changed. I didn't know it then but that day would come back to haunt me.

That experience aside my mood was buzzing and I was back in my element. It rapidly became clear the risks we had run in my previous employment in order to stoke the collective ego of Rethink. Unlike when I had been at Community Support before we now had access to records and an electronic system to record our work. I had rarely if ever seen a risk assessment in my time there before; now they wouldn't let me do anything without being fully informed.

At the end of my first month there was some confusion when neither Rethink nor the Trust actually paid me. It was later admitted by HR that despite being given my bank details weeks before I started they had lost them. But it did get sorted out fairly quickly and I sailed serenely on in my new venture.

On 6th May, Blair won his historic third term. The majority was cut massively but he still had a comfortable majority of sixty six. Brown was still calling for him to step down which didn't make sense. Despite the victory, Labour had the lowest recorded share of the vote for a government with an overall majority. So we were in for a few more years of the New Labour experiment. Who knew what the future would hold after that? I really couldn't see them going on to a fourth term if Blair bowed to the pressure and backstabbing and stepped aside.

Back in the obscure Kent backwater where I resided I was about to take my next step in my epic recovery journey. Society expects so much of us to conform but so little in my life was normal. How many Cambridge graduates were earning so little, lived in shared houses, and at the age of 35 were not married and childless? My friends kept going in the world to which they were destined. But my life derailed for so long by my madness was very far from theirs. That said though I loved life now and was doing something I felt was really important. There were still doubters some of whom had suggested to JB if not me that I had wasted my life. But they did not know of my madness. In reality I had achieved something very few others did. And that was to get off long term benefits.

I was still earning a very low income but it might just be enough to get my own place. That great step that many take in their twenties still eluded me. But as with so much of my life something came up that took me in a different direction.

Tom, like so many of my friends, had come to me through James. Actually I had met him some time after I had met the others. He had not experienced the great summer of 1995 as he was away. But we knew each other by reputation and when we finally did meet his friendship meant just as much to me as with the others.

He had made a very successful career in IT and was perhaps the highest earner of my immediate circle. He was the first to buy a house just off the High Street at the other end of town from my parents. He was currently living with his girlfriend who would eventually become his wife in London. They kept the cottage in the quiet seaside town as a weekend retreat.

We met from time to time for a few beers when he was down. It was during one such meeting in May that I suggested if he ever intended to rent the cottage out to let me know. As chance would have it he had recently been thinking precisely that. Quickly we worked out a rent level and a date. He did not want a deposit, merely that I cover the cost of his mortgage. The rate of £370 was within my grasp although I knew it would be struggle with the bills. But I was determined to go through with. Another step into the real world.

As spring turned to summer I set about packing up and making preparations to move back to where I had come from. I had some apprehension but was on the whole excited by the prospect.

The day I moved was a truly mad day. Only I could arrange to move house the day I was offering training to Home Start. The previous year had been so successful that I now had a regular slot there. Full of triumph after a good session, I packed up what was left of my possessions and moved out of JB's for the last time. Anders had given me some help to move but I had yet to accumulate the clutter that we all inevitably build up if we live in the same place for too long.

The house needed a good clean but I finally had a home of my own. It was small, just a one up one down cottage but it was mine. The position could not have been better. Set in the street behind the long High Street I had five pubs, two curry houses, two kebab shops, a Malaysian restaurant, a supermarket, Mandy's fabulous butcher's shop, and a host of other things within a two hundred yard radius of my front door. The nearest pub was actually right opposite my front door although I didn't frequent it very often. At the other end of the town from the pub at the bottom of the hill I settled instead for a pub in the middle of the High Street. That was when I met Sue and Duncan. It would become my new local and another second home.

There was also a taxi rank just outside so transport was great. Every Sunday I visited my mum and dad for dinner. Back home I set out on a great culinary adventure. Soon that small house would become a food mecca for my friends. The party began the very first weekend; it would continue for many months to come.

All seemed great in my little world. I had the job and I had the house. Now I was doing normal things. There was but one cloud on the horizon and that was that I would have to re-apply for my own job that autumn. Confident though I was if that failed I would lose everything. But that was a couple of months away. As June turned to July, the party just carried on.

Mark Edgar

Chapter 17
The Day Before You Came

Thursday was a good day for me during that point of my journey. There were three main reasons for that. We had our team meeting in the afternoon, a chance to catch up on the wider picture and let my voice be heard. Of course I was also party to the nutters' grapevine so really knew more than they did. Perhaps that would give me power should I choose to use it. Now much more overt in my actions I certainly seemed to be making a mark on the world of mental health in East Kent.

Secondly, it was that much closer to the weekend. I was extremely well on the whole but my sanity was still very much dependent on not getting too tired. By Thursday I was usually close to exhaustion but salvation was near. In the new house, most weekends I slept as long as I possibly could. That I was wise to do so would be born out in the future; but that was far away.

Thursdays were also good as by accident of fate, or perhaps by design, I could usually get an extra half hour in bed. My first visit of the day was down on Romney Marsh and I lived between there and the office so I could set off a little later. Coupled with this the man I visited down there was not much of an early riser; I guess we shared that in common. So by mutual arrangement I visited at 9.30 rather than any earlier.

He was an interesting man who lived in a crumbling and ramshackle bungalow with his brother. Somehow they got through their lives in a rather chaotic way. When I was sent to visit him they told me he rarely spoke and feared going out. But I seemed to have made some progress in my short time and twice a week we would go for a walk along the beach. He also opened up showing a sharp if flawed mind and a passion for films.

There appeared to be nothing unusual on that particular Thursday. I woke up feeling tired, dazed, confused, and grumpy. But that was normal. I quickly made a pot of very strong coffee and lit a cigarette. With the BBC Breakfast News on I settled down with my coffee and cigarette and as usually happened the fog of my mind cleared quickly. Nearly the weekend, two more days to go. This always provided me with extra impetus. When I had finished my coffee I went upstairs to my substantial bathroom that seemed almost out of place in such a small Victorian cottage. I washed, put my lenses in, and brushed my teeth.

At about 9.20am I left the house and climbed into my car for the short journey down to the Marsh. The radio was playing quietly as I drove but I was taking little notice. I have a vague recollection that during the travel news there was a throw away comment about there being problems on the tube that day. Nothing new there then.

When I arrived I parked, walked up the overgrown path to a house that had seen better days, and knocked on the door. After some strange shuffling sounds the door was opened by my man's brother. In a funny sort of way I wondered who was in more need, him or his brother?

Roused he stumbled down the stairs looking about as dishevelled as I had done an hour or so before. He made coffee and we retired to the main room to play cards. We always played two rounds then went for a walk. I've never really understood cards but by then I had grasped the game we played and we usually came out evenly. With that we headed out into a bright and sunny summer's day for the short walk to the beach.

As we got there we chatted about films and mental illness - again that was normal for us. We always walked slowly and he loved to skim stones off the surface of the calm water. When I had first met him I had commented that "I used to do that when I was a kid." His splendid response was that "I have always been a kid."

It was fairly quiet down there as it was still early. He became more nervous when there were people around but on that day it was okay. As we walked our conversation was interrupted by the bleep of a text message coming though. This was slightly unusual in that people rarely contacted me when I was at work.

I took the phone out of my pocket and found a message from my sister Miriam. Very short it simply said "I'm not in London today". Slightly baffled I wondered if the message had been sent in error. She should be at work and she never contacted me from there unless it was an emergency. I had forgotten that very occasionally she worked out of the London office. Still rather mystified we continued our walk and the cryptic message slipped from my conscious mind.

As our allotted hour began to expire we headed back to the house. Once inside we arranged another appointment for the following week, I got back into the car and drove back towards the office. The sun was still shining on what was looming up to be another lovely summer's day.

Then it happened. The radio had been taken over by the news. The four young men who had been lurking in the shadows raging at the West emerged and seared themselves into our minds. They blew themselves up on three tubes and a bus in Central London. When all was told fifty two innocent people had been killed, hundreds wounded, and London paralysed. I had long predicted that the bombers would come to us one day. And that day was 7th July 2005. It was almost four years after 9/11. All four bombers died and in their view were headed to paradise and seventy two virgins. Who knew what the real truth was? But four young men had been radicalised enough to take their own lives and those of others. Their leader had been a teaching assistant in a school. It later transpired that he had been photographed by the security services but not deemed important enough to be followed up.

With that Miriam's bizarre text suddenly made sense and it occurred to me that I had better try to get hold of my many friends who lived and worked in London.

Back at the office we pretty much all set about doing that. Through phone and email I was able to ascertain that all my friends were safe although Tom usually travelled on one of the tubes that had been attacked. I got hold of Beka late in the afternoon as she struggled through the chaos on foot from the Oxo Tower to her then home in North London.

Very little work was done that day. We had our team meeting as usual but it was dominated by the bombing. Apparently word had come out of London that volunteers from elsewhere were needed to help people deal with the psychological impacts of the devastation. I volunteered but in the end nothing came of it.

When I got home I sat glued to the news coverage. Reports were often confused and chaotic. But that is always the case in war. And we were at war. It struck me what an awful irony it was. Just the previous day London had been awarded the 2012 Olympic Games.

That had been against the odds and the Games would return to these shores for the first time since 1948. The morning after the night before. The day before you came. From triumph to disaster in twenty four hours.

I went out that night with Beth to the pub in the middle of the High Street. It was a regular routine now. I can't remember if it was food night or music night, they alternated the two. But it was a sobering and sombre day that day.

I guess I always knew that would not be the end of it. Precisely two weeks later on 21st July a second attack was foiled only because the bombs failed to go off. No one was killed until later that day. With the would-be bombers escaping a young Brazilian electrician left his house to go to work. He knew not that he was being watched and followed. On a tube at Stockwell station he was shot dead by armed police. He was entirely innocent just as the victims before him had been. His name was Juan Charles De Menezes. The war claimed another victim; this time to friendly fire. Within a few days all of the real bombers had been caught. The war on the home front had begun.

Chapter 18
That Little Urn

On the face of it there was nothing remarkable going on in my life during the summer of 1989. I had just completed my first year at Cambridge. Much as I was loathe to admit it for all the triumphs of that first year I had been very lonely. Integrated though I was through my rugby, American Football, and singing, I still felt distinctly self-conscious at the many parties I attended. The big mistake I made when I got there was to hang out with friends I knew already rather than meet new people. Perhaps I should have braved the 6 o'clock starts and taken up rowing at the beginning.

With the term now over I faced the long, boring, and lonely summer back in Kent. There I was even more isolated than I was in Cambridge. In a house where war could and did break out at any moment, it was the last place I wanted to be. I yearned for the autumn to come and take me back to Cambridge. In retrospect I was probably depressed then, depressed but not mentally ill.

Little did I know during that long summer that in a few months Rachel would enter my life, turn it upside down then ultimately almost destroy it. Mental illness was far from my mind during that summer.

Of course in the real world huge changes were taking place - the Berlin Wall would most unexpectedly fall in a few months. But I didn't care about that; I was too wrapped up in my loneliness.

I went to Trieste for two weeks to sing but it was perhaps the least memorable of my many tours. But it got me away from home for a while. The other thing I did that summer was do a lot of driving practice. My test was scheduled for 1st September. This pissed me off slightly as it prevented me going on a short holiday with a couple of friends from school. That, however, was life.

But there was one thing that was remarkable about the summer which stuck in my head; it was an Ashes summer. The pinnacle of contests in the world of cricket, since the 19th century England and Australia had fought over a small urn that was kept at Lord's. It was alleged that the urn contained the ashes of the bails which had been burned to mark the passing of English cricket following a defeat by the Australians. Contested every four years in an English summer and two winters later in Australia, England were the holders going into the 1989 series. They had won it in Australia, a rare occurrence back in the winter of 1986/87.

That summer the contest was eagerly awaited and much of the cricket world felt that England would retain the Ashes. History would prove us all wrong. Australia thumped England in humiliating fashion and started a long reign of dominance.

Fast forwarding sixteen years my life was completely different. Following my devastating breakdown just after I had left Cambridge, I had barely survived. But now I was in recovery. I had Risperidone, Rachel had come and gone in my life, I had a job, I had a house, but more than anything else I had hope.

The summer of 2005 heralded the start of a new Ashes contest. So there I was, with many things going on but the Ashes to fall back on away from my crazy work world. And God did I need that. Against that backdrop I embarked on the next part of my strange journey.

At work I was still making my mark; I wanted to be noticeable this time. The new STR role was emerging driven on by the trendy recovery model. For some I was the epitome of recovery. Few of my friends barring James had got anywhere near as far I had. For some time recovery as a model had made me uneasy. What was the real motive behind it? Yes we wanted people to have better lives but was it realistic that they would appear to the world to be "cured"? From my perspective schizophrenia and bipolar could not be cured. Neither could what I had whatever we chose to call it. So were we looking for something else?

But I was perhaps in a small minority of "professionals" who saw the limitations. In its purest sense we would look to integrate people into all of the world, not just part of it. All of the world meant work, independent living, and no longer being a burden to the others who paid tax. Perhaps the payment of tax was the work thing that bound together the real world of recovery. Yet I was very nervous that something new and radical was being driven by financial motives rather than to actually help them live better lives. Maybe I had spent too long in the clutches of Supporting People.

Having said that I liked the more targeted, fluid, and short term interventions that the new model of care asked me to provide.

Those who for years had been utterly reliant on the efforts of Community Support were very pissed off. But the world had changed and we had to move with it.

Dan too embraced the new world more vigorously than some of the others who had been there for years. Both of us relished the challenge of working with people in crisis situations, the greater responsibility, and being more valued than we had been before. I came across the usual problem word of boundaries but I was determined to get it right through my experience rather than by what the "book" said. I didn't care how we did it, I just wanted the best outcomes.

My bipolar friend who had been so depressed for so long fell victim to the insecurities of the System. When I arrived back in the spring, word of what I had done for her at Rethink was well known and they allowed me to keep her. But it didn't last and her depression continued until the following spring.

Whilst people generally trusted me to get the job done I was still the lowest of the low in psychiatric pecking order. That was okay, as Heather had told me "you have to start at the bottom." My ambition was clear to those above me though and perhaps they sensed they would not keep me forever. It was a happy, well run, coherent team that summer.

Whether they feared losing me or not I feared losing them more. However good I was I was still only on a temporary contract and along with Dan was expected to re-apply for my own job in the autumn. Anxiety was never really a big part of my illness but as the summer progressed, fear of losing everything fuelled a rising anxiety about the future.

Away from the mad world, anxiety aside, life was good. The Ashes had got off to a most disastrous start as Australia hammered England at Lord's but we were fighting back taking an epic pair of tests at Edgbaston and Trent Bridge. Now it was a question of whether they could hang on.

At home my house was turning into a renowned party house. That was actually just carrying on the tradition that Tom and his sister Kate had set when they had lived there at separate times. I always had people coming and going. Thursday night was always my night with Beth when we went to the pub in the middle of the High Street then returned to mine for strong coffee, cheese and grapes, and Rioja on my part and vodka on hers.

Virtually every Saturday I cooked for friends. It might be one person or it might be ten but it happened every week. Marie often came down at weekends which was fun. I became so well known for buying unusual ingredients that the owner of the nearby fruit and vegetable shop once asked me which restaurant I worked for. Mandy kept me supplied with a wonderful selection of meat usually bought as I staggered in hungover at lunch time on a Saturday just before she closed. It was a popular place.

This did not go un-noticed by others. There was a taxi rank just outside and with so many people coming and going at all hours rumours began to circulate that I was running a brothel in there. And thus the legend of the Chapel Street Brothel was born.

On Sundays I nearly always went back to see my mum and dad for dinner. I don't think my mum ever came to Chapel Street and my dad only came a couple of times. But the Sunday arrangement suited me fine. I had my own life now.

Life was not all parties that summer though. I had undertaken the mammoth task of trying, as a complete unknown, to get my book published. From the advice of others it became clear that the key was to get an agent who would do it for me. Throughout the summer I slowly ticked off the list of every literary agency around and sent off to two or three at a time the required chapters, synopsis, and biography. As the summer progressed, each time the manuscript came back with a weighty thud and a short, terse, but pseudo polite letter telling me to fuck off. But every time I was rejected I carried on sending them out.

Those who read the manuscript raved about it but those who mattered, the faceless ones with the power didn't appear to care. Way back three years beforehand when I undertook the epic journey of writing it I knew the hardest part would be later. The literary world really didn't care about a nobody like me however good the book was.

But life went on as the summer began to wane. It was a most unexpected event when I came back to the office one sunny afternoon and Chris asked me to go out for a coffee with Dan. Slightly mystified by this request the two of us walked the short distance to a coffee shop owned by an acquaintance of mine, we got our cappuccinos, and sat down to talk. It was a revelation. Unknown to me, prior to coming to Social Services Dan had applied to train to be a psychiatric nurse at the Maudsley. Unexpectedly he had just been offered a place and was not sure what to do. My response was simple:

"Take it, you don't turn down the Maudsley".

And so I was set to lose a close friend but it was definitely the right thing for him to do. I would face re-applying for my own job alone. That made me more uneasy.

At the end of that first summer in my own little house, I turned 36 in the usual decadent style. Perhaps not quite as decadent as it might once have been but I still loved to party.

England held on to win the Ashes courtesy of Kevin Pietersen's maiden century when he scored 158 at the Oval in blistering style to force a draw. Finally, after sixteen years, the Ashes were back in England's hands. Many said it was the greatest Ashes series of all time; I did not argue with that.

It had been a memorable summer. Truly I had found where I was at the time. The question as I entered an uncertain autumn was could I hang onto it all?

Mark Edgar

Chapter 19
The Autumn Wind Blows Chilly and Cold

By the autumn of 2005 I was permanently carrying 3 mg of Risperidone with me. This was in response to a very unpleasant experience at a wedding the previous April. My old friend Jody who had been so helpful in the writing process of A Pillar of Impotence married in Nottingham. It was still the time of births, marriages, and deaths in my life. Jody's was the second of three weddings I attended in the space of a month. I travelled up by car with Beka and another friend Michael and stayed in a hotel for a couple of days. The wedding wasn't until quite late in the day so the three of us took lunch in a nearby pub. It was during that lunch that the subterranean lift crashed through the floor and the voices returned.

It had taken a single sentence from Beka said in all innocence. But the strange mechanisms of my frazzled mind exploded into action, made connections that to others would not have been obvious, and the psychosis switch turned on. My Risperidone was back at the hotel. Powerless I fought my demons throughout the day; I did not succeed very well. Feeding into the chaos was the belief that I was ruining Jody's big day. There was much relief when it was all over; I took a hit of Risperidone and calm was restored later that night.

This terrible event proved once again that I should fear a return of my madness. Ever since I have always carried an emergency stash of pills just in case.

Whilst that event came out of the blue, I knew that there were certain triggers I had to guard against. Sleep was essential but so was managing my stress. As summer turned to autumn that year I knew my stress would rise under the pressure of maybe being out of a job by the end of October.

So in the time that I normally enjoyed with the coming of the NFL and the autumn rugby internationals my mind turned to securing my future. The application form was already in and I now just had to wait.

The weeks running up to the interview disappeared in a rapid cyclone. Then I found myself once again in a room facing a panel of four people. This time I knew them all. It was the same service user as before; I was still very much in her good books which was a necessary need in those days. Chris was not on my panel. But Jill one of my colleagues was. She had told me previously that "you are very good at interview." I knew that but there was a senior manager chairing and he was man I had no time for.

The questions kept coming. There was nothing I did not expect. But unlike last time, I was asked to clarify some of my answers. The manager appeared most harsh although at times the counter questions of the service user were quite helpful.

With it all over I left in an unexpected confused mood. I wondered why on the earth the manager had been so harsh. But as I had learned before, what is done is done; none of us could ever change our pasts.

Fortunately I did not have to wait long to find out. I got my secured post and was due to be joined by two others. Kirsty was a woman I had known from Rethink. Whilst we didn't work directly together she worked for a service that used the top floor of our old office. She was a bundle of energy verging on the manic most of the time. We would also be joined by a woman called Lynne whom I didn't know. She would be part time. Of course both would have to work out notice in their other jobs and planned to join us at the end of October. None of us knew then that something so familiar to me yet alien to Lynne would one day draw us together.

With the stress put to one side and no need to take any emergency Risperidone hits I got on with the day job. Life was once again idyllic in my world. We were very busy as we no longer had Dan to help us. He was embarking on his course. Needless to say the amount of work did not reduce so we all had to do a little bit more. But that was fine with me.

September turned to October and the weeks flowed by until Kirsty and Lynne were due join us. There was nothing untoward on the horizon; the Chapel Street Brothel carried on in its usual vein.

That all changed when the weather turned colder at the end of the month. I was used to living in houses with central heating. In fact it never even crossed my mind that I needed to look for that when searching for somewhere to live. But Tom's house did not have gas central heating. When the weather turned I switched on the electric heating. It was not very effective but was at least slightly warmer than outside. I did have small gas fire in the front room and each evening I used this to augment what I had.

Cold and irritated I took each day as it came. My mood began to slowly sink as each day progressed and it was nearly time to go home. It was no longer homely.

This had been progressing for a couple of weeks when I woke up from a bad dream one night and went downstairs to have a cigarette. As I sat there in the gloomy darkness of the early hours I heard a strange whirring noise. Baffled I stumbled around in the darkness trying to find the source of this strange sound. My ears took me towards the cupboard that housed the gas and electric meters. Shining a torch in I saw the electric meter going round so fast with all the consumption it was actually making an audible noise. Knowing I could not afford to keep it like that I immediately shut the inadequate heating system down.

The next day I did a quick calculation and worked out that the one storage heater was actually costing me nearly £50 a week. There was no way I could do that, especially considering how little heat came out.

I called Tom that evening and he said he would immediately look into getting central heating put in as soon as possible. That would take time though.

As the last few weeks of autumn came and went my life took on a strange duality. Kirsty and Lynne had joined the team at Halloween. The former was like a fire ball consuming us all. Her infectious enthusiasm rubbed off on all of us. Lynne was more circumspect and kept a fairly low profile to start with.

It was still a happy and cohesive team even after our original manager had left to start another service. Her temporary replacement was in my eyes just as good. All was well at work.

Yet at night I returned to the gloomy cold of what had once been such a joyful house. There was little joy now. Each week I waited for news on the heating but none came. I was driven to seek shelter in the pub in the middle of the High Street more and more.

My mind's response was to sink ever closer into depression. I was depressed but not ill.

Adding to this was a rather strange incident that occurred around that time. I received a call one afternoon from an unknown senior manager demanding that I attend an interview with her and that I had the right to bring a union member with me. I was not a member of the union. I was baffled as to why this would occur but it was pretty clear that I had no choice.

She arrived in the office one afternoon when no one else was there. I still had no idea what she was there for. What transpired startled me. She more or less accused me of sending threatening letters to the fool who had been so arrogant in the health and safety training day back in the spring. Clearly someone had taken umbrage with his outrageous attitude and done something very foolish in response. And they seemed to think it was me. Raging and powerless I did what I could but she seemed unconvinced. As she left she told me she would let me know the outcome of the investigation. She also demanded to interview Dan. I told her that he had left the organisation and so was unavailable. She was not impressed by that.

The next week I complained to our new team leader. She was furious too commenting that "I will not have a witch hunt in my team." The interesting thing was that the OT from our team who had also attended the training was not contacted. So why me? I never heard any more about it but it sowed the first seeds of doubt in my new life working with the enemy. Could I trust them?

That all added to my depression as the final few weeks of 2005 began to wane and the cold really began to set in. I was in for a tough winter.

Chapter 20
The Frozen Tundra

As a young child I had spent very little time at home. I went away in 1978 having just turned 9 and did not really return until the infamous summer of 1991 when my life completely fell apart and I ended up in the place I called The Archbishop's Palace. As a family we moved from near Bristol to Kent in the summer of 1979, just a few weeks before my 10th birthday. From what I recall of Bristol it was often very wet. Kent was totally different. Being so close to France we had an almost microclimate more akin to that on the continent than the rest of the UK. Summers were often long and glorious with the weather holding on until October. Winters were usually fairly mild but when it did come in a bad way by God was it bad. Snow was rare in my part of east Kent but when it came we were usually cut off from the rest of the world by six foot snow drifts. I vividly recall the winter of 1981 the only year in my life that I have seen a white Christmas. That year it was so cold the sea water froze as the waves broke on the beach.

Unfortunately for me in my unheated house winter took a terrible revenge as the last few weeks of 2005 waned. Life took on the grim feel of fighting for survival. Each morning I woke up and sat in front of a small electric heater just to warm up. I had taken to wearing extra layers at night. I went to work each day and continued to thrive. But my mood was ebbing away with the return to the freezing house. Along with the cold came the damp. Spare pillows were getting mouldy, I couldn't dry my clothes when I washed them, and condensation on the windows froze to sheets of ice.

I tried as best I could to maintain my mood. I was still doing all my normal things but I had the feeling as we got to Christmas that it was only a matter of time before I became ill mentally and quite possibly physically.

For reasons I've never quite fathomed I asked for and got two weeks off that Christmas. In retrospect that was a big mistake. On Christmas Day I went to my mum and dad's as usual. It was a most sober affair as was their norm. By 5 o'clock I had had enough and walked the mile and half or so to my house. In a cold, dark, and gloomy end to the day I sat in an empty house and drank. Later I went to the pub but saw almost no one. A very sad day. But the following day beckoned for better things.

In my small part of east Kent the Boxing Day Run at the Castle Hotel in the village at the top of the hill was one of the social events of the year. It was also the heaviest drinking day of the year. Those who had moved away to get on with their lives usually returned to see their families over Christmas. Then we would all gather at the Castle for all day drinking. The run itself had been the brainchild of Tom's father Tim. Each year I joked with Tim that one day I would do the run. But as yet I have not done so. The only running on my mind was trying to force myself through the vast crowd to get to the bar.

As darkness fell on Boxing Day I finished in the pub and went for a curry. Heavenly to have been in the warm for most of the day. When the pub in the middle of the High Street closed it was back to the frozen reality that had become my life.

Just a few days later the long feared relapse exploded in my head. For three days I shambled around like a tormented ghost as I fought off my demons and voices. I increased my Risperidone by 50% and took my maximum dose of Trimipramine. It worked yet at New Year I was still but a shadow of my former self; there but not there. My psychosis when it came often took days or weeks to heal itself even after the voices stopped. It proved to be a New Year memorable for all the wrong reasons.

That first week of 2006 I yearned to return to work where at least I would be warm for much of the day. On the Sunday before I was due to return I woke with a very sore throat and terrible shivers. Once again I was struck down by a virus. Was it because of the cold or just coincidence?

When I finally returned to work a week later than planned I was still in low mood and very irritable. A simple question from a colleague on how my Christmas went was answered with a snappy recall of the terrible days of the holiday. That was not like me at all.

But there was one good thing on the horizon that January. My old friend Helen who had been so kind, generous, and helpful during the years of my madness would turn 30 at the end of the month. And there was a big party planned.

Just before the party Jayne phoned from Cambridge and said she planned to come along and surprise Helen. Owing to the cold in the house I advised her to deviate from our normal practice of one night at her friend's and one night at mine. Instead we arranged to go out for lunch the day after the party. But I knew there might be a problem as her ex was planning to come to the party. As Beth had once said "it was great around here until everyone split up with each other". My town was littered with broken relationships and it was so hard to not choose sides. I let Jayne know that he would be about but she said that was fine.

On the day of the party so many old friends gathered to eat and drink. All went well until we got back to my house. We huddled about ten people into my front room and carried on in the cold. Unfortunately some people I know are not great drunks and sadly on that evening Jayne's ex was one of them.

It was in the end a relief when everyone left. I called Jayne the next day but she said she wasn't able to meet. I didn't know it then but I would not see her again for near three years. A schism brought about by alcohol. Fortunately Helen was oblivious to all of this and enjoyed her night.

As January turned to February I was still battling through the cold. Tom eventually got a quote for the heating early in the New Year. It was twice what he expected and he couldn't afford it. So we were back in the round of getting quotes. Each week ticked by but still no help. It didn't get any warmer either. It was indeed a bitter winter.

It was not until March that it began to warm up. Maybe the coming of spring would lead to good things after my long dark winter.

Mark Edgar

Chapter 21
Us and Them

Throughout history people have strived to describe madness through the word, the image, and the sound. During the later years of my madness I had devoured such depictions. The books like Girl Interrupted, The Bell Jar, and Prozac Nation. There was of course a film made of the first of those books and along with such dark, disturbing, and frightening depictions as Repulsion. More latterly we have witnessed Black Swan. In 1999 I had journeyed to Amsterdam specifically to see Van Gogh and had marvelled at the late images such as The Raising of Lazarus and The Plough and the Harrow.

I too in my own lost and childish way had tried to describe my madness through my as yet unpublished account A Pillar of Impotence. Only time would tell whether that would ever see the light of day let alone be read by anyone not connected to me.

Yet there was one depiction that was to epitomise the world of the mentally ill in my era, Pink Floyd's haunting and iconic album Dark Side of the Moon. Released in 1973 when I was 4 it would be years before I connected the whole album together and realised what it was about but I did hear so many snippets through the media. All that at a time when Glam Rock was in vogue. It was so different.

The songs that always struck me on the album were Us and Them and Brain Damage. Who could resist the allure of a song that talked about the lunatics are in the hall, you lock the door and throw away the key, there's someone in my head but it's not me, and rearrange me till I'm sane? That song had become an all encompassing anthem for us lunatics.

Us and Them also was a very powerful image for me; my experience was so dehumanising that it did not reduce my isolation but stigmatised me more. That had changed though.

In the early spring of 2006 who had I become? I was doing what I swore I would never do and was working for the enemy. For a year it had felt at times as if my employers had been trying to get me to switch sides. There had always been a barrier up between those who used services and those who provided them. I was both which at times felt most uncomfortable. But what I liked about the STR role was that it provided important support at the right times yet was not too far into the System. I did not feel they owned me but I sometimes felt pressured to step further into their fold.

To me working for them was a means to an end. What that end was I didn't know but it was an important step. These were the ethical battles that lurked quietly in my mind. Did I have a loyalty? Well yes I did and most of the time it was to my people. It is for others to judge how good I am at what I do but the evidence suggested it worked even if at times it was an uncomfortable place to be.

Early that spring those thoughts were no more to the fore than usual. But they were about to take a more prominent position in my thinking.

When Dan had left the previous summer we had shared out his work until the reinforcements arrived in the form of Lynne and Kirsty on Halloween 2005. By that time the model of short term work was well established if still resisted by some of the old guard. Effectively we dipped in and out of their lives as and when it was needed.

What started as an apparently inconsequential walk triggered a chain reaction in my life. I was asked to do some short term input with one of Dan's old charges. She was very bright woman in her late forties who had a habit of disappearing when the going got difficult for her. She was a student on Open Door and for a couple of weeks I was tasked to help her re-establish herself at the college.

As we walked the short distance from her flat to the college rightly or wrongly I mentioned that I had been one of the first students on Open Door. Her response came rapidly without thought.

"Do they treat you as one of us or one of them?"
"Oh they look after me pretty well." I had paused slightly in my response as I knew it might be a comment that would be frowned upon by others.

But it was true, I was treated differently. I was still seeing a psychiatrist once every six months or so but could get help if I needed it very quickly. When I went to my blood test for my

Risperidone, I did not have to queue. My file was kept separately from those of my friends. On occasions with the electronic system we would later use there was the ethical pressure of discovering things about people we weren't supposed to know. I only did what was pertinent to my cases but I'm sure others were sometimes tempted.

That night when I went home my mind mulled over the curious duality of my life. I was party to so much of people's lives. I had access to files many of which did not reflect the people I knew. On the other hand I was well attuned to the jungle drums of the underworld that was mental health in East Kent. Very little happened without me knowing about it. I would usually hear about the overdoses and deaths long before my colleagues. Sadly that period of death was still in full flow then.

It was a very strange place to be and knowing what if anything to do with information if I had it. I did have a rule that I would not interfere with anything about my close friends unless I absolutely had to.

I'm not sure my special position always sat well with my colleagues but they were always happy that I could get access to funding from Rethink whereas they would not have known where to start. I was also at times able to fill in blanks for them and I guess I was appreciated for that. But I was still at the bottom of the food chain.

As March turned to April I reached the top of my pay band. From then on I could only progress if I undertook an NVQ III in Promoting Independence. In my eyes and those of many I worked with this would be a completely pointless exercise. But it was one I would have to do. In the strange world of mental health what really qualified any of us to do anything? I was not certain of the answer to that but I also knew it was very unlikely I would learn anything useful. But that would wait until the autumn.

Pay rise aside the other significant thing that happened that April was finally getting some heating in the house. I decamped to Sue's for a couple of days and when I returned the house was in carnage but at least I had heat. Over the following weekend I righted everything and cleaned up the mess. Although I didn't really need it I put the heating on for a few days just because I could. It was slightly off putting the smell emitting from the new boiler which reeked ominously of gas but I was reassured that that was normal with a new boiler. As things would transpire it was lucky I only smoked downstairs.

Now that it was warmer the party returned to the Chapel Street Brothel. Good things appeared to await us all in the coming summer. Work seemed good on the whole despite my reservations. I continued with my mind re-invigorated, my energy restored, and my passion for the mentally ill still burning.

There was not much expected on the horizon as the weeks passed by and what we hoped would be a glorious summer began to appear.

But as had happened too often in my life events beyond my control would once again engulf me in an unexpected maelstrom. Foremost of those was to be a severe testing of the them and us scenario that would lead me to question everything I was doing. Yet at the end of May I had no idea what was to come. As I had always said to my charges "we can't change the past or predict the future. But we can try to shape that future." Sometimes though our futures are forged by the actions of others.

Chapter 22
Prescott's Whore

Politics is a strange game that I do not profess to understand. By that summer the great New Labour project was in its ninth year. The man I once described as an obscure political figure had achieved something none of his Labour predecessors had done and won a third term in office. But all had not been well with the government for a long time.

Each step of the way Blair clashed with his chancellor Brown. There were other dark and dangerous figures in the party like Mandelson. He flitted in and out of government due to scandal and public disgrace. He was still a powerful figure who would later describe himself as the "Third Man". But was he really the third man?

Another figure with links to the past also loomed large in every sense of the word on the skyline. Prescott was the sop to old labour. He was a trade unionist through and through. He initially held two roles, as deputy prime minister and transport minister. He had made such a mess of the latter that that had been removed from his portfolio long before. But he remained as deputy PM and seemed to be a go between for the warring parties.

In the past he had been significant in my life as it was to him that the infamous Supporting People had reported. Effectively in my last job I had worked for him and it had not been a good experience. That summer I thought I had been away from him for over a year. But Prescott was about to re-enter my life.

Whilst Labour fought itself, a new man was rising from the shadows on the other side of the House. David Cameron had been elected leader of the Conservative party the previous December. He like Blair before him had once been an obscure political figure. But not now. Young and dynamic he might have been more Blair than Blair. And with him came the prospect of a change although it would be some time until the election battle would commence.

Elsewhere, the battles were far more real and dangerous. The world was aflame. Iraq stood on the brink of all out civil war. Sunni was killing Shia, and Shia was killing Sunni. Above all everyone was killing coalition soldiers. Thousands of civilians were still being killed every month and no one seemed to know what to do. Why did Al Qaeda need to fight in the west when the West had come to them? Would-be jihadists were pouring in from all over the world. In the south some were even whispering that the mighty British army had been defeated by an Iranian backed militia. They would eventually cede the city of Basra.

Further east in Afghanistan things were changing for the British. Based in the fairly quiet north since 2001 the British had suffered very few casualties. That summer they shifted area and took over the southern province of Helmand. A single battle group would go to support reconstruction over a vast area. When the move had been announced back in January, John Reid the defence minister had said "I hope it will happen without a shot being fired". How wrong he was. That summer the British army faced the toughest combat conditions since the slugging war that was Korea. There would be casualties; big casualties.

I lived a world away from all of that and it only hit me through the news and the fears that I had for the various relatives of friends I had who were in the forces. I lived in a quiet, forgotten seaside town and made a living trying to help out my people who fought more personal battles when their demons got on top of them. Whilst I was well and content not all was well with my friends; there was always someone struggling.

Two of my friends in particular were deep in trouble. Both had bipolar and both had stopped taking their medication. The inevitable happened and by June one was in hospital under section and the other one needed to go in. I had worked with neither but it made me feel most uncomfortable hearing the efforts that were being made to detain the other one.

But there was a need. It was always a sign when he started dressing in combats and generally causing chaos. He had a history of carrying weapons and posed a significant risk to others when he was unwell.

That June each team meeting brought more news of the fears of others. I saw him around but I certainly wasn't going to be the one who set in train the measures to deprive him of his liberty.

The knock on effect was that sleep that was so precious to my survival became harder to come by. Two weekends in a row I failed to sleep. That made me distinctly nervous. But it was about to get worse.

At the next team meeting we were told emphatically that if any of us saw him in public we were to immediately leave and call the police. The risk was simply too great. The following night, sleep eluded me once again.

On the Saturday night I was with friends in the pub at the bottom of the hill. Tired though I was it was a good evening and I still hoped for more sleep. My friend was far from my mind.

It was then that my phone rang. The call was from another friend Katie who was one of our secretaries at work. When I saw the number come up I was quite pleased to hear from her. But what I got was a very frightened voice.

"I'm in the pub and he has just walked in. I can't get out, he has me trapped. I'm hiding behind the bar. Please call the police quickly."

I tried as best I could to calm her down and promised to call straight away and get back to her.

With that I walked into the backroom of the pub that I was in and called 999. I asked for the police and explained the situation. The response I got was beyond belief. I was told that it was not an emergency and that I was wasting their time. I had to call the local station instead. Even trying to explain how dangerous he could be they didn't want to know.

After that I called the local station and explained the situation and they too did nothing. I called Katie back and she kept pleading to know if they were on their way. I couldn't answer that. Filled with fear for her safety I kept trying to convince her to get herself out of there. Eventually he left and she emerged utterly shocked and in fear. I felt an overwhelming sense of powerlessness. That was a very bad sign.

When I got home that night once again sleep would not come. I called Katie the next day to see how she was. She sounded okay but was I? I could feel the mental whirlwind beginning to build in my mind. Was I on the slippery slope back into the depths of my madness?

Unknown to me whilst I was in turmoil my friend who had trapped her walked into the local police station with weapons and demanded that they arrest Sarah our consultant for murder. They took the weapons off him and let him go. They knew he needed to be hospitalised and did nothing. Could I rely on anyone anymore?

Back at work on the Monday I checked to see how Katie was and recounted the story to others. Katie seemed to have come out of it reasonably intact. I was less sure. The others were shocked by what had happened. I didn't really think it could get worse but that week I became aware of two things that would take me to edge of the precipice.

At the Thursday meeting my world started to collapse. It was the day that Marie's case was referred from the intake team to the enhanced mental health team that I worked for. I knew her better than anyone ever had and had nurtured her and willed her to get better for so long. But now I was struck by a hammer blow. In the referral she was deemed by the consultant to have a personality disorder. I knew this was wrong but could do nothing. The word of an STR worker or a consultant psychiatrist; who held more power? I knew from that moment she was doomed and would be deemed beyond help. They rejected the referral.

Something else happened during that fateful ninety minutes that had even more impact. It was that day that I learned that unbeknown to me my post was being funded by Supporting People and they were about to take over my life once again.

Only I really knew the folly of that momentous decision. It seemed that the mental health team thought they were getting money for nothing. But Supporting People had now put their foot down and completely changed the ethos of what I was doing. I raged openly and inwardly about that decision. But like everything, what could I do?

Floating support as it was known was the very antithesis of what STR was. They wanted us to completely change people's lives in two years. I knew they would drive me into the ground but no one else seemed to heed my warnings.

My soul had been sold to the devil and that devil's name was John Prescott. I had been prostituted to a political entity that fraudulently claimed to help the vulnerable but in reality was trying to get them off the books.

I for one wanted no part of it and decided that night that I needed to move on. But where? As June ended and another week was over I was losing my balance on the edge of the cliff. The time was set for mental meltdown.

Chapter 23
Ferry Ride Across the Styx

Is there a place more lonely than to be locked in the madness of one's own mind? The place where no one hears one's cries and all around is utter darkness. In the comparatively early days of my own descent people talked about being in a dark lonely tunnel where they sought light at the end. Once when I was talking to my bipolar friend John I had tried to describe my visualisation. I was not walking in or standing on the hard floor of that tunnel but floating in an abyss where I had no anchor points. Emotionally I was utterly dead save for the deluded and chaotic relationship that I had with Rachel, the one whose voice so utterly haunted me. At that stage I was still seeing her for real from time to time. That all stopped on a day in 1995 when we had a pleasant and quiet drink on the banks of the Thames. I certainly had no inkling I would never see her again. Maybe she did but gave no hint. Strange how our lives are so changed by unlikely twists of fate that defy logical thought. After that her voice still haunted me until that momentous day a week before 9/11 when I found the Holy Grail that I had sought for a decade.

The truth of madness is that it is created of our own minds and is unique to each of us and the lives we have lived. To me it was an underworld where we were neither alive nor dead. Many faiths have a concept of the soul and an after life of sorts. My understanding of the faith that had been forced on my life was of a wonderful heaven and a tormented hell. But through my madness I lived in my own personal tormented hell. And it was an utterly lonely place.

After I found the salvation I sought in this life I forever feared a return to that underworld, the world of the mad. I had glimpsed it on occasion but the power of Risperidone had brought me back from crossing the boundary into the underworld. The ancient Greeks had had a defined boundary to the underworld; the river Styx. Was a descent into madness about crossing the Styx? Perhaps the image is an apt one.

As June turned to July that summer I knew there was a coming storm. I was physically exhausted from overwork and lack of sleep. I was mentally exhausted from the challenges of having a foot in both camps, that of the madman and that of the curer. The strain of that summer and working for the enemy had been building but the final straw was the realisation that they had betrayed me and sold my soul to the devil. Pink Floyd had used the words if the dam breaks open many years too soon...and if cloud burst, thunder in your ear, you shout but no one seems to hear for that moment of crossing the Styx.

The dam of my mind finally broke on the first Friday of July 2006. I had left work a little early that day as I had to go to my surgery to drop off my repeat prescription. The intention was that I would go in a little late on the following Tuesday to pick it up and collect new pills to replenish my very low stocks. That evening I went to the pub at the bottom of the hill to celebrate my friend Donna's birthday. Only a year younger than me I had met her at a low point in her life having just left a very unhappy fifteen year marriage. I was never really sure how it had come out but my inquisitive mind had coaxed some parts of the story out over the years. Later she once said to me "do you know why I don't come round to your house very often? Because you can see into my soul and I don't like it". But on that day she was happy.

We sat at the bar but my mind was elsewhere; it was aflame with the vortex of the coming madness. I said little, I shrank on my bar stool and my eyes narrowed to the slits that were the only viewpoint for my craziness. They were what hid me from the scrutiny of the world. It was all going wrong.

"For fuck's sake will you cheer up, you're doing my fucking head in." The words of someone who knew so little of my underworld.

I mumbled a response of a few words. But I knew I had to act. I asked for a glass of water from the bar and took the small pill box that had been my constant companion since the previous year out of my pocket. I took the three Risperidone tablets one by one with a sip of water. With that I prayed that they would kick in and bring me back from the brink. Within an hour they had slowed my mind but not enough to save me.

Feeling very unsafe and paranoid, and not wanting to ruin Donna's night I took my leave early and headed back to my cottage. When I got there I rolled a spliff and opened a beer. I was hoping they would help but they did little but cloud my mind more. When I was too tired to stay up any longer I went upstairs and trebled my anti depressant. Then I climbed into bed and slept the sleep of the dead.

I woke up late but I was still firmly in the darkness of my underworld. Alarmed I realised that this was something very different to anything I had experienced since 2001. It was going full blown.

Alone in the house I wondered where her voice was. She was nowhere to be heard although Rachel was dominating my conscious thought. Neither did I hear the man's voice. Who was he? I didn't know the answer to that but the thoughts that prompted him to come were also very prominent. Suicide was once again my constant companion. In retrospect the Risperidone was holding the voices off but I was at that stage where psychosis seemed inevitable. I was in the fuzzy grey area between sanity and insanity.

Throughout that Saturday I stumbled about the house in a cocooned daze. Thoughts kept coming and those thoughts were only of a way out. I feared the reaction of others so stayed in until the evening. I knew that if I wasn't there people would wonder where I was so I went to the pub in the middle of the High Street. I said almost nothing and what I did say was short and devoid of meaning. Yet all the time I surveyed the world through my narrowed eyes. When I had worked at Rethink one of the women that I worked with had described her depression as like being behind a glass screen through which she could see but neither speak nor touch. She thought I was the only one who had ever ventured through that glass barrier. She was of course right. As I sat there I knew I was behind that screen, I could see the world but I could not touch the place beyond. And all along the lure of suicide kept dragging me deeper into the abyss. But this time I was resisting. For all the mental collapse I knew I had the weapons to fight it now.

The next day nothing had changed. The trebled medication was holding me but only just. With that came thoughts of running out. I was down to two days' supply. It was too terrifying to contemplate what life would be like without Risperidone for even a couple of days. I knew then that I had to call in sick the next day and go and see my Doctor. My Doctor, the brilliant Claire who was one of the few GPs I had ever met who had even an inkling of my madness.

In the evening I went to see my mum and dad for dinner. The silence continued. It was a relief to get home, take the pills and go to bed.

The last thing I needed in that state was having to get up early in the morning. But that was precisely what I did on that Monday morning. I called work about 8.30 to tell them I wouldn't be in. I knew it would be at least a week so I told them I would update them as and when. Straight after that I called the surgery to try to get to see Dr Claire. Sadly she was not available that day but they offered me an appointment with someone else. Having little choice I accepted on the spot.

Later that morning I went to the surgery and met a charming young Asian Doctor. I think Dr Claire must have put a warning sign in my notes because much to my surprise he was most interested and attentive. He gave me a new prescription which solved my immediate problem and told me to come back in a week if I needed to.

Whilst that was a nightmare for me missing a week of work I knew I had to face the reality of my situation; there would be no quick fix this time.

Each of the coming days brought the same. I shambled about a shadow of my former self and tried to look normal. But my thoughts did not shift all that week. They just became darker.

Worst of all was the astonishing sense of failure and emptiness. It felt as if all I had achieved had been for nothing. I was back at the bottom of the psychiatric heap. It was not supposed to happen to me. I was the one who had got out; the one who proved that recovery was possible; the one who showed an example to the others. And I had failed.

With that came waves of expectation. Some of these came from others but most I piled on myself. I may have been brilliant at bringing others out of their madness as some would have had me believe but I was completely incapable of bringing myself out. And I was too proud, stubborn, and arrogant to let anyone else help me. In reality I had gone back to being one of us. Everyone who really knew me saw it and did what they could but nothing shifted.

By Friday I knew I would have to go back to see the young Asian Doctor and ask for a sick note. That in itself would be an admission of failure - I had not done that since I started work at least not for those reasons. In my head it was okay to be ill with the flu but not okay to be mentally ill. I had come too far to admit that. But what choice did I have?

When I saw him I asked for a sick note for a week. He wanted to sign me off for two weeks. That rather surprised me and further damaged my fragile ego but he persuaded me of the sense of that option despite the confirmation in my mind that I had failed. I came away in a very mixed state but finally submitted to his advice.

The following day I chose to go into work to give them the sick note. I could have sent it in the post but my old suspicions that they thought I might be faking it came to the fore. With the exception of Sarah, only two of the team had ever seen me ill, Andrew my old CPN and Lucie who had got her first OT job there in the old days of the Day Service.

As I went in there were stunned looks as they took in the enormity of the transformation in me. I will never forget the looks on their faces as this shambling wreck of human being walked slowly through their midst. I spoke briefly to Suzanne our then team leader. She told me to take all the time I needed and promised to phone me the following week. But I was determined I would be back and challenged myself that I would return after those two weeks.

For the rest of that week I fought my demons and the knowledge that the longer I was off the harder it would be to return. And if I didn't go back it would confirm my terrible sense of failure. Failure was not an option though.

As the days passed the extra sleep, the increased Risperidone, and the cutting out of stress slowly brought me back from the gates of hell that awaited me if I got worse.

By the second week I felt more myself. I decided on a change of scenery so headed off on a boat trip to France. I never really got off at the other end but merely bought supplies of cigarettes and tobacco. It was whilst I was on the return journey that Suzanne called. I explained that I couldn't really talk but that I planned to go back the following Monday. The thought crossed my mind that if I was well enough to go to France I was well enough to go to work. As always happened when I was getting better I felt even more of a fraud. Another demon to fight.

Yet fight I did and made my return as planned on the fourth week of July. My pride and foolishness stopped me taking the option of phased return and I achieved nothing that first week. But going back was enough to bring me out. I was alive again and back on the road at the end of the month.

The whole experience had been stunningly unexpected. I knew I needed to learn from it and determined never to go there again.

I mused over the rest of the summer about my vulnerability. I marvelled too at the power of Risperidone to make me recover. Before that it would have taken months if not years. It had held the voices at bay throughout and had brought me back to life. But life was different now and I needed change. At the end of August I turned 37; time once again for a new beginning.

Chapter 24
Tapas, Tinto, and Thieves

My musical talents had taken me to many places over the years. At 10 I had sung for Prince Charles. By 13 I had met the present emperor of Japan and sung in that extraordinary country. My 14th birthday was marked by a post concert party with the Governor General of Australia present. By the end of that tour I had sung in Sydney Opera House a total of six times. The next few years took me to many of the great cathedrals of Europe including the Duomo in Florence, Sacre Coeur in Paris, and the astonishing former mosque in Seville. After I got ill I still toured each Easter until 1993. My last choir tour was in the summer of 1996, a trip on which I had suddenly gone psychotic during Zadok the Priest in the middle of Chartres cathedral. That was my seventeenth and final choir tour to date.

In the days after my madness started I continued to tour. The final trip before my complete breakdown had been a wonderful if disturbed visit to Barcelona. By that stage my mind was in chaos leading up to my final term at Cambridge; that trip had been my final hurrah before I collapsed completely mentally.

I had been abroad on a few holidays but they were far less frequent than my working travels. Money had simply not been there too often. But when I did have money I liked to go for short holidays, sometimes with others, sometimes alone. After I found Risperidone I had a couple of times tried to recapture some of my lost time by going to older places. After I started work in 2002 I revisited Seville. By the summer of 2006 my mind was once again reaching to far away places.

Even before my recent relapse I knew I needed a holiday and I settled on a return to Barcelona just as summer turned to autumn. With my birthday occurring the week of the August Bank Holiday it had become my habit to book two weeks off each year. My plan now was to travel that first week of September to try to recharge my batteries in the run up to the mayhem of work beginning again. I had really hoped to go with Beth but sadly she was unable to take the time off work. So once again I would go into the unknown alone.

I should have taken it as an ill omen when the flight cost much more than had been advertised. Since the advent of the internet everyone seemed to think it was easier to get a cheaper holiday by doing it oneself rather than through an operator. With my very expensive ticket in hand I set about getting somewhere to stay. I didn't have a computer or the internet at that stage so there were frequent visits to my mum and dad's to use his. Each time I tried to book a hotel it fell through. When I eventually got one the cost was huge for a very mediocre place. But I was determined to go and was all set by early September.

The night before I flew from Gatwick I stayed at Tom's place in London as it made the travel easier. His then girlfriend and now wife had a flat in Earl's Court. They had a dog which disturbed me - I had never been a fan - but I could put up with that.

Quite early the next morning I got ready, took my bag, and walked to the tube. I got lost and my stress began to rise alarmingly. Fearing I would miss my flight I fought through the crowds to Victoria. From there having paid an exorbitant amount for a ticket I took the Gatwick Express making it with a little time to spare. What confronted me was one of the biggest queues I have ever seen. A couple of months before a jihadist plot had brought the airports to a standstill with the threat of liquid bombs. The backlash of security was astonishing leading to all liquids being banned on flights and bringing about huge delays.

After three hours queuing I finally went through the gate and waited. But my unusual anxiety did not abate. I became convinced that my bag would get lost and I would be left without my precious Risperidone. Anxiety had never really played much of a part in my illness except in my dealings with the DWP. But now it was rampant.

Fortunately in those days they still had small smoking areas so I sought refuge there until boarding. I had had to throw away my lighter before going through security as it was deemed a risk. I had to borrow a light and decided that the first thing I would do when I got there was to buy another one.

When I finally got there my bag emerged unscathed and my anxiety subsided. I took a taxi to the hotel, a place just overlooking Sagrada Familia which I had visited in 1991. Having briefly settled I stepped forth into the late afternoon to check out the scenery, and in my world that meant bars. I found some good ones where I ate fine tapas, drank cervezas and tinto, and smoked endless Fortunas from the soft packs I so liked. As the evening drew to a close I sat in the small bar just down the street from the hotel trying desperately to communicate with the barman who spoke almost no English. We had but one common ground, football. Spain was due to play Northern Ireland the following evening and he very kindly asked me to join him to watch. As I lay down to sleep it was on my mind, the kind gesture of this stranger. Tomorrow would be a good one.

It was a beautiful and warm autumn day as I emerged late in the morning in search of café solo and Fortunas. Settling in a nearby bar I took a while to get back into the world. I took a leisurely lunch of tapas in another bar washed down with a cerveza. With that I made what for me was a very brave decision and headed for the metro. One of the few remnants of my illness that still affected me was a chronic loss of direction; I feared getting lost more than anything else. But I made it to the Ramblas and wandered around taking it all in. Memories of all those years before flooded back, some good some bad. I looked for the bar near the beach that we had frequented back then but could not find it. Settling elsewhere I ate more tapas in a haze of cigarette smoke.

Late in the afternoon I sat in a relaxing bar whilst I contemplated what I would eat that evening and the promised football match. Nothing seemed out of place.

Leaving the bar I got back on the metro and headed back to the hotel. The plan was to go back, shower, then set up a fine meal. As I got to my room I felt in my pocket for my key. I found the key but my wallet was gone. Barcelona is notorious for its pickpockets and it seemed I had been yet another victim. I subsequently checked with the last bar I had been in to see if I had left it but to no avail.

Overcome with panic I went down to reception to ask their advice. I called Visa to cancel my card then somehow managed to get hold of my dad. After that I headed out for the police station to report the theft. They were very helpful but didn't hold out any hope. Having spent a couple of hours there I went back and for the first time realised how hungry I was. But I only had the change in my pocket so there was little I could buy; my fine dinner never happened.

As the evening drew on I was exhausted. Remembering the invitation from the barman I went along the road and watched the remnants of the match nursing the single cerverza I could afford. Northern Ireland upset Spain and won a famous victory. A good day for them, a disastrous one for me. I slept very poorly that night.

Most of the next day was spent at a high level of stress. I managed to get hold of Tom and my dad both of whom offered to wire me some money. For someone who so feared technology the joys of email were a Godsend. By late in the afternoon I knew that 200 euros would be wired to a Western Union branch just round the corner from the hotel the following day.

With that sorted I had a look round the Sagrada Familia to do the tourist things. It was packed and uninviting if impressive. In the evening I spent the last of my change on some food and settled in for another uneasy night. I had long held the mantra that I would never believe anything until it actually happened. Until I had got that money the stress would not subside.

In the end I picked up the money late in the morning. I only had two days left to try to make it a good holiday. For those two days I cautiously partied. I tried to find the cathedral I had sung in all those years ago but my fear of getting lost got the better of me. I did manage to find La Boqueria, that Mecca for foodies like me. With that the memories came flooding back.

On the last morning I went to a tabac and bought a few cartons of Fortunas. I had planned to buy enough for several months but with my card stolen I was stuck. I headed to the airport early and found it remarkably deserted. Unlike Gatwick there were no queues and I had no real need to check in early. I regretted going in early as the promised smoking area did not seem to exist.

The flight was okay but tinged with regret. With the money I had lost four nights away had cost me nearly £700. And for what? It had been disaster. I was certainly not refreshed. I was facing a tough autumn and winter in a job I was trying to leave and the unenviable task of insurance claims. I had never fared well in those and true to form they charged me the earth and still failed to make a complete pay out.

All seemed set for another cataclysmic slump in my mood. But then something most unexpected happened; my mood rocketed upwards and stayed there for months. I never did anything crazy when I was like that but I did become even more arrogant and annoying than normal. For me though it as a very good place to be.

Mark Edgar

Chapter 25
The Team Implodes

Stress is a very strange thing. Do any of us really know why it affects different people in different ways? It has for years been a strange comment that covers a multitude of sins and is a favourite on Doctor's sick notes or as they are now called fitness notes. After I found Risperidone all my stress such as it was disappeared. Work had never really been stressful after that; I was merely talking to my people as I had done for the past eleven years but now getting paid to do it. That all changed when I went to Rethink. I was fine for ages when I started but when Supporting People were intent on grinding me into the dust odd things began to happen. I had a couple of really nasty viruses in the autumn of 2004 which were probably related to the pressure. I also put on weight. At the time I wasn't sure what it was. Maybe middle age spread. I certainly wasn't eating or drinking any more nor was I doing less exercise.

As soon as I left Rethink I lost three quarters of a stone almost overnight. That improved my mood no end along with the joy of being away from Prescott's dominion. But the stress would come back in another form. I don't really recall when the nightmares began. I had on and off been affected by strange dreams throughout my years of illness. Yet by that autumn they were an almost daily occurrence. I was up at least three times a night, sometimes five times smoking cigarettes downstairs and watching the sun come up. I didn't feel very stressed at that stage but clearly something was up.

The stress of work such as it was was not confined to me. The team I returned to that September was slowly sinking to its knees. It had been in almost open warfare with the area manager for months. Chris had been redeployed to focus on the dreaded Supporting People agenda. We were facing a new locality manager whom I had not yet met but I knew her reputation amongst service users; not good. Sickness rates were soaring and people were starting to turn on each other. That combination was tantamount to disaster in a mental health team. And still the work kept coming.

Not much of this mattered to me during the strange mini high that struck me unexpectedly after the holiday debacle. I was sailing serenely on full of energy and only partially affected by the nightmares.

With Chris having moved elsewhere I now had a new supervisor. An experienced part time social worker she proved the only professional who ever recognised the upper end of my mood. As she pointed out quite early "I know when you're not well as you speak very fast, you're very opinionated, and difficult to talk to." She was of course right and she knew I was in that stage now. Such a state didn't really impact on me in a negative way but later it would lead to disaster. It would also later transpire that that had something to do with my break with Jayne. But all that was in the future.

The other big change in my life at work was my return to my former college to do the long delayed NVQ. I considered it a complete insult to my intelligence but I was required to go through the hoops to get paid more. Every other Thursday I went back to my old haunts. My new supervisor also suggested that I work from home on the other Thursday so that I could get it done quicker. It was a strange experience going back. I worked in mental health in the community, everyone else on the course worked in learning disability residential units. So our worlds were very different and when I did talk about my work they all seemed alarmed at the apparent risks I was taking.

They were all pleasant to be with but what made it even vaguely interesting was that our lecturer had previously been a senior support worker at Social Services in mental health. So at least she knew something of my work.

September turned to October and all around me my colleagues were succumbing. NVQ and Supporting People apart my life was good. I loved the elevated mood even if it pissed some other people off. I anticipated the usual autumn. I was still vaguely looking around for other jobs but not really knowing where to start. What I didn't realise was that three things were about to happen that would take me on a new course.

I was still getting rejection after rejection on my book but kept going. That October it crossed my mind that the makers of Risperidone Jassen Cilag might be able to help. Why I didn't think of it before I had no idea but I spoke to their drug rep and he suggested I email it to them. I did this and quickly got a very positive response with the news that it was going on up the hierarchy there. They seemed to think it was great. So maybe there was hope.

A week or so after I went on a two day workshop entitled "Psychosis Revisited". It was being brought over from Sussex by a psychologist called Mark and he planned to use service users to help. This was unheard of in my experience in Kent. Yes I did such workshops but only privately. When I went it was revelation to me and seemed to invigorate my colleagues. It was unusual for STR workers to go on such training but it proved most helpful to me. Meeting Mark and his colleague Ruth proved key elements in my journey. I chatted to both of them and talked a little about my own experience of psychosis and they suggested I might like to come along to present at a future event. Now that was an idea I relished.

Just as things seemed to be coming together in other places I finally made a breakthrough on the job front. I'm not sure what drew me to the Guardian website in the first place but looking one day the job was staring me in the face. A university on the outskirts of London was looking for a Mental Health Advisor. And they were offering almost half as much money again as I was making at Social Services. Hurriedly I sent off for the application form and job description. They were demanding quite a lot but I knew I could do it. In fact it seemed quite straightforward. I filled in the form as best I could making great play of my lived experience. There was one bonus to having a disability in that employers were obliged to interview the disabled if they met the minimum requirements. I could not see any problem with that. They were not asking for a qualification I didn't have so I thought I had a guarantee of an interview. Suzanne seemed to feel the same too and was delighted to act as referee.

October seemed to end on those high notes; hopes for change. But it did not go as expected. The date of the job interview came and went and I heard nothing. Somewhat confused I called them. All they told me was that they had had many applicants. What had happened to a guaranteed interview? The law was there to protect yet in this case it had clearly been flouted. Annoyed I called the Disability Rights Commission. They were quite helpful but I decided not to pursue it; surely that would jeopardise any future attempts. And attempts there would be in the coming months. It seemed many universities were looking to fill such posts.

Back in what passed for working reality the infighting and casualties continued as autumn gave way to a wet winter. The one thing that was holding the team together was our occasional evenings out for a curry or a meal in the pub. These had reached almost legendary status amongst us and the public who saw us. On one famous curry occasion with three of our team dancing on the table a fellow diner asked me who we were. When I replied that we were the local mental health team he commented that it looked a fun place to work and he would know where to come if he had any difficulties.

Of course these events were the exception and one of the few cohesive parts of our working life. It was far from a fun place to work then. But in my elevated mood I was having fun.

In the run up to Christmas all of my STR colleagues were either off long term sick or in one case on a six week holiday to Australia. I faced Christmas alone but buzzing. It was around that time when I met one of my greatest success stories. Norma had been in hospital for six months and I was tasked with getting her reacclimatised to the world. So started a fantastic and twisting journey that we would share and continue until well after I had moved on.

The staff Christmas party took place in Canterbury on a wet December day which forced us to drive through floods. The night was up to our usual standards of partying although the food was poor. Sarah's credit card took a hell of a battering. Not what she was expecting but she took it with her usual good grace. In grim times it was good to unite even if it was only one night.

Away from work I went on a mad spending spree. For some reason I decided to get all my friends presents. A sign perhaps of my soaring mood it seemed the right thing to do. I also invited everyone to my house in the evening of Christmas Day.

When Christmas finally came it was the finest one I could remember. I went to the pub in the middle of the High Street on my way to my parents' house. We ate lunch and did presents. Feeling very full I left and walked home at about 5 o'clock. I had a bath then started drinking in earnest. My friends arrived about 8 o'clock and we drank champagne long into the night and ate tapas. It was a magical day.

Boxing Day was also a great day, the run, good beer, and a curry to finish. Of course I was merely providing moral support to all those brave runners; forcing my way through the crowds was the nearest I got to expending any energy.

I had to work a couple of days between Christmas and New Year but with my present energy that was no problem. I went to a party on New Year's Eve but did not enjoy it much so I got a cab and went to the pub. There I partied long and hard and contemplated what the future held. And so I entered a decisive year of my life. 2007 would take me to an unexpected place. But being mortal and flawed I could not see beyond the horizon of my present.

Mark Edgar

Chapter 26
Wanderings in the Land of Limbo

Is there really any better way to understand a field than through lived experience? It was at times a lonely place for me in the mental health world of east Kent. I was the one who had got out whereas many of my friends were just as stuck as they had ever been. Us and them still existed. There were some who almost lauded my abilities in the field as I was supposed to really know. Others derided me as almost selling my soul to the devil. I didn't really see it as that. I was merely using it as a stepping stone to go somewhere I knew not. I had been working full time for four years by the winter of 2006/07. I had found mental health by accident as they had given me a job when no one else would. Many had suggested I should train to be a social worker. But that idea was flawed on two counts. Firstly having gone virtually bankrupt training to be a teacher only to be rejected over and over again, I simply couldn't afford to retrain again. Secondly that would draw me further into the realm of the enemy and would in my eyes really be switching sides. There were pressures to do so even in my current role. During my madness I had sworn I would never work for them. Many had wanted to train but few did. That was precisely what I didn't want to do but circumstances had taken me into uncharted and unexpected territory.

As such I was placed under enormous pressure from both sides of the divide to take a firm stance one way or the other. I certainly enjoyed working with individuals but struggled with all the other bullshit that goes with being employed. I was the lowest in the food chain and so was the least paid. But what did STR workers really do? It was us that did much of the difficult dirty work when people were in crisis. For good or ill care co-ordinators spent little time with their charges and way too much time bogged down in paperwork. But they were paid more because they held greater responsibility.

So what did I really know? I knew all about medication having taken so much over the years. Hospital too was familiar to me. I had a trail of success working with people with long term illness not how to cure but how to live with them. But above all I spoke our language. And I knew how to listen and bring in similar experiences from my years in the wilderness. People told me far more than they ever would others as they knew I would understand and I had no power. I had the energy and drive to be successful most of the time. And I was tuned into the grapevine knowing far more about what was really happening than my illustrious and more highly paid colleagues.

That made it hard at times working out what to share and what to keep. This in itself added to the pressure on me. I was after all one of the few openly mad workers in the region. It was so far from anywhere that the thought that others had made it out like I had seemed a remote possibility. My eyes had been somewhat opened to the possibilities that others existed through meeting Emma and Ruth. Emma helped service users get into work in the Trust in South West London. Ruth was as well working for Mind although she told me even there she was discouraged from disclosing.

It was still frowned on when I did disclose in my area but not by the service users. That old dirty word boundaries surfaced still on occasion but often when the shit was hitting the fan they would call me in despite my connections. Suicide was the one we all feared and by God did I know about that. It was still so fresh in my mind the mechanics of how I had got there. More importantly I knew how to come back across what I called the line in the sand. Some revered me for having that talent.

But what was it all for? Without the piece of paper that described this or that, how could I possibly move on? And move on was what I wanted to do. I had already outgrown what I was doing.

Coming across the university roles had been a Godsend but so many of them would only consider a social worker, nurse, or psychologist for such a role. There were jobs almost weekly but I couldn't apply for any of them. And those I did apply for rarely if ever got back to me. So much for the Disability Discrimination Act 1995 (DDA 1995), (now superseded by the Equality Act 2010) and the protections it was supposed to offer.

Yet none of that really mattered to me that January. Unlike most people with a mood disorder there was no particular seasonal pattern to my shifting moods. With the exception of the freezing winter of 2005/06 Christmas cheer had usually kept me afloat until after the Super Bowl in early February. If there was a time I found difficult it was during the cold, wet darkness of February and March. I had been riding the crest of my mood wave since the unexpected events of September. Yes I wanted to get a new job but I was still enjoying my elevation even if others didn't. No one except my supervisor commented on that. In fact no one seemed to notice.

In mid January I got another ego boosting jolt when Ruth phoned and asked if I would like present my story at the next Psychosis Revisited workshop in Canterbury. There was a small fee of £175 which certainly would aid my sometimes complicated and precarious financial situation. More important than that though it was a chance to have my voice heard. That had been so rarely listened to in my years of "treatment". The only downside was that it was due on the morning after the Super Bowl so I would have to get up very early. I had in recent years been in the habit of taking that day off so I could travel to Miriam's to watch with my brother-in-law. This year I would take a day of annual leave but for a different purpose.

Ruth was proposing to stay with a friend in Folkestone and travel up early the next morning on public transport. But that made no sense to me so I offered to come over and pick her up.

On Super Bowl Sunday I spent a pleasant evening with her in the underground bar that had been my local when I had lived there. I watched as much of the Super Bowl as I could and recorded the rest.

Getting up absurdly early the next day I went to Canterbury via the circuitous route of Folkestone to pick Ruth up. Parking aside it was an amazing day and the delegates seemed to find my story most interesting. It was also fun to see them trying to draw psychosis in one of the exercises. My picture was rooted in self with a sad eye crying tears of blood and speech bubbles telling the world of my voices. Some found this disturbing but then again it should have been; my psychosis was deeply disturbing. Yet so long ago now.

I came home exhausted with little sense of the people who were there. Ruth called in the evening to say how helpful they had found it. So another ego boosting success. I watched the rest of the Super Bowl contented and upbeat. But could I sustain it in forthcoming dark months?

Unfortunately such places cannot last for ever. What goes up must come down and even though I did not go into freefall as I had the previous summer my mood lowered throughout February and

March and I found myself unhappy but not depressed. I was not ill but in a kind of limbo of nothing.

The infighting at work and the pressure continued; with so many people off sick the work did not lessen. It just meant that those of us who were there had to work harder.

Our new manager proved utterly unapproachable and pissed off almost the entire team by trying to change a well trusted system. We may have been flawed along with the System but at least service users had a named contact which meant consistency. Since the services had integrated smaller sub teams existed called pods which meant that it was comparatively easy to cover when staff were off. But the new manager wanted to do away with that and go to a traffic light system. Fine until someone we hadn't seen relapsed and we didn't know. The great strength of our two previous managers was their open door policy. More than once I had been able to see either of them at the drop of a hat. But no longer.

With each passing day of the winter I came home more disillusioned and angry. I was still getting rejections on my book as well as from universities who simply wouldn't look beyond the farcical paperwork and recognise I could do the job. I knew if I could get an interview I could shine. But where would it come from?

In the meantime I just tried to keep going. My amazing friends usually helped. Beth still came every Thursday, Saturday I would always cook for people, and Sue and Duncan in the pub proved a great support. Yet how long could I sustain this? And where would the break come from?

It actually came in the form of a partial book success. Janssen Cilag was still making encouraging noises and it was I'm told up at board level being read. A friend had come across a publisher in Brighton and on a whim I decided to send it off. Until then I had focussed exclusively on agents. This publisher unlike most others would accept manuscripts directly from authors and look at them so I sent it off.

About a week later an envelope arrived. It had my writing on it and was the return advice. But this time it was not a big fat envelope padded out by the returned and rejected sheaves. The letter inside was asking me to send the complete manuscript. Finally a little opening. Who knew where it might lead?

The answer came pretty quickly. I was aware that as the publisher was not in the mainstream I would have to pay something but Miriam had already offered to help if she could. I had not by then heard the rather distasteful term "vanity publishing". When it arrived the answer was yes. They wanted to make changes and edit it as they felt it was a little too long. What they were offering was a five hundred book hard back print run with accompanying editing and promotion. But at the end there was the catch; the cost was £10,500. There was no way I could afford that but knew I had to find some way to get it done. My hopes lay initially with Janssen Cilag. But there must be other avenues of sponsorship to be had.

With that the buoyancy of my mood shifted upward and counteracted my increasing disillusionment.

What I didn't know was that somewhere to the north of London in a place I used to drive past before my madness, a plan was in motion that would affect my life. The plot had been hatched during that long winter. I had been vaguely aware of it through the press but had ignored it due to my apparently flawed education. That would change in the coming months of warmer times.

Mark Edgar

Chapter 27
The Tripos

Shrouded back in the mists of time someone decided to call Cambridge degrees the tripos. I have no idea if the name of said person is recorded in the annals of Cambridge University but it has ever been thus. To the uninitiated it might seem an odd and meaningless name. Back in my very early days there when I was singing I had wondered what it was. I would quickly learn that the tripos was a three legged stool on which scholars sat during their studies.

The idea of a tripos stuck with me over the years and when I found myself firmly rooted in mental health it seemed an apt way of describing my field. Three things made it up. The System, which like so many others I had found to my cost was utterly flawed. The people who worked in that System. They too are fallible. So much of my life had been dominated by the flawed decision in 1993 to write me off as personality disordered rather than mentally ill. And finally the money that runs it. Few service users I met really understood the intricate balance of those three components. In reality money or lack of it drove the whole thing. If a service was not funded it would not happen even if it was needed.

For those of us working we were bound by all three. We couldn't operate outside the System and the pot of money was finite. The way the System had evolved through the Care Programme Approach meant that there were in theory two levels of care, standard and enhanced. What it did was to create an almost premier league of nutters, the haves and the have nots. Without being on enhanced CPA one could expect almost nothing. The intake team as they were known acted as a screen and barrier. Those with the most needs would then be passed on to the enhanced team for whom I worked. Then people would get something. Arguments often ensued in our team as to who would qualify - resource limitations rather than the needs of people. We always talked about need but didn't often take any notice of what people said. We ourselves made those decisions.

Ironically enough I was in the System in two ways, as a user and as a provider. What it meant for me was that I saw a psychiatrist twice a year and that was that. By the spring of 2007 I had tried and failed to get a specific diagnosis other than personality disorder.

But if there was one thing I knew of psychiatrists they rarely contradicted their predecessors and told it as it was. That spring another consultant came on board. I asked him the question but he said it was all too long ago to be certain so he too sat on the fence. What he did say though was that the report from the man I knew as god was utterly offensive and contradictory. But he could not help either.

The one thing I had over so many of my friends was that my life was no longer defined by my illness whatever we wanted to call it. There were now many aspects to my identity whereas once I had simply been Mark who was mad. Work was one thing but I was now able to do so much more than that. True I was unhappy at work and more than a little disillusioned but I was well and life away from there was good. My house was still a party house. I entertained regularly and was generally very happy. Another of those strange paradoxes of the mental health world, the duality of being both happy and unhappy at the same time.

Work didn't change much for the better but I kept going and lived for the weekends. The pinnacle of my culinary escapades came on Easter Saturday that April when I spent a whole day barring stopping to watch the Boat Race preparing an elaborate Chinese feast of some ten courses for twelve people at Beth's house. A huge success the party went on late into the night. It would prove to be one of last great events of my time in Kent.

For it was just after that that I became more aware of the plot that had been hatched north of London. It was just a few weeks after the feast that I saw an advert for a Mental Wellbeing Advisor at the University of Hertfordshire. This was not actually the first time it had been advertised. Back in the winter I had seen it but they wanted qualifications I didn't have. This time they had expanded the requirements out to include qualifications in education. This I had through my PGCE. There was a number to call if further clarification was needed. I eagerly called and was told by the woman on the other end of the phone that they didn't really know what they wanted.

Seeing their confusion it seemed an opportunity to have another go. I felt I could do it but they were asking for a great deal. More so than the many other jobs in the field that I had seen. And they were offering far less money. But what they were offering was about a third more than I was getting at the time.

Over a couple of nights I constructed a carefully written application although I did have to stretch my experience at times particularly when talking about policy writing and the legal context. With that all done I sent it off and wondered what the fates would bring me.

At almost the same time I did my first public talk on mental health. Something I had wanted to do for a long time came to fruition with an invitation to speak at the Rethink carers group meeting. Word soon got out that I would be speaking and the news spread like wildfire. Colleagues said they would come, many of my friends planned to also. So did my parents. That was the tricky part. Not content with that they also invited along the priest from their church. With such a turnout expected I had to think very carefully about what I was going to say. My mad life was still one thing that had been largely kept from my mum and dad. They knew I had written a book but had not read it. That was something I had feared all along - how would they cope with it if and when it was ever published. I thought long and hard on what was safe to say.

In the end I decided to divide my talk into two parts. Firstly an outline of my story. Secondly I would talk about the role of an STR worker and explain the complex nature of the tripos that made up mental health. I planned to speak throughout without referring to notes or using MS-PowerPoint; I had seen way too many speakers just reduced to reading from MS-PowerPoint and I wanted to be different.

When the day arrived so many people turned up at the Mind Centre to hear me that we had to collect extra chairs from upstairs. Nearly forty people sat down in great anticipation. Very carefully I told a sanitised version of my story for half an hour or so. Then just as carefully I tried to unravel the great mysteries of the strange field in which I worked.

The response was astonishing. They were utterly mesmerised as I spoke. My colleague Josie brought her young daughter along and she sat there wide eyed as this amazing story came from my voice. At last I had a voice and a command of an audience. The night was talked of long afterwards. The little girl wrote a school project on my story, my parents learned more in those brief moments than they had in the previous seventeen years and my friends finally got to hear what it was like on the inside. They also knew that I had not switched sides.

Flushed with the buzz of success I went back to my life with new found energy. Maybe my luck was changing and I would move on.

The next stage happened shortly afterwards when I came home from Mind one Wednesday evening to find an envelope embossed with the stamp of the University of Hertfordshire. I quickly opened it to find an invitation to interview in mid June. The time of reckoning in my career had come - someone with the power to help would get to hear me speak. Another summer beckoned.

Away from the forgotten piece of east Kent that I called home change was happening as well as spring turned to summer. A new strategy was afoot in the Middle East. What became known as the surge was about to change the course of the chaos that had become Iraq.

Closer to home, the man of New Labour Tony Blair gave up his post and his seat. The arrogant Brown took over without even being voted in. Labour was now once again unelectable. But we would all have to wait our turn to get to the polls. Brown finally had his wish but he had doomed his party to defeat.

Chapter 28
Fast Train to Somewhere?

Is it really possible to prepare for an interview? If one is required to give a presentation as I had been at my PGCE interview that is straightforward. But as none of us can really predict what is going to be asked how can we prepare? I had always held the philosophy that the most important thing was to be myself. In the myriad interviews I had had for teaching jobs different things came up at different times. One school had suggested afterwards that I needed to read some more syllabuses, but which ones? History was so vast that it was nearly impossible to decide where to start.

Back in the days before mental health found me, clearly my philosophy had not worked. Of the one hundred and fifty jobs I applied for I didn't get a single one. Who knows whether that meant I wasn't a very good teacher or were schools just too reluctant to take a risk on someone with my history of mental illness? Later when I did find myself teaching occasionally the feedback was astonishing. But that was all still to come.

Why mental health found me I have no idea. What I do know is that once I had the first interview back in 2002 I had succeeded every time. I had done no preparation and relied instead on my knowledge by experience. And that experience had served me well.

By June 2007, faced with another interview it was hard to know what if anything to do in preparation. What I did know from the job description was that I needed to know something of the law. By then the Mental Health Act promised so long before after the conviction of Michael Stone had come into law. But it would not be applied for another year. I knew enough about the 1983 Act to get through as well as having a very minor knowledge of the new Mental Capacity Act. I also knew a little of the DDA. But would it be enough? Only time would tell.

What was clear from the job description was that they wanted some sort of superstar who could do everything they could possibly think of. I felt I was up to the task although my dad looked most alarmed when I showed it to him. Yes I would have areas I would struggle at but I seriously doubted that many competitors even if more highly qualified than me would really know anything about policy writing. My thought was that that was easier to learn than to know what I really knew about the mad world. The only part that worried me about what they wanted was a rather strangely worded section on mental health promotion. Notoriously hard to do, I knew most people would run in the opposite direction as soon as I mentioned the word mental in public. That said all the candidates faced the same difficulty.

Few people at work knew that I was looking for another job. My supervisor knew as did Suzanne who remained my great supporter despite my increasingly vocal opposition to Supporting People. Away from work a small number of my friends knew. I had no intention of making things very public until I had secured a job if indeed I did so.

So it was just seen that I had booked three days off in the middle of June as me wanting to take a breather from the chaos of life in a busy CMHT. I had decided to take a couple of days off after the interview as well; more time to catch up on sleep.

It was very early in the morning that I drove the five miles to Folkestone Central station for the journey up north. Little was on my mind but my confidence; if they didn't like me I would have lost nothing. As I got to King's Cross my phone bleeped a couple of times with good luck messages.

My destination was not really very far and when I got there I took a taxi which dropped me off at the back entrance to the former Hatfield Polytechnic. I had never been there before but I had driven past it many times in the days before my madness.

Following the instructions I had been given I went to main reception where they asked me to take a seat in a small waiting area. I picked up a copy of the Times that was on the table and gently scanned the pages. There was another man in a suit there too. Older than me I assumed he was another candidate. I didn't fear any opposition though. After a while a woman with striking hair came along and led the two of us into a large room where three people were seated. Each of them introduced themselves although their names and jobs passed me by at the time. When I looked back it was clear that they represented Disability, HR, and Occupational Health.

The woman I had spoken to when I thought of applying explained a great deal about the job and structure of the University most of which I failed to take in. She explained that each of us would have three interviews, two for case studies and one for the formal interview.

My first set of case studies started in utter confusion when I was given the wrong set of instructions. Fearing a trick question I bullshitted before the error was spotted. There was nothing in them that I didn't really understand although I did point out to them that the study of a psychotic Chinese student would almost certainly never make it to the advisor until after as I knew the huge stigma in the Chinese community around mental health. With the first part complete I was led to a small office which I was told would be the office of the successful candidate.

As I sat quietly I contemplated what would come in the main interview. Where might my life go if I was successful? It was not a long wait before I was led into a smaller room in the next building along to be confronted with three women and a man. One of the women was a wheelchair user and in my naivety I falsely assumed she was a Disability representative. She was in fact the Head of Counselling and it quickly became clear she had a very sharp mind. The others were the Head of Equality, the Dean of Students who would chair the interview, and his equivalent from the University of Essex.

For the next thirty minutes I was bombarded with questions far harder and more intense than anything I had experienced trying to get a teaching job. Each answer I gave was followed by a qualification question. It seemed to go on for hours but as they had told me how many questions they would ask I was able to count down.

I emerged shell-shocked and exhausted. As a parting shot the Dean of Students had told me that if I was offered the job I would need to move to Hertfordshire - I knew that anyway - but gave the sweetener that the University paid up to £5,000 in removal costs. I hadn't expected that but it would make my life so much easier.

My third and final interview was far gentler. I sat with two women, one from the Student Union and the other a Disabled Students Co-ordinator for what was supposed to be another case study. In fact we went in a completely different direction when they asked me what my background was. I came clean and told them of my illness. Suitably impressed the case studies were never mentioned.

It was late on a sunny June afternoon as I waited for a taxi by the back exit to the University. At last I could smoke a cigarette. At the station I bumped into the other candidate whom I had met earlier. We chatted as the train went the short distance to London. It transpired he had once been an Approved Social Worker but had been so badly injured during an assessment that went wrong he had left the field. He was currently working with furniture in London but thought the job at the University might be a gentler way back into the field. He made a passing comment that they were offering very little money for the role. It was indeed less than many other universities were offering but to me it would be a huge pay hike.

At King's Cross we parted never to meet again. I headed to Charing Cross feeling I had done the best I could but not sure after such a tough interview process. When I got home I had a bath, ate, then went to the pub. I was pleased if tired. The phone did not ring that night.

Nor indeed did it ring the next day. Expecting to have heard by then I assumed I had been unsuccessful and just tried to enjoy a day away from work.

I awoke late the next morning as I was wont to do when not working. I turned the TV on, made a strong black coffee and lit a cigarette. Switching my phone on it immediately rang with an answerphone message. Unusually for me I answered straight away to the voice of the Dean of Students asking me to ring him. Fearing that I might be wrong in my belief that I had got the job I delayed calling back. When I did I spoke briefly to him and he confirmed that the job was indeed mine if I wanted it. He had to go to a meeting and said he would call me back later to discuss details.

It was not until the evening when we spoke. I was in Folkestone and had just parked the car when the phone rang. We spoke for a while and sorted what we needed to do. Much to my surprise I would have time to prepare for such a huge move when he suggested I start in September. We agreed a date of 3rd September. There would be much to do. But it also gave me another summer by the sea.

I had finally done it and got a serious job. Someone had decided that my experience was as good as any qualification. It was time to move on.

When I got back to work I told my supervisor and Suzanne but kept it quiet for a while. At the next team meeting in the any other business section I almost forgot to make my announcement. Prompted by Suzanne I gave my triumphant news to a sea of stunned faces. I never worked out whether they were stunned that I had got such a job or stunned that I wanted to leave. But there was great delight.

With my mood highly elated I told the world and partied hard. What I didn't expect was the anxiety that was to come and almost cripple my life during those short months of summer.

Mark Edgar

Chapter 29
I Love the Rain

Rain held an almost mystical place in the symbolism of my illness. A simple throwaway line from Rachel on a wet day in June 1991 would become woven into my psychosis when it finally destroyed my life. Back then it was but a couple of days before I realised that the only solution was suicide. Suicide had lurked darkly in my mind for many months but I had not been able to say it out loud or internally. That would change sitting in the Granta pub the day Rachel left.

She had come to see me in Cambridge after she had finished her exams and I was about to graduate. For the first time since the break exactly a year before we had really talked properly. When we had arrived in Cambridge from Sussex soft rain was falling in the pale light of dusk.

"I love the rain."

When the voices took over fully it was usually her voice saying things that she had said in person or in her many letters. Whenever it rained those words came back to me and haunted my very being.

Three years later on FA Cup Final day I had stood on the banks of the Thames wondering what it would be like to hurl myself in. It was raining hard and her voice was screaming I love the rain, I love the rain. Then out of nowhere came the second terrifying voice. A man I knew not, he kept saying time to die, time to die. Years later when I met Ron Coleman he suggested that it was the voice of my illness, in essence my own but detached from the conscious.

Throughout the terrifying duet of the two pillars of my madness I was at the end. How I survived I don't know but somehow I did.

In the post Risperidone world I rarely heard voices. But the symbolism of the past still crossed my mind from time to time. How hard it was to escape the symbolism that was woven into the fabric of my madness. Contrary to the dismissive comments of a myriad shrinks the sounds and sights of my madness were not typical of a depressed or personality disordered mind. I did not think these things were about me. More it was that I attached to certain things that described my pain better than I could. Those representations became part of me but were not about me. Not even I was that arrogant.

Whilst symbolism was still at times significant what had never been a great issue was anxiety. I had experienced a glimpse of what it could do whilst in Barcelona but I had never considered anxiety to be a mental illness even though it was identified in various guises in the "psychiatric bible" DSM IV. True I expected the worst most of the time and never believed anything until it actually happened but these attitudes were merely a reflection of bitter experience. I had battled the System and the DWP for way too long.

But as I faced the countdown to my new life in the summer of 2007 both symbolism and anxiety came increasingly to the fore. It proved to be a very wet June as I tried to get my head around the enormity of what it is like to give up one life and move onto another. Just the mental side was hard enough to deal with. But when it came to the practical realities of what needed to happen I found myself overwhelmed with anxiety at times.

Slowly I started to collect boxes and pack up the happy home I had in the Chapel Street Brothel. My life was being packed away for pastures new. Yet of course my life at work had to continue. It meant coming to the end of my time with the amazing Norma whom I had so successfully nurtured and tried to teach the finer parts of living with a mood disorder and being able to stay out of hospital. To the others there were the goodbyes to deal with. Word quickly spread on the grapevine that I would be leaving and not everyone was happy about it. I tried in this period not to take on too much more work but to prepare people for my departure.

In the background to this was a team on its knees that was busy turning on itself. I had not been immune to this when I had had a nasty falling out with my friend Lynne. I was so surprised by this that I thought she too like me may well be mentally ill. Time would prove me right and we did return to a new place after I had left.

After each day I went home to the forlorn existence of the cottage in which it was barely possible to move. Yet I had to keep going. People kept asking me if I had anywhere to live but how was I supposed to sort that out from so great a distance? True I looked continually on property websites which reported an alarmingly high standard of living in Hertfordshire. I had always thought property and rentals far too high in my part of Kent but Hertfordshire was a different world. True I would have a much higher income but looking on the web it seemed I would certainly need it.

A wet June turned to an equally wet July. And with that time was running out; only two months to go. There was more to do than just pack up and find a new place to live. I needed money to pay for everything and to keep the receipts to claim back. I needed to sort out all the bills such as council tax and the utilities. Each of my calls to various people gave advice that in the end would prove erroneous and come back to haunt me. I needed transport to move all my stuff. I needed to sort out insurance and change of address for the post office. Not all of this could be done straight away as I didn't yet know where I would be living. As it transpired something would go wrong almost every step of the way.

Whilst all of this was happening I was in constant communication with the University over such things as contracts, supervisors, and management lines. HR sent huge sheaves of paper explaining so many things. They were still waiting for references by the middle of July. I was also in regular touch to try to find somewhere nice to live. As things transpired I would only have a very short window of time to do that as I planned to use what little holiday I had left just before I moved.

Much of the paperwork sent by them was not too clear. In my anxiety I was almost crippled in my capacity to deal with this just as I had been in my psychosis back in 2001 when I had finally got my first job. With each passing day that anxiety grew. One of the few things that did seem to be clear was that the promised removal costs of up to £5,000 appeared to have stipulations very much in favour of people buying property rather than renting as I would be forced to do. What I really needed was money for a deposit for a flat; all my previous places had been rented from friends so did not require a deposit. When I saw the advice I phoned up HR to query it. I was told that as long as I provided receipts it would be covered.

As had happened back in the summer leading up to my PGCE time seemed to fly by. And with each passing day the anxiety grew and grew. It was not just anxiety but mood shifts too. I was really looking forward to the job but terribly fearful of the actual move itself. My sleep was hugely disrupted and at times I was so anxious I could barely eat. I remember one Saturday walking up to my parents' house and having lunch with them. But my hands shook so violently I could barely put the food in my mouth.

It was of course all mental, the fear of what might happen rather than what would happen. But even though I had by and large defeated my illness I hovered on the brink with so much on my mind.

Slowly, very slowly things fell into place. I managed to get an extended overdraft from the bank and a credit card to tide me over. They turned down my request for a loan as I had no credit rating. One of the great paradoxes of finance seemed to be that as I had never asked for credit before I must be a risk.

I thought I had some transport for the actual journey and Beth had promised to help if she wasn't working.

As July slipped quietly into August I had a supervisor sorted out via my new manager and they had also arranged another member of staff to mentor me during the first year. I had not expected that nor indeed felt I needed one but as things turned out it proved very useful.

Yet with things coming to fruition I still couldn't mentally tick off the list. Each night after saying goodbye to more and more of my charges I returned to the cluttered and forlorn chaos of the cottage.

There were occasional distractions and people sought to help me celebrate my success. Various people took me out for celebratory meals including my parents. I had one memorable night out with Tom when he came back to the house and we carried on late.

None of these could distract my mind from the fear. As had been the case back in my illness I still had to wake up to the reality of my life in the morning. And each was another day closer to the day of reckoning when I would give up life as I knew it and venture into the unknown.

With summer rapidly waning I booked my final leave for the end of the month. In any normal year that was when I would book off two weeks for my birthday. Now I was constrained by the limits of the time available and my resignation letter. I had two things directly linked to work that I had had been unable to resolve. My contract phone was a deal through my employer so that would change. My computer was also through work with the payments deducted monthly before tax. However much I phoned they seemed unable to advise me on those two.

So it was that I was in for a shock on pay day as they took what I owed from my last salary. Suddenly the need for money hit hard and I had to take a loan from Miriam.

Everyone seemed rather sad that I was leaving both amongst the staff I worked with and the clients we helped. I hoped to have a leaving party. Many were on holiday so I expected a fairly small affair. In the event only two people turned up. Perhaps that was the final stab in the back from a team at war with itself. I certainly would miss individuals in the team but not working in such an environment.

As I left I was still confronted with my fears. I had about a four day window to find somewhere to live. I needed to complete the final details of the move including a vehicle as I had been let down by another friend.

What a week to face leaving the world I knew so well. I would turn 38 that week. There would definitely be a party for that. And of course the party in the pub in the middle of the High Street to mark my leaving. I knew people would come to that. There had to be a send off.

But still the anxiety kept me in its grip. And all along the rain continued to fall bringing with it faint haunting memories of Rachel. Could I really escape my past?

Mark Edgar

Chapter 30
Beyond the Boundaries

People have repeatedly told me that two of the most stressful events anyone can go through are divorce and moving house. I had never been married so I had never had to go through divorce. But I knew all too well the pain and consequences of relationship breakdown. I had however moved house twice in the previous four years. These were comparatively easy moving small amounts of possessions over short distances. What I faced now was a whole new scenario.

That final week of the summer of 2007 I was free from the constraints of my old working life. It was now or never time on the move to a different world. Many times I had thought of calling the University and asking to delay my start date by a week. As that Monday morning arrived my mind was still full of anxieties. As things stood I would be starting work again in precisely one week.

By that stage I had identified two possible flats that I could just about afford. So it was that I set off to Hertfordshire on another wet day to meet the agent. He arrived shortly after me as I stood in the rain. He was polite but pompous. Fortunately for me the very first flat he showed me seemed perfect. Set in an oak wood it was an annex to a large and expensive house in perhaps the nicest area of that town.

I indicated to him that though small it would be perfect for me. We did go and look at the other one although it proved to be not very nice. I offered to pay the deposit by cheque that day so we went back to his office and filled in reams of paperwork. He seemed to balk at the idea that I smoked even though I was quite happy to do so outside. For reasons I didn't know he advised me not to mention it on the forms. He called the owner to tell him that he had identified a possible tenant. The owner asked to meet me but unfortunately I could not stay long enough for him to finish work. So I would have to do another trip the following day.

As the agent dropped me at the station he made a reference to hoping my cheque would clear in time and references asked for would be okay. This did not inspire confidence in me with such a short period of time until I had to be there.

The following day it rained again as I took another slow train to London and the fast train to Hertfordshire. We met at the house and he showed me round again. We got on okay and he struck me as very charming and polite man. With everything bar the paperwork done he dropped me at the station for the journey home. I called Suzanne from there to tell her the news that I finally had somewhere to live.

I was exhausted when I got home on that rainy August day. But even with that part complete my anxiety did not lift. I still had to get a vehicle to take my possessions for the planned move on the Sunday. It was a crazy plan to move to a new area on a Sunday and start a new job on the Monday. But I had a reason for doing that - there was a great party planned in my honour on that Saturday night.

I took the following day off. It was after all my birthday. 38 years old. Young to many but for someone who should by rights have died of a drugs overdose at the age of 21, it was some achievement. My parents took me out to lunch as was our usual practice and in the evening I drank myself into a mild oblivion with a few friends. That was the only way I could block out the anxiety. The real birthday party would take place on the Friday evening.

Friday, a mere three days to go. We managed to acquire the very last van available. Beth would drive and my dad would navigate. She too had to bring her license - more bureaucracy. And of course yet more money. Money anxieties aside, a new anxiety had appeared in my delicate mind. Although I had a print off of how to navigate my car, I had no faith in my sense of direction. I was convinced I would get lost.

By the time I was ready to go out that evening there was very little else I could do towards the move. It just had to happen now; time marched ever onwards despite my fears.

We partied hard that night just as I had done so often in recent years. The lonely isolated young man was no longer. Instead there I was with many friends who had been the backbone of my recovery from mental illness. What I didn't expect was just how many people would come to mark my final hurrah in the small insignificant seaside town in east Kent the following night.

Nothing could prepare me for that. They came from miles around. Dozens and dozens came to see me off to my new and strange world. It was somewhat overwhelming and so reminiscent of the party we had had for my 26th birthday. Beth brought a cake she had made and there were so many cards and presents. I marvelled at who I appeared to have become.

It was a night of true chaos and laughter. It was very late when I left the pub in the middle of the High Street which for one night only was bedecked with photos garnered from many over the years. When I got home I rolled what turned out to be the final spliff of my life and slept the sleep of the dead. My time in Kent was over.

The sun shone on that Sunday morning. I was tired, hungry, and anxious. Beth and my dad arrived late in the morning and we loaded my life into a hired van. Other parts came with me in my little car. With that we set off at midday on the hundred mile journey to what would be my new home. There was sadness in my mind as I left my beloved little house for the last time.

Much to my surprise both vehicles arrived unscathed at the annex in the oak wood two hours later. Michael my landlord very kindly made us coffee. We unpacked and Beth and my dad left. I was once again alone in an alien place.

Michael's mum took me on a quick tour of the town so I could orientate myself. At her suggestion and with her directions I drove down to the University so I knew where I would be going the following day.

It was when I got back that it occurred to me that I hadn't eaten a thing all day. In the pale light of an early autumn twilight I walked the mile or so to the town centre and took a seat in a Chinese restaurant. The proprietor commented to me that I ate like a Chinese. I got free tea and made my first friend. Tiger would be a regular part of my life for the next few years.

When I had finished I went into a pub round the corner and had a couple of drinks before heading back in the darkness to a new place.

As I lay in a new king sized bed that night I was finally able to reflect on what an amazing journey I had been on. During the years of my illness I had been dismissed and dehumanised by a flawed System and by those who had run it. I was on the outside, one of them, who had had to be kept in place by that great tenet of that System, boundaries. Us and them was maintained so stringently by the enemy.

In those days I had sworn I would never work for the enemy. But fate conspired against me and somehow I had ended up doing what I did not expect. I was the poacher turned gamekeeper. But I was very clear they were just my employers and a means to a greater end.

Almost from day one I had been a maverick, determined to get it right where so many had failed me. My entire practice was based on doing the opposite of what was done to me.

This did not always sit well and that word boundaries had been thrown at me. But what no one could argue with were the successes I had had. By being open and acknowledging where people were really at I learned far more than my more highly decorated colleagues. The field was not hard to me, I was merely talking to people in my language as I had done since I was first thrown into the System in the summer of 1991.

The great paradox of the boundaries bullshit was that by rights none of my colleagues should have had any contact with me outside of work as I was still a service user. They quietly ignored that on our nights out though. I was both one of us and one of them.

Some had me believe that I had sold my soul to the devil by working for the enemy. Others revered me as some sort of genius. I was of course neither. But I was different. I did not switch sides. I merely climbed to the top of barrier that divided us from them and looked both ways. I had become a hybrid.

But what was more important for me was that I had gone beyond the boundaries, done things my way and I had won.

When sleep came to me on the night of Sunday 2nd September 2007 I had finally arrived in a place where I could do it my way. The job had never been done before and I had in front of me a blank sheet of paper. Create from nothing as I saw fit. I was in control of my own destiny for the first time. Not perhaps what had been expected of someone struck by psychosis on 16th June 1990, who had been written off in July 1994 as untreatable and likely to commit suicide within six months, but had found salvation through the magic of Risperidone almost exactly six years before. It was a night of endings and beginnings.

Chapter 31
St George and the Dragon

Many people over the years have deigned to tell me how lucky I was to have been part of a world famous choir as a child. Others have gone so far as to suggest how privileged I was to have lived that life. True it had taken me to many places, had granted me lifelong recordings of fine music, and ultimately it brought me back to Cambridge as an undergraduate. People have suggested that that was a privilege too. In my time a great myth perpetuated that one had to be rich to go to Cambridge. My family was anything but rich. The reality of Cambridge in my life was it was very hard to get in but easy when one was there. I went to Cambridge because I had talent and intellect. Not through some back door deal. That all changed when I got ill.

Years of psychiatric treatment in which I was regarded as delusional tried to take away my legacy. But I would not let them. I still had talent. The older I get the more abnormal I see my life as having been rather than privileged.

It was the singing as a child that had the most impact on my mental breakdown rather than any pressure of Cambridge as so many have tried to convince me. The reality of that anonymous fame was far more bleak and brutal than many care to acknowledge.

Our world then was one of exploitation, extreme hard work, and intense pressure. A world of hangers on and shadows cast over others, particularly siblings. It was tainted by the fear of the violent reprisals simply for making a mistake in a piece of music. Often hungry and tired we were worked into the ground. All for the sake of a famous name. We never knew when the explosion of rage would come and rarely thought about it until it happened. When it did, like all victims of child abuse we accepted it as normal as we didn't know any different. And all this was orchestrated by a man who became a knight of the realm.

What may have been worse though was the insidious culture of bullying and turning one child against another. Rigidly enforced through the one to sixteen order that took away our names but rather gave us numbers and surnames. Perhaps most insidious of all was the ruthless initiation known as the Star of Bethlehem which was inflicted on newcomers in the run up to Christmas. All as a means of control.

As I got older I fostered thoughts of retaliation. On the choir stalls we had candle holders with electric lamps underneath encased in glass covers. The dark thoughts of using one of those as a weapon if it happened to me again sometimes came to my mind. In fact he never hit me again so I never got the chance to see if I had such courage to fight back.

The regime changed in 1982. To me it was little better but at the end of that academic year I left for pastures new in Sussex. The scars could rarely be seen although sometimes they came to the fore in the form of an increasingly angry teenager.

During the years of my madness it was often thoughts of those days that precipitated my descent into the hell of psychosis. Anger turned in on myself would invariably trigger a freefall of the subterranean lift that was my life back then. With that came the psychotic jukebox, then the voices, and with them the overwhelming desire to kill myself.

Subsequent conversations confirmed to me that the abuse that went on in my choir school was also rife in at least two others. I wonder how many casualties there have been from that world in the 1970s and early 1980s?

By September 2007 as I stood on the brink of a completely new world the dragon in my mind that was child abuse was well and truly shut away in its box. The more immediate dragon to slay was my fear of utter loneliness. I had worked so hard over the later years of my illness to create a place and identity that was firmly in the real world. I had so many friends in Kent. Now I had given all that up to pursue a career of strange twists and turns in the world of the mad. Finally I could say fuck you to those who had tried to destroy me with their claims of delusion. I had got to that place through hard work and talent. How many unqualified people got to such a place in the world of mental health? Time would attest that very few had done it. But that new place would for a while be very lonely. Hopefully my new place of work would provide the first of what I hoped would be many friends.

On Monday 3rd September 2007 I set off in my little car to drive the five or so miles to the University of Hertfordshire for my first day of a new life. I got lost on the way but still managed to get there well before the prescribed time of 8.30. I knew that would be a time of struggle for me given the considerable sedative powers of my medication. As I got there I found that not only my immediate manager but also the head of department were on holiday. For that first week I would be guided round by a colleague whose office was directly next door to mine. It seemed strange to have my own office; was I really that important?

That first week was a blur of meetings, induction, huge amounts of information leading to utter confusion. A programme of people to meet had been set up but there were so many I quickly forgot who everyone was and what they did. Even from day one it seemed as if everyone expected me to remember everything that was said. It quickly became clear that this was a vast organisation with many competing agendas. More frightening though was that everyone seemed to have a view on what I should be doing for them.

Each evening I returned to the quiet empty annex in the oak wood and tried little by little to piece together a new home. I had to get cable TV as there was no working aerial there. Along with that came a phone and the Internet. Beth and my dad had set up my computer when they had helped me move - I was just too inept with technology. Fairly quickly I was able to get going although I did worry somewhat about the cost. On the plus side it meant that for the first time in my life I would be able to watch regular live NFL games just as the season started.

I cooked in a tiny cramped kitchen and sometimes went to visit my friend Tiger at the Chinese restaurant. Some evenings I visited the pub I had been to on the first night. It transpired it was a former bank. But it was not like the pubs I was used to in Kent. There were few if any regulars to get to know so my visits out were just as lonely as my staying in the flat.

On the very first weekend Michael's father was having an 80th birthday party in the garden of the house. Very kindly Michael and his family invited me along. I proved something of curiosity to those gathered. I couldn't stay long as I had arranged to visit Beka in her new flat that weekend. It was the first of many weekend trips away.

Michael proved to be a charming landlord although he kept himself to himself most of the time. The anxiety that had led up to the actual move had mainly dissipated but a strange new one evolved. After the odd exchange with the agent about smoking I got it into my head that I would get evicted if Michael found out I smoked. I had no problem smoking outdoors and I became a regular sight sitting on the bench at the end of the road. But it felt a very shameful and secret experience.

With the coming of week two the pace quickened. It was still a round of eternal meetings but at last my managers were back. What rapidly became apparent though during that week was that all was not as it seemed in my new department. They were under review with possibility of major change soon. It was like coming into a great play scene as an unknown. The meetings continued to baffle me as I knew not what had come before. It was also clear that we were a team of specialists in unique jobs and as such we were by our nature quite alone in the organisation.

I was utterly confident that I could handle any mental health cases that came my way. What I was not clear about was how on earth I was going to change attitudes or worse to get involved in policy. That latter part seemed alarmingly big in the grand scheme of things; the organisation was awash with policy. Even then I knew that it fitted very uneasily with the realities of the mental health world.

When I finally got round to meeting my ultimate manager, the Dean of Students, I was somewhat relieved to be told that there were plenty of people who knew how to write policies but what they needed me to do was advise them on relevant detail. He also told me that it would take an entire three year cycle for me to truly understand the University. These proved to be most prophetic words.

Slowly students started to come and see me. It would take a while to realise it but I was completely fooled into thinking that they would by necessity be high functioning in order to be at University. I also completely misunderstood the levels of complexity that I would face within the role; some would prove riskier than anything I had seen in the wider world.

Of course the many confusing meetings were not just confined to employees of the University. I needed quickly to establish links outside. Had I been given a job in Canterbury I would have been ahead of the game in that I was already well known. In Hertfordshire I knew no one. Some of the ground work had been laid already. My new supervisor Jacek was a consultant with the Early Intervention in Psychosis team. He proved an absolute Godsend. I managed to establish links with inpatient facilities fairly quickly with help of a local charity Viewpoint. They proved a very useful ally to have and things quickly moved on in the voluntary sector. There at least I received overwhelming support.

The big sticking point though was the local CMHT. I arranged a meeting there and was told "we don't quite know what you will get out of this meeting as we only work with people with severe mental illness and you won't have any other those at the University." They seemed to be forgetting that they had had to assess and detain a student on the very first weekend of term. As far as I could see they wanted me to manage things so they didn't have to.

As September moved into October, the chaos of a large university exploded as the students arrived. Nothing could have really prepared me for that. Confusion seemed to reign all around. But it did pass.

My overwhelming sense of my first month there was that it was a workaholic environment where people were business-like rather than friendly. People were not unfriendly but didn't in the main want to get too close. There were exceptions such as my amazing mentor Kym who kept me sane. The chaplain, who shared my passion for American Football proved a great supporter and ironically so did someone I met from HR. I was accepted quickly into the mental health academic community and was most intrigued by the University's Centre for Mental Health Recovery. Generally it was discouraged that I disclose my own life, there it felt safe. I was quickly asked onto the service user and carer advisory group as one of them. The activists in Hertfordshire differed little to those in Kent.

Although things went well early on despite my confusion, it was not the sort of set up that helped me to slay the dragon of loneliness. That was the one I was expecting but I kept telling myself that it was early days.

Sadly another dragon appeared very quickly. I simply wasn't earning enough to live there. All the attempts I had made to make arrangements over bills in Kent came back to haunt me. Almost every day brought calls saying I owed money from there. Even the local authority took council tax erroneously leading to me to being fined for going over my overdraft limit. Of course that would be sorted out as soon as I submitted my receipts. But in the meantime I had to keep going. True I went to the pub and to visit Tiger, but fighting the loneliness dragon meant going out and that cost money.

I had actually suspected it might be a struggle. The job offered less than other equivalent jobs I had seen. The cost of my housing had gone up 60% with the move and my student loan repayment trebled. It was not until a couple of years later when I did the figures that I realised I was actually marginally worse off than I had been in Kent despite a third increase in salary.

It was hard fighting two dragons at once. But it was then that a third appeared. And this one meant facing the past. In October I received an invitation to Cambridge for Remembrance Sunday. A new requiem was to receive its UK premiere. And it was to be conducted by the composer and a figure from all those years before. The man who had terrorised us all.

I could have just thrown it away. Why would anyone sane or otherwise wish to see such a figure again? It had been twenty five years since I had last seen him. True I had my defence mechanisms now that in the main stopped my descent into psychosis. Not sure how to respond I was nevertheless curious. What would that man look like now? Was he still abusing children? That I doubted as I suspected access was far more restricted than it had been. Would he even remember me? Lots of thoughts and questions.

I'm not sure what switched the confused balance in my mind but I quickly decided I would go along to Cambridge and see what happened. I had faced the past many times before and was still standing so what would another time be to me? I had come so far.

It turned cold early that year. In fact it snowed in October and the oak wood looked magical in its whiteness. Snow aside that month my travels took me to many places. I went to Loughborough for a meeting of the University Mental Health Advisors Network (UMHAN) which was most enlightening; it seemed that I was not alone in my feelings of bearing a heavy weight of responsibility in a lonely place. The reality was that at all universities such specialists as us did not always fit easily into the structure.

I also visited the Universities of Essex and Bedfordshire to meet my opposite numbers. And with each trip I learned more.

The run up to Cambridge went very quickly as is usually the case when one feels some apprehension. On Remembrance Sunday I took the train up. It was a direct line which took just under an hour. On a cold day I went to the chapel I had known for over thirty years - it had not changed much.

As the service began I stood mesmerised by that figure from my past. He seemed to lack the presence of the former days. The music was beautiful and my mind tried hard to remember why I was there on that day. I should have been remembering the war dead but my mind wandered to casualties closer to home. That service had always been one of my favourites of the year. It was one of the few I would consider going back into a church to hear long after I had given up on religion.

The acoustic took away the final sublime notes and there were smiles all round. But the bit I feared was what lay ahead. For afterwards we were to dine and combine. And that meant coming face to face with this apparition from my ruptured past.

I was most cautious as we combined after dinner. A few there I had seen more recently. Others I had not seen for years. And then the time came. We spoke. He looked older and less imposing. He had lost weight and was no longer frightening. He didn't remember me until I told him my name. He enquired of my health and me of his. Little more was said and I had passed a test of time. As I left I just saw an old man.

On the train home the encounter echoed round my mind. It had not been bad. I had not felt compelled to harm him although in past times I might have done. Nor did I feel the need to ask him if he still abused children; that question had lurked for a long time. More importantly I had faced the past head on and not been harmed by it. I'm not sure if I had slain that particular dragon that day but it was one more step on my journey.

The following morning I woke early and went to work. It had been two months. I felt none the wiser about what I faced in the coming months. What I did know was that the twin dragons of loneliness and poverty were unchanged. I prayed that would change in time. But I also feared that they would bring me back down to the depths of my despair; madness is still madness even when partially controlled.

Chapter 32
Storm Gathering in the West

When I had moved to the Chapel Street Brothel in 2005 Chris my then manager kept suggesting to me that I would be much better off getting a mortgage and buying a flat. My response was swift and categorical, I couldn't afford it. Property prices there were way beyond my means. Back then it was pretty easy to get a 100% or even 125% deal on a mortgage. But I knew I would struggle to pay rent and council tax let alone a mortgage and all the attendant upkeep costs.

Some time after that on a night out with JB and the karate people I was talking to a young man who was a mortgage broker. We talked of the cost of property and how hard it was to get on the ladder. He told me he could get me mortgage no problem at all. The key question was whether I could afford to pay for it. The answer was still no.

By the time I moved to Hertfordshire I had long suggested that the cost of housing could not sustain itself at such absurd levels but no one seemed to take any notice. When I moved I was in for an even bigger shock. The price of buying there was about 50% higher than in Kent. On the immediate level this didn't really matter to me as I intended to rent. But from the perspective of the University it was significant; I still vaguely remembered the paperwork that aided buyers rather than renters in the relocation costs. Yet I had my reassurance from HR; it would be okay as long as I provided receipts.

As the weather turned colder I submitted all the receipts and hoped and prayed that they would pay me soon. Money was exceedingly tight. I had had my credit card cancelled over a bill I never received and their failure to set up the direct debit I had requested. The phone calls kept coming from Kent for hidden costs. In the shops the price of everyday things I bought was rising alarmingly. This was made doubly difficult for me as I no long had Mandy's special butchery deals to help nor could I just cross the Channel at the drop of hat and buy precious cigarettes and tobacco. Petrol too began to rise at an alarming rate. That was not too bad as my mileage had been reduced dramatically by no longer working in the community.

At the flat it turned out the gas fired central heating - so needed after my misery of two winters before - did not work. I was paying a flat rate for bills and I was lucky enough that Michael provided an electric heater at no extra charge.

For all the financial worries that fluctuated in my mind I was still trying to find my way in this new job. The meetings kept coming as did the jargon. Still it baffled me. I yearned for the few precious hours in the week when I could sit with my students and do what I was best at. Following the UMHAN meeting it quickly dawned on me that I was being asked to do something no other advisor was; and that was to work with staff as well.

Referrals trickled in during that first term. The staff ones were rare but interesting. Many of them were not mentally ill per se but put under huge strain by events in their lives often beyond the University. These were leading to increasing levels of depression and anxiety. This was also what afflicted many of the students I saw although there were small numbers of people with psychosis and bipolar. There was also emerging a tiny fraction of that category that I so hated and that we all struggled to work with, that of personality disorder.

For all that I knew I did well there was so much else to learn. I never really worked out why I had been placed in the Equality Unit but it brought a whole new agenda to me. We had always wondered why on earth we were being pressured to ask people's religions when I worked at CMHT. Prior to that when I was at Rethink Supporting People had forced us to put a list of all places of worship in our brochure for clients. We had no idea why. Slowly it began to emerge now though.

It transpired that October was Black History Month. I had been to a number of events on this same theme all of which were good. What I didn't understand was why people from BME communities were most insistent that they were more discriminated against than white people with mental health difficulties. No one seemed to accept that discrimination against the mentally ill happened in all communities. I had experienced years of it in my life and would almost certainly have been working at one of the four other universities I had applied to had the DDA been properly implemented.

But equality was not as straightforward as that. It seemed we had anticipatory duties as well. I wondered how we could anticipate something we didn't know about. Yet this all underpinned the strange and confusing policy work that came across my desk. Everywhere was jargon.

The other part I struggled to get to grips with was the varying ways in which we treated different groups of students. We treated our younger ones in a different way to our mature students. Internationals were different to home students. People from different racial groups differed in their levels of attainment. And there was a whole new world when it came to people doing professional type courses in health care and teaching. They had to be deemed sane to qualify and worked much longer hours and terms than everyone else.

This was all new to me. And I thought they should all be equal. What made it really hard was that people continued to assume that I had a complete grasp of their department's needs when in fact I was drowning in a sea of information overload.

In direct contrast to that was the lack of being told what I needed to know to support my students and staff but also to advise the University on mental health. There no one told me anything. In the real world of mental health so much information is shared. Rarely do referrals get made to other services without risk assessments being passed on and backroom conversations had. Yet at the University I faced a wall of silence. I attended meetings at which we all knew who we were talking about but no one used names. There was a great deal of concern across the sector at the very small number of students declaring mental health difficulties. At our place I was not even told the names of those who did as this was deemed too confidential for me to know. In my eyes it was madness.

We lived in fear of suicide or worse yet we never spoke to each other. Perhaps that was why they had really employed me. I knew that if catastrophe struck then we would get hammered in an enquiry. All the reports from investigations into mental health homicides highlighted the chronic lack of information sharing. Yet we did none of that. So I was working alone and bearing the risk myself. How could I respond to a situation if no one told me the known facts?

Of course after each day I returned to my lonely flat and cooked in the cramped kitchen. Most weekends I went away as I could not stand the loneliness. Marie came to visit but she was the only one. She had been there the day England lost the rugby World Cup Final.

The few friends I made worked in restaurants and pubs. I had joined the local rugby club and on rare weekends I was home I often went down there. But no one spoke to me. And with each weekend I worried more about money.

As we reached the end of November I thought some sort of financial restoration would happen. But on pay day I was in for a huge shock. The University turned down over half of what I had claimed for. The information I had been given was clearly wrong. They completely refused helping with a deposit for the flat, the thing I most needed. I would go on to challenge that on equality grounds but apart from a small amount they refused to move on the issue. They even turned down a request that they might loan it to me on the grounds that I might leave and not pay it back.

Facing financial ruin thoughts of leaving came strongly into my mind. But where could I go? Where could I afford to go? Already in debt before I even set foot in Hertfordshire I faced a very uncertain future as December came. I even doubted my decision to make the move in the first place. Yes I was moving on in my late starting career but it seemed that only oblivion awaited me.

Somehow despite the fear my mood held as the weeks ticked by to the holiday. The University would be shut between Christmas and New Year so I could have a break without using too much of my precious and limited holiday time. I decided to take as much time as I could and head to Kent where at least I would be warm and amongst friends for a while.

In the run up to Christmas there were some fine moments though. My two mad New Zealand friends Sarah and Tori invited me to a Christmas party. They were sisters and at the time working for their brother in London. It was a great night apart from the complete inaccessibility of the toilets owing to all the cocaine users. I stayed at Sarah's flat but a stone's throw from Borough Market and the Hotel California where I had stayed for four months in 1994. I made it to bed at 6 o'clock in the morning and didn't surface again until 3 o'clock in the afternoon. I was getting too old for that.

Michael too took me out. We went to a fine if eccentric pub in the country for steak and kidney pie. Michael it transpired had a passion for pies. Comically our quest failed when the landlord came over to tell us that he had fucked up the pastry that day so we would have to make do with just the steak and kidney. It was very fine but not quite what we had ordered. That evening out was quite significant as it allowed my anxiety about being evicted to dissipate.

In the final week of term we all headed out to a local hotel for the Dean of Students' Christmas dinner. For the first and only time I saw immediate colleagues outside of work. I tried to be myself and was relieved that at least some of them were not entirely business-facing away from there. I ate so much I was sick but soon recovered and had an enjoyable night. Sadly I would never witness such a night again.

The night of the party was the end of term for me. The next day was the first day off after an exhausting, confusing, and difficult first term in my new life.

I drove to Kent into a low, blinding, setting sun the last week before Christmas. I did not go straight home but rather to a hotel in Folkestone. Sue and Duncan's daughter Donna was getting married that day. I met Marie in a pub by the harbour in the late afternoon. We were pissed before we even got to the reception but it was a memorable night.

The following morning I arrived back in the quiet forgotten seaside town in Kent. I had been away three months. Now I hoped I could forget about the financial chaos that my life had turned into. I was back at home with friends.

The generosity of those friends helped me to party hard through that time. Boxing Day was the usual epic event even if Christmas Day had not been great. That day brought an old friend back into my life. I had met Ali back in the heady summer of 1995. But she moved to London not long afterwards and I had not seen her for years. She would become my next visitor to the annex in the oak wood.

Deep in my mind lingered the fears of going back. How could I afford to carry on?

On 27th December the freefall of my mood that I had so feared finally happened. Darkness began to take over. It was lifted slightly on New Year's Eve but then went back down again.

The coming of 2008 was a portend of things to come. In the Middle East the so-called surge appeared to be bringing dividends. Further east the Afghan debacle continued to get worse. There were still plots against Western targets - in the run up to my move an attempt had failed in a spectacular fireball at Glasgow airport.

At home the arrogant Prime Minister continued in his aloof manner. Totally unelected some said he had made a big mistake by not calling a snap election.

Yet it was further to the west that the most serious storm clouds were gathering. For those in the know and with an interest in economics the property bubble was beginning to burst. Despite what I had predicted we were told in low-key terms that there would be no crash. The arrogant one continued to claim that his time as chancellor had eliminated boom and bust economics. How wrong we all were. 2008 would bring a day of reckoning.

I limped slowly and hungover into 2008. My mood remained low as I headed back to Hertfordshire. When I got back to the empty flat there were ominous puddles of water on the carpet but it was not clear where a leak was coming from. Michael was still away when I got back but had very kindly left me a bottle of Rioja for Christmas.

The University was almost deserted when I got back. Deserted and cold. Had I made a big mistake?

Chapter 33
Left on the Shelf

Does anyone really care about the unknown people of the world? Most of us are complete nobodies. Our media bombards us with images of the rich and famous. The cult of celebrity surrounds us most of the time. Yet Joe Public like me just carry on in obscurity. It had always struck me as strange that people would want to be in the public eye. In reality if the world wanted to know about any of us it could find out pretty quickly who we are and who we have been. One only needed to look at the press in the days and weeks following someone's elevation to fame for good or ill. That of course is as true for a winner of Big Brother as it is of the evil celebre of a serial killer.

It is true that in a democracy we the people do have a say in the form of a vote. But did the arrogant one really care about me, my friends, or those others who populated my world? He was too busy trying to be important.

In my little world I was having a strange flirtation with fame that almost certainly wouldn't come but which might come through my actions. As the world stumbled into 2008 I had been trying to give a voice to the mentally ill ever since I had had my breakdown. I had known all along that I had to write a book about what really went on. Ever since I had started writing six years before I had been aware that there were three possible outcomes. Firstly, I could write a book and no one would want to publish it. Secondly, I could write it, someone would publish it but no one would want to read it. Finally, I could write a book, someone would publish it, and everyone would want to read it. The third option was of course what I desired yet it was also the one I most feared. In the unlikely event that that did happen my life would no longer be my own. By necessity if one puts work in the public domain it would be judged; and that might not be good. Criticism could well trigger an avalanche back into my madness.

I had lived through rejection after rejection and survived. But could I go on? In the chaos of my life, A Pillar of Impotence had very much taken a backseat. True I had the offer but I didn't have the £10,500 needed to proceed. Janssen Cilag the makers of Risperidone had been gushing in their praise but had quietly withdrawn with a short and rather terse email the summer before I had moved. I was in a limbo between the first two options. That had all been forgotten until I received a letter from the publisher that suggested the deal was off as I couldn't afford to pay for it.

That was the last thing I needed in the first couple of weeks of the New Year. My mood was low enough without having what seemed my final hope taken away from me. Hurriedly I wrote them a letter explaining that I had recently moved and had not even looked at the book. In reality I was begging for more time. There was one last option for funding through the Arts Council England. With my mind still aflame from my descent into the depths during the holiday I set about trying to get that funding. But I certainly wouldn't be holding my breath.

My response to the risk of meltdown was to reluctantly increase my Risperidone. I had a very nice GP who I saw from time to time. He let me do what I wanted with my medication. The increase did pay dividends by late January and my mood scale looked a little healthier. But it was nowhere near the plus two I liked to be on my scale. He was quite happy for me to do that but didn't really want it to be a permanent thing. He did however agree to refer me to secondary services. I had had a consultant for sixteen of the seventeen previous years. Now with my life in turmoil I needed to be known.

It was hard to tell what was driving the volatility. Was it the sheer loneliness of trying to reinvent my life in what I perceived at times to be a hostile environment? Whilst many perceived that my job was going well, I was still utterly confused by it all and hugely disappointed not to make many new friends.

Four months in I felt all at sea in the job. I was too frightened to reach out to say I was struggling. When I reluctantly did my manager was actually quite reassuring by suggesting it had only been four months. Despite that I lived in fear that I would relapse. My take on the absence policy was that people in their first year who took more than a month off sick would after that have their pay diminished. If that happened it would all fall apart. There was no way I could afford to carry on if that happened. My fate then would be to be back with my parents.

In reality I couldn't afford to be there anyway. The pay was just too low. My foolish naivety had been deceived that with such a huge increase in salary I would be okay. There seemed few if any chances to improve that.

There was one small hope although there was no timescale on that. One of the senior academics had approached me early on suggesting that I might consider becoming Head of the Centre for Mental Health Recovery. She seemed to think I was an ideal candidate for that. It would mean a huge raise but I had no idea when or if it would happen. But a little hope was better than none. She had also mentioned the University had its own publishing house and might be worth considering for the book.

One other good thing happened in those early weeks of 2008 and that was that people started coming to see me. Still baffled and switched off by much of my work, I knew I was good at working with the mentally ill. Slowly they kept coming out of the woodwork. It was the tip of a very large iceberg.

I was still completely lost as to how to do the other parts of my role. The policy parts kept coming in but they just led to more confusion. I only had one thought on the promotion side of things and that was use technology to assist me. But I was very frightened of technology. I had an idea to start blogging but I didn't know how to start. Then fate shone on me when I went on a short course on how to do it. Thinking it would be useful I toyed with the idea in my mind but was reluctant to start. That would have to wait.

Yet for all the small successes as that second term wound on towards the end of winter, each night I went back my small and lonely flat. The puddles kept appearing as if from nowhere. My fears of being evicted made me think twice about speaking to Michael. It seemed the whole world was against me. And accompanying my loneliness was the relentless anxiety of having no money.

Each continued to trouble my mind as it teetered on the brink of meltdown. In the main the Risperidone held the potential freefall but the swings remained volatile. And if meltdown happened the result could be cataclysmic for me. It would be the end of what had once been a promising career. Would I really end up back where I started? Did hospital or suicide beckon? It had become a day-to-day existence. But did the world care? Probably not. When I did eventually get to see a psychiatrist they foolishly sent out a junior doctor who was utterly baffled as to why I had come. The consultant did speak to me briefly and informed me that I was far too well to need them and to give his secretary a call if I did go into freefall. I had been around way too long to have any faith in that. A random nobody phoning up to speak to a consultant; I didn't think so. That would in fact change in time as I became better known. But that was the future and I faced a bleak uncaring present.

To the wider world I was a nobody. It was too preoccupied with the financial meltdown that would engulf the world. The previous autumn had seen the first run on a British bank since the 19th century. Northern Rock had collapsed into chaos leading to the hurried privatisation by the government. Each day there were more and more fears about complete financial breakdown. My poverty was a complete irrelevance compared to the wider picture.

Still the commentators said there would be no housing collapse as had happened before. How wrong they all were. Far worse was yet to come.

As I staggered towards an early Easter holiday in which I was due to attend a friend's wedding, my quiet and largely forgotten life marched on as spring came. Was I any better off here than in Kent? It had been seven months since I had undertaken that momentous move. Financially just like the move away from benefits in 2002 it had been a disaster. I had had to have another bailout from Miriam. I hated borrowing money from anyone and I knew I had no way of paying any of it back. But without it I would never have stayed afloat.

My move had left a legacy of debt, fear, anxiety, and utter loneliness. I was regretting ever having given up what I had known. Was this the price of trying to build a career? As always happened in my life I failed to celebrate the good and dwelt on the bad. It meant nothing how far I had come. Yes I was one of the few who had got out of the world of madness. But for what? I knew the darkness that might engulf me. Each day I seemed to be lapping at the margins of that darkness; the blackness of despair.

Chapter 34
A Great Crescendo

The coming of spring heralds the start of many new things. In past times the coming of spring and of the lengthening days was something that I feared. With my illness mainly under control during that spring of my first year in Hertfordshire it promised fewer demons. True the end of the NFL season had happened. That other stalwart of fighting my way through my life, the Six Nations rugby was also drawing to a close. I had described them as the "pegs on which I hung the mantel of my madness". But no more. A summer in the oak wood was but a few months away.

It had been an extremely rocky baptism of fire with my move. My mood had been very variable. At times I coped, at others I didn't. Despite my fears I had avoided mental meltdown although I was still taking increased Risperidone as a precaution.

The big change had been getting a second bailout from Miriam. It was the last thing that I wanted to do but I had no choice really. Lurking bleakly in the back of my mind was how on earth I would ever be able to pay the money back.

Elsewhere in the world life was also moving on. In Iraq, the Iraqi army had moved into and taken the city of Basra from militias loyal to Iran. The British in whose area Basra was situated had withdrawn the previous September. Some talked of humiliating defeat. Maybe so but I guess only history will let us know about that. Further north in the American sector the tide of the insurgency had shifted. The tribes which had been the backbone of the original insurgency in Anbar had switched sides and were now trying to evict the Al Qaeda radicals from their lands. General Petraeus' policy of surge, backed up by huge financial incentives had turned the tide.

The news from Afghanistan was less promising. Body bags kept coming back in ever greater numbers.

The financial world was still plummeting although none of us mere mortals knew quite how bad it would get. Banks were in big trouble. It was not a good spring for those in the money making business.

That was of course all beyond my control. There were other things that I could control. Back in the day job there was a sudden surge of activity. It was not that the number increased dramatically just the nature of what I was doing.

My great efforts early on to get known were now coming back to me. Whilst it still felt somewhat isolating clearly some had great faith in me. Those sent were coming from a variety of backgrounds. The number of staff members I saw stayed low but they were often quite needy and I found myself having to do some outreach work for the first time since I moved. This was fine as my modus operandi had always been in the community. For all my discomfort of the policy of staying safe in the community when I was at CMHT, at the University it never seemed to have occurred to anyone that working off campus did bring some potential dangers. Yes I knew what I was doing but I did insist that someone knew where I was. In the end we negotiated with security that they would cover me if I went elsewhere.

Security and its concentration was one of the things that shocked me when I moved there. Back in Cambridge we had the porters who I suppose in their quiet bowler hatted way had done that. There was rarely any trouble, just boys will be boys type of things. Here it was different. There had been two incidents earlier that year involving knives. In both cases a young man would eventually be jailed.

I was also most alarmed that we had a police woman permanently based on campus. I was probably naïve to think we wouldn't need that but I was wrong. After all it was a large community which in many ways resembled any other community. As that spring unwound I did from time to time have to have contact with the police.

Amongst the student population those visiting me were from a cross section of all six faculties we had at the time. Yet there was a huge imbalance between those doing business and humanities and those doing creative subjects such as art and students seeking to become health care professionals. In a way I was not surprised by that. Many I had met in long journey had been curiously creative and found great solace in art.

Neither was it surprising to me that people were seeking professional qualifications. How many people over the years had wanted to train as a nurse, social worker, or OT? I had sworn never to do that until the strange quirk of fate which had led me into the arms of the enemy. Of course I was unqualified but the University had taken a gamble on that.

Nurses were the most needy of all the groups I saw. That was true as much for the Counselling Centre as for me. What I hadn't expected was the stringent regulation of such a profession.

Perhaps there was resistance from the profession to accept service users. It was very easy to make inclusive statements on what they could bring to a Trust but I knew from my own experience it did not always seem to sit comfortably with others. That old term boundaries was a favourite of nurses whether they worked in mental health or in other branches.

There were two things my nurses feared; that their Fitness to Practise might be questioned; or worse than that was the further step of Professional Suitability. I struggled to understand the differentiation and the plethora of governance that lay behind nursing.

As March gave way to April exams were looming ever larger for students. For some reason they were extremely early at Hertfordshire, far earlier than I had been used to at Cambridge. But with that backdrop I became more and more enmeshed in the difficult world of Fitness to Practise. Some students alarmed me but I had no power to do anything about that; I simply wasn't important enough. What was clear was that the academics were most fearful of something going wrong in students' later careers and that it would come back and bite them on the bum. After all, someone had to sign the form saying they were Fit to Practise.

Others I was less concerned about. I was actually forced to attend a Professional Suitability panel with one student. She had in my view acted foolishly but trying to get her disbarred seemed a very great step. I was very struck by what she said at the panel: "mental health nursing is not ready for people like me". This did not go down well as a defence but it did have a very clear resonance with me.

I cast my mind back over my time at CMHT and Rethink. They had constantly harassed me but what was clear was that they found it most difficult to deal with the friendships and relationships that were part of me. Had they tried to get me to change side? Yes of course, but they would never succeed. Doing it my way had always worked even if they found that hard to handle. I was a maverick and intended to stay that way. My priceless gift of language had never deserted me.

Perhaps the difference between those students and me was that I had learned to play the System whereas they had not. My meetings with external agencies reflected a widening set of beliefs. Viewpoint was very much driven by its members all of whom were or had been service users. The Trust was much more wary. Way too many students across the spectrum refused to disclose their difficulties for fear of discrimination. It was very hard to help those we didn't know about. But I never really felt certain that students who asked me about disclosure would really be safe doing so.

Keeping up with all that felt at times as if it was taking its toll on me. But there was another sudden pressure put on me that April which I had not expected. I was therefore somewhat stunned to get a message from two different sources that those at the top of the University were taking a very keen interest in what I was doing. Why would such important people be interested in a mere minnow like me? Well as ever it was down to money. They wanted their money's worth - even if what I was paid was very low - and so wanted to know what I was doing. Yet again I was being asked to justify my existence and to do that most difficult of tasks, to quantify what is unquantifiable.

We resolved in the end that during the summer I would write an end of year report and work out my statistics. I hoped this would keep the wolves at bay.

That April also brought me my first plunge into the delicate world of mental wellbeing promotion. To coincide with Depression Awareness Day I finally launched my "Does university do your head in?" blog. What I really wanted to do was challenge myths and to offer up a hand to those students who might be struggling mentally. It was not just intended to get more people to come to me but more to let them know contact points such as Counselling, the Chaplaincy, and various external agencies. I didn't know then but I had unleashed a monster that would threaten to overwhelm me in the coming months.

At more or less the same time I received a rather nice invitation. The Student Union with which I had formed a good bond offered me two free tickets to the end of term Ball. So long since I had been to a Ball - the last two had not exactly been wonderful. But my life was different now so without hesitation I indicated that I would like to go. So the stage was set for a celebration of sorts to end a tumultuous year on a Friday night in late May.

Since Boxing Day I had stayed in touched with Ali, the girl from the summer of 1995 who had disappeared then come back into my life. I asked her if she would like to come with me and she agreed straight away. She told me she had never been to a Ball but would use her passion for sewing to create a dress for the occasion.

That thought remained during a difficult and intense May. Whilst many of my students disappeared at exam time, the nurses kept coming. The other challenge for those who did professional courses was that their academic years were much longer. Thousands of hours of placement had to be completed so they too would be there much of the summer.

Many of those around me assumed that I would get months off during the summer. In fact that was a long way from the truth. I only got five weeks a year. Those on academic contracts got much longer. I wondered in my place in the Equality Unit how equitable that was. But the unions had not been able to overturn it. There would be a shift later but only in favour of those on higher pay grades than me; another way to lose out.

In the event those final weeks of May sped past. By the time exams were over it was time to party at the Ball. Some would have to retake exams in the summer and I would carry on on my lonely journey the following week.

It was a beautiful early evening as spring ended when I picked Ali up from the station. I cooked us a curry and we changed into our finery. Michael very kindly gave us a lift to the University. Unbeknown to us we had VIP tickets and did not need to queue.

We entered a vast throng of people. Few were properly dressed in black tie, it seemed many did not know what it was. From there on in we ate and drank with abandon. Catching up on all those years it transpired that Ali's life too had not been without her battles with depression.

Late on as the night turned cold we went indoors to find yet more to do. That was a relief on a cold night.

When we had both had enough we caught a taxi back to the little annex in the oak wood. It was getting light as we tried to sleep. Michael left at about the same time to catch a flight for his holiday; we heard him but did not speak.

That Saturday morning we got up late and wandered into town in the sunshine. It would be the first of many trips that Ali would make to the oak wood. She stayed the whole weekend before heading back to London and reality.

I too had to face reality. It was in essence all over that first year. What would the long summer bring? One thing I did know was that it would involve a lot of policy work; that aspect of my life I found so hard and disliked so much. But on that Sunday evening I didn't worry. I had survived year one.

Chapter 35
A Desert Stylite

The roots of Mediaeval monasticism lie in the deserts of Egypt in the fourth century. Holy men would go out into the desert to contemplate God and live humble and deprived lives. Perhaps the most significant of these Holy men was St Anthony whose works gave rise to the great monastic orders of the Middle Ages.

The problem for those early Christian pioneers was that as news of their aesthetic lives spread in an increasingly Christian world, people ventured out into the wilderness to marvel at their meagre lives.

With the conversion of Constantine and the shift to a Christian empire based in Constantinople rather than a pagan empire based in Rome the importance of these Holy men grew. And so they moved. They moved into the heart of the city and stood and lived on tall pillars from where they would preach and advise. So the aesthetes became civilised and thus distracted from their contemplations. They were the stylites of the Byzantine world.

In my brave new world that first summer my mind often drifted to those stylites. They lived in isolation until the world came to them for advice. Isolation, I knew that very well. How different was that from my life in the University? Whilst I was certainly not holy I existed in the isolation of such a huge organisation and dispensed advice to those who wanted it. Then it was back to the solitude of my office; standing on my own pillar.

The euphoria of the Ball faded quickly and within a week my mood was in freefall. I had feared this would happen. Deep down I knew that the summer would be filled with policy writing. It was an area I neither understood nor truly believed in. For reasons that I never really digested the University had committed itself to having a staff mental health policy in place by that September. And that task fell to me despite what the Dean of Students had told me way back when I had started.

We had an existing student mental health policy that had some merit. My thinking was that the needs of the mentally ill were the needs of the mentally ill whatever their circumstances. I had grave doubts about the validity of any policy when it came to my field. There was simply too much we couldn't predict or plan for.

But as a starting point it made sense merely to reword the existing policy. Sadly although I was the alleged "expert" no one else agreed with me. It was felt by others that the needs of staff were different and I had to run with this.

So week after week as the summer progressed I sat alone in my office working away on draft after draft. Each was dismissed as not fit for purpose. How could I write a policy if the goalposts kept changing? With each dismissal my mood fluctuated into the lower regions of my at times troubled mind. Day after day it went on.

There were some distractions on occasions. Although the numbers were much lower I continued to see some students and staff. Each of these meetings provided a welcome break from my otherwise confused life.

I did manage to break things up in other ways too. I attended a couple of conferences and my face became better known. I had also been co-opted onto a working group which was planning for a major recovery conference that October. They had all the big players in place but they were looking for others to run workshops on the theme of mental health and employment. This did not go down well with many in the Centre for Mental Health Recovery advisory group. Some simply refused to entertain the idea that employment was important. The promised job as Head of Centre had never materialised partly as no one was able to agree on a job description.

That said I liked the idea of running a workshop at such a prestigious event and put in a proposal based on my experience. It was quickly accepted and I had something to look forward to in the autumn. In the meantime though I had to get through what was an increasingly forlorn and depressing summer.

At the same time I started to attend a series of lectures in the evenings run by our Social Work Department. I had had some contact with them during the year concerning a few of their students. I was at that time still oblivious to the role I would play with the social work students the following year. Once a month they ran a lecture as part of a series entitled "Working in Social

Professions". Some were excellent and worth the late working; others were less so. As a result of attending, the programme lead approached me about possibly giving a lecture in the future. I agreed in principle although it was as yet unclear on the content. But being open to professionals from right across the county and London it would be another good way of networking.

Diversions aside though as the weeks of June passed by I was becoming increasingly disillusioned. This was not what I had signed up to do nor was it any great strength of mine. True many people had met with me to advise on the policy but as each draft came to me it was rejected one after another. With so few distractions I found myself living for the weekends.

These proved somewhat better despite my meagre resources. At the end of the month I attended an Old Lancing dinner back at my old college in Cambridge. It was a memorable evening at which I renewed acquaintances and saw some for the first time in years.

On other weekends friends came and weather permitting we were often to be found in the garden of the oak wood house drinking cold Pimm's and passing the time of day. Ali came several times that summer and Marie continued her more or less monthly visits when she had received her DLA that was actually funding her quite well in those days. But for every weekend there was another week to get through after that. And sadly as it had been the year before it was another wet summer.

Some weekends I did go away but with less frequency than I had earlier in the year. Some thought I was a party animal at the University but that wasn't really how I saw myself. Even after getting well I still at times felt most uncomfortable at parties.

June moved on into July and little about my day job changed. With each passing week I sat on my pillar typing away knowing full well that draft six would be rejected just as the first five drafts had been. But there was change coming up.

In August I undertook the review of what I was doing and wrote my report. Some of the data rather shocked me. I had seen a total of forty one students and staff since September. The breakdown was kind of expected with about 15% having psychosis, 10% with bipolar, a lot of depressed anxious people, a small but alarming number of PDs, and some unknown. The surprise though was that I had seen three times as many men as women. This went completely against the expected grain.

In my world men were notoriously difficult to help. They simply didn't come forward with problems. Despite this trend or perhaps because of it suicide rates amongst men nationally were three times as high as for women. Yet women made three times as many attempts as men.

With my unexpected data complete I set about writing the report itself. That was one thing I knew I could, writing was now well within my blood. It took four days to write the report and much to my surprise it was welcomed largely unaltered. Finally an acceptance of something I did do well.

Reflecting did help me to start believing again that I was doing something important. It didn't always feel like that at the University.

Despite that high my morale remained low as those weeks of August went by. But I didn't care as I was counting down to my holiday. I certainly needed it by that stage.

I set the precedent that year that I would go to Kent for my holiday. Better to have a birthday surrounded by people who did care rather than loneliness of my working existence. For two sadly short weeks I forgot about my disillusionment, lack of money, and doubts as to what I was doing.

Those two weeks flew by. I was now 39 years old and away in the land of people who had yet to take me to themselves. I faced semi eviction from my flat as the men were about to commence work on the puddles. When the insurance assessor had finally looked, it transpired that the built in shower had been leaking for years. It had gone on so long that it had seeped under the wall and led to the lakes of water in the main part of the flat. It would take several weeks to dry out and as a result I would have to move into the main house which Michael generously offered. The real bonus was that for the time being I would not have to pay rent.

Since my bailout by Miriam I had become far less stressed about money but continued to spend beyond my means. Throughout my year in Hertfordshire prices had rocketed. As the world stood on the cusp of autumn 2008, official inflation was almost matching the reality. For me this was good as the University had agreed to a rise in line with the RPI calculated that October.

Cushioned by the lack of rent I might finally be able to claw back some of my debts and get back in control.

But in the wider world financial catastrophe was engulfing us all. Banks were being bailed out on both sides of the Atlantic. The money we supposedly didn't have appeared to bail them out. The coup de grace of a full recession was about to happen.

Life was changing too in the political world. The despised George W Bush was in the final few months of his second term. There had been a bitter struggle for the nomination to contest the presidency. Now we faced the very real possibility that a black man would ascend to the White House. Although not naturally a Democrat follower I quietly wished that Obama would triumph and sweep away such discrimination against those who did not share the same colour of skin as I had. For all the chaos of the world, that would have a seismic effect on all of us.

There was therefore some hope. In my quiet part of the world I would face year two of my quest. Did I really want it? Could I cope with the still prevalent loneliness? Time would tell but I was not very hopeful as that September began. The policy lay unwritten and abandoned.

Chapter 36
Whispers in the Ether

Back in the spring of 1994 when I was in the special hospital where they treated the untreatables like me the man I knew simply as god had asked me if I had lost all my friends. When I confirmed that for all intents and purposes I had he responded that that was "inevitable". Perhaps he was right but over the next few years I slowly started to regain them. My reintegration with the Cambridge crowd was complete in the winter of 2002. It was then at a party in London that a friend had inadvertently given me the ending sentences to the as yet unwritten memoir A Pillar of Impotence.

I didn't often see them all but it was good when we did get together. Yet the wonderful thing about Cambridge is that old loyalties tied us all together. We had arrived in October 1988 as passionate and arrogant dreamers. Now twenty years later we had all been through a great deal but were still very much alive.

To mark the twentieth anniversary of our matriculation, the college organised a reunion dinner on the second weekend of September. I no longer had the fear of what to say to people. I may not have been the MD of this or that as all my friends were but I had a job, a life, a home, and recovery. And that was a huge change for me.

Of course by then I had many other friends as well, some sane and some insane. I had reluctantly joined Facebook just before I moved to Hertfordshire. Much to my surprise people were looking to track me down. I was never interested in the competitive side of it, the numbers of friends didn't matter to me. What mattered was re-establishing links to my past. These people after all were the background to my now relatively good existence.

But one friend had been particularly welcome back into my world. Lynne, my former colleague with whom I had fallen out in the run up to my move had got in touch via Facebook. I always hated losing friends so to re-establish contact was really important. But Lynne had changed significantly in my eyes during that lost time. For shortly after I left she was diagnosed with bipolar. She had crossed the Styx from the sane to the insane. I had been right when we had fallen out that she was ill but I just didn't know what she had.

Unlike me, she was having a very hard time working for CMHT with that diagnosis. She felt very strongly that she was being pushed out. We talked often and she seemed to find my thoughts helpful. What I couldn't predict as I came back from my holiday was that Lynne would be in touch shortly with terrible news. I could not predict the future so for the time being we just chatted as friends.

For all my friends in many parts of the country I still had very few close at hand as I stood on the brink of my second year at the University.

Having been perched on my lonely desert pillar for most of the summer the start of September came as something of a shock. Suddenly people began to come and see me in droves. There was no sign of the now defunct policy work that I had so struggled with. Instead it was down to real people. Of course they were needy but that was my reason for doing the job. It had always been about the people, finding them in the wilderness, speaking their language, and working towards a move back to reality.

With this sudden influx of people my mood shifted accordingly. Very quickly I moved into one of my mini highs, the ones in which my mood is up, my speech is quicker, my mind sharper, and the less pleasant side of my arrogance comes to the fore. True I might have pissed some people off when I was like that but I loved it.

Buoyed by need induced euphoria I caught the train to Cambridge on the Saturday of the dinner. It was an unusually warm day and somewhat uncomfortable on the train. I was irritated to discover there was engineering work going on that weekend and I had to catch a bus from Royston. But it delayed me very little and having dumped my bag in the college I quickly made my way down to the Eagle. Yes, the Eagle, purportedly the best pub in Cambridge but one which was closed for renovation for our whole three years there.

For much of that afternoon people arrived and we wound back the clock. The beer flowed and talk moved lyrically on. My banking friend Anna told me more of the financial catastrophe that was engulfing us. The latest bank in the news Lehman Brothers was as she put it "fucked".

Later we moved to the Granta and sat by the river in the sunshine drinking more. Not much had changed on that front for most of us. With the afternoon winding down I headed back to college to shower and change for dinner. By then most of us were pissed.

Dinner, as ever, was a most grand affair. Cambridge knows how to look after its own. Excellent food and drink followed by witty and succinct speeches. Then we all adjourned to the bar going on into the early hours. Many friendships were resumed and stories told. On the whole most people's lives had worked out well. Mine had too although it took much longer for it to get started than for most.

It was good to catch up with an old friend Scott from my PGCE days. He was not studying but had become bar manager at the college some time after I had returned to the obscurity of Kent.

After the bar closed we retired to someone's room and kept on drinking. I have no idea what time I gave up but I did find myself back in those familiar rooms in Old Court to sleep the sleep of the dead.

I awoke late the next day to find the place deserted. I made a few calls but got no reply. With a slightly saddened heart I headed to the station for my journey back to Hertfordshire. It would have been nice to have said goodbye. As I sat on the coach half way to Royston a text came through to say they were all in the Eagle for Sunday lunch. It was too late to go back now. Despite that little setback my mood remained high and buzzing. Life looked good for me if not for the rest of the world.

The following day Lehman Brothers went under and set the tone for the chaos of many years to come. The coup de grace had been delivered. The financial world was fucked. And by extension so were we. On that day though I didn't care; I was alive again after my lonely summer in the desert.

Back in the reality of my now blooming world I was preparing myself for the big entry to the wider realm of mental health. I had always been determined to make a name for myself and the forthcoming conference would provide just such an opportunity.

It was at this precise moment in the build-up as the weeks of September passed before the start of term that another opportunity presented itself. I had an email from one of the social work academics whom I did not know to come and speak to the whole of the second year cohort on mental health law. That would not be very interesting but when I learned through further enquiry that it was part of a series of lectures on a module around engaging service users I sensed another opportunity to tell my story.

The offer had come about purely by chance as their usual speaker had dropped out due to illness. I spoke to the module leader and she thought it would be an excellent idea for the students to hear another real narrative story.

It was on the Wednesday of the as expected chaos of induction week that I stood as an unknown before a room full of eager social work students that I first told my story to people who might in the future be able to do what I couldn't do, change the System. Speaking clearly and without notes I delivered the story of A Pillar of Impotence to a stunned audience. They laughed of course at the "what the fuck have you done to the dog" comment. As I surveyed the sea of faces I could see people genuinely being moved by my tale.

When I had finished I took any questions they wanted to ask and continued to control an entire room. It was like the singing of the old days; my voice had come back.

With the interesting bit done I briefly went over my somewhat boring handout on mental health law then promised to send it to them. As time ran out the room exploded in applause. And it appeared to be genuine. Finally I had an audience with potential power. I had delivered my first sermon on what I knew best; me and the world of madness.

The following day I was approached in the corridor by an unknown student. She had attended my lecture and was full of praise. But then she said something really curious.

"We were talking afterwards and we all agreed what a shame it is you don't teach anymore."
"I think what I do now is far more important than teaching year 9 on a Friday afternoon." Stunned that I had said that it made me reflect. Yes it was more important. I was making a real difference to

people's lives. I was infinitely better at the mad world than I had ever been at teaching.

I never saw the student again but it was the start of my belated teaching career. Mood flying I started to prepare myself for the next voice giving, the conference at Newmarket.

A few days beforehand I had a call from Ruth asking if I could get her a free ticket. I explained that that would not be too much of a problem but I would have to ask Michael if it was okay to stay as I was still staying in the main house. Graciously he agreed and so the night before the conference I picked Ruth up from the station. We ate in the former bank and drank perhaps more than we should have done.

It was way too early on a cold October morning that Ruth and I walked through the oak wood to the pick-up point barely five minutes away. I was armed with a list of names and numbers for those who were coming on the bus. With the company all accounted for we set off up the A1(M) towards Newmarket race course. I cursed my mild hangover as I focused on what was to come.

We got there to some grandeur, with coffee and Danish to eat. Food seemed good at that point. I was not nervous but I was determined to get it right. It would be a small group to which I would speak, perhaps twenty or so if they all turned up.

All the great and the good of the recovery movement were there; figures far grander than I was. I took very little in during the morning session despite the inspirational nature of some of the tales I heard. But I was zeroed in on one place.

After lunch I went to my assigned room and waited. Slowly people shuffled in. Then the rush came. By the time I started to speak there were some fifty people crammed into the room. All the seats were gone and people were sat on the floor in the aisle and the entrance.

I held no fear as I told my story. Again I used no notes. As I spoke I surveyed the mesmerised faces of the vast throng and they absorbed every detail of my story. Being about employment I extended it to look at how far I had come and how hard it had been to get to where I was now.

When I finished the story I asked them in groups to work out why the mentally ill should work and what was stopping them. Much to my surprise I had complete buy-in. They loved it. The responses at times overwhelmed me. In the end we ran out of time. A huge round of applause awaited me.

Utterly drained emotionally I went outside for a few minutes afterwards. In the cool air of an October afternoon I just sat there and smoked.

The rest of the day was a blank. I simply didn't have the energy to listen. But I was happy.

When we got back home Ruth and I once again retired to the former bank and drank more. But there was good reason. My voice had finally been heard by those who might make a difference. I had arrived on the scene.

For so long I had whispered in the darkness of my madness. No one had wanted to listen. I had never changed my story but it had taken ten years for one person with power to hear it. Now the wider world wanted to listen. Apparently I had something important to say.

Throughout the rest of October amongst the chaos of an extraordinarily busy first term in year two at the University my mood was flying. An autumn buzz abounded in my mind. I had made the right move. The nobody had become a somebody even if it was only on a small scale. But where could it go from there?

Chapter 37
The Black Night Descends

My last five years of living in Kent had mainly been a time of huge progress. I had done what few others had done, namely to get away from the DWP and steadily rise up the mental health ladder. I had been to many weddings and so many of my friends had had children it was hard to keep up with them all. But there had been a darker to side to my time there. It was a time marred by sudden deaths. The funeral count during that time stood at an average of five a year. Way too many for someone who had not yet reached the age of 40.

Yet that was part of the life of being mentally ill. Life expectancy was much lower for us. There were many ways to die other than the obvious one of suicide. I had become aware that Risperidone almost certainly would shorten my life when I had met a French locum GP in the autumn of 2005. He seemed most worried that I was taking such a drug yet it was that that had prevented my anticipated suicide. My reasoning was that it had given me back a life, a life so much better than before.

Fourteen months into my new life in Hertfordshire, the world had blessed me with no further funerals. As I sat in a pub near King's Cross just days before the greatly anticipated US election with two old friends, death and funerals were very far from my consciousness.

It was always good to see old friends. I had seen neither of them for several years. Tory, the astonishingly bright girl from school who had got into Oxford at such a young age that it put me to shame. She was at that time pregnant with her second child and about to take leave from her high powered job at ITV. She had chosen the pub, a mere stone's throw from her office.

Richard whom we all referred to as Professor Steve was equally bright although in a totally different field to the two of us. He had not gone to Oxbridge but had chosen instead to go to university far further afield. He had completed a PhD in London and, for the past seven years he had been teaching and researching at the University of Pennsylvania.

It was a meeting of very old friendships interrupted by the vagaries of our present-day lives. As we ate surprisingly good food our thoughts inevitably turned to the upcoming election. A mere six months before I still hadn't believed America was ready to elect either a black man or a woman as president. But my thoughts had changed after Obama's innovative campaign using the Internet to target young voters who would be voting for the first time. I was convinced that he would win.

Professor Steve had taken a keen interest in American politics long before he had gone over there to live and work. He still believed that old prejudices would win out and bring to power the Vietnam War hero John McClean. That seemed inconceivable to me after the debacle of Bush's two terms. In the end we agreed to disagree and see what happened.

At the passing of a very pleasant evening we all headed our separate ways back to our lives. I would not see Tory until three years later. I have not seen the Professor since.

Ultimately my conviction was proved right and history was made on 4th November 2008 as Barak Obama was elected the first black president of the United States of America. It was a mighty day for those in the equality business as well as for so many people from BME groups.

I smiled at the news. In fact it seemed I had a great deal to smile about. My mood was exultant, I was doing what I loved, and my voice had finally been heard. True the world was in freefall but the impact of that on me was still some way off.

Going into the Remembrance weekend there seemed few if any clouds on the horizon. But all that was about to change.

On Remembrance Sunday itself I was sat in my still deconstructed flat watching the NFL as I always did when there was a knock on the door. It was Michael.

"There's no easy way to say this but I'm going to have to sell the house and you will need to find somewhere else to live."

I was stunned. I'd known that business was down where he worked and he had recently taken a significant pay-cut. But he had a small property portfolio and it never occurred to me that he would be forced to sell the main house. It was only later that he admitted to me that he had never really been able to afford the mortgage on the house even when business had been good and his income was supplemented by me lodging there.

There was no real rush to get out, it could take months to sell. But I was aware that appointments to view would not fit in easily with my need to sleep at weekends.

My mind went into immediate meltdown. Stress and anxiety took over rapidly. The rest of the night I was back thinking about what it had been like over the summer in which I had moved. I envisioned that doing a short distance move might be less stressful but that did not relieve the crippling anxiety.

As I returned to work the next day it was very hard to concentrate. My diary was still overwhelming but that paled into insignificance. I just had to get on with it. My thoughts turned to finding another place. It was clear that the rental prices had gone up even further in my short time there. I never had been able to afford living there without an increase in pay. I was only really being kept afloat by the fact that with the flat still uninhabitable I was paying no rent. At least this would give me some leeway with a deposit and rent in advance.

The next couple of weeks went by in the same way. I looked at one or two places but they were unsuitable or unaffordable. I was also aware that I would have to pay astronomical agent's fees too.

Then I struck lucky as the days of November began to wane. One of the agents called and said they thought they had the perfect place for me. It was in the next village where there was a much greater sense of community than where I was now. It would come furnished and was only marginally more expensive than I was paying already.

I visited and it seemed perfect. I paid the agent's fees which did not seem to make sense until I found out part of that was for setting up utilities and others things. Expensive though it was that might at least keep the anxiety down a bit.

The following weekend after my viewing I travelled down to Kent for a bit of a break. Nothing much eventful happened, just old friends and too much drinking.

On my return I walked back from the station with my bag over my shoulder. It was cold and November was nearly over. As I turned into the oak wood my phone rang. Pulling it out of my pocket I was somewhat surprised to see Lynne's mobile number appear on the screen. Sensing something might be wrong I answered straight away.

"Mark, it's Lynne. I have bad news, Andrew has had a heart attack."
"Is he okay?"
"No he's dead. We're all stunned."

That voice hit me like a blow from a hammer. Andrew had been my CPN in the late 1990s. I was very distrustful of him at the time but as my life began to resolve itself Andrew had come back into my world and was my greatest supporter.

At CMHT he had always maintained that I was the best qualified of any of us to do that kind of work. I had seen him barely a month before when he had said to me "you don't fancy coming back as a senior practitioner do you?" I'd thought he was only speaking in jest but he had been serious. He had had faith in me, faith that one day I would rise to great things.

I swiftly finished talking to Lynne. She promised to keep me posted about the funeral arrangements.

When I got home I tried to reflect on such stunning news. It did not make sense. How could a man of 42, just three years older than me who didn't drink, or smoke and who kept himself very fit suddenly die of a heart attack?

In the coming days there were several phone calls each bringing the news that I already knew. Sadly, no one gave me a date for the funeral. Andrew was buried on 4th December 2008 in my absence. It was I'm told one of those rare occasions on which the us and them came together as equals. The CMHT never really recovered from his death.

Still reeling I had to get back to reality. Work was still flat out but at least I had somewhere to move to. My anxiety had diminished a little with some certainty to my future.

On the day I was planning to go in to pay the deposit I received an unexpected call from the agent. She was most apologetic but the news was not good. The present tenant had changed his mind and had decided to stay put. There was nothing I could do. They did promise to keep looking for me and to return my fee. In the end I had to fight for that.

Girdled in a blanket of darkness my anxiety went through the roof and my mood fell through the floor. It had been a very black few weeks. And each time I went home it was back to a building site. Work had begun on what would soon become my ex home.

Through the despair I went back to flat hunting. On a whim I called a number in the local paper the following weekend. A charming sounding woman answered and confirmed that the flat was still available. It transpired that it was in fact her partner's flat. He was a military man and was soon to go on deployment to Afghanistan. I arranged to meet him the following week.

It was in a place I did know although not well. There was a parade of shops including a Co-op, a Malaysian restaurant which I already knew, and a Chinese take away. Over the road there stood a church and a pub. I had been warned about that pub but had never really taken any notice.

On a cold December evening I met him by the shops. He showed me the flat. It seemed fine for what I needed and I confirmed my interest. It was at that stage unfurnished but he could rectify that. He said he would call me.

When he did he agreed for me to have it. He and his girlfriend came round on the following Sunday, I paid a month in advance by cheque and got relevant bank details for a standing order. He did not want a deposit or references both of which I would have been happy to give. The rent paid all in including the bills was just £50 more than I had been paying in the present flat.

With the holiday coming up we arranged to meet the day after I returned from Kent. He and his dad would furnish it in the meantime. Then I could pick up the keys.

Back in my forlorn flat I lamented what might have been. I had not expected to move twice in fifteen months. Having somewhere to go only reduced the anxiety by a few degrees.

Flat, tired, low, and, in despair I went to Kent for Christmas and New Year. It was a desolate time in which I was not very good company. I was actually quite glad when it was over.

Back in Hertfordshire I knocked on the door of my manager's house to tell her my plans. She too lived in the oak wood. We arranged an extra week off so I could complete the move.

That first week of January was bitterly cold. Snow lay on the ground as I packed the last of my things. A former colleague helped with a van and my dad came up one day to help me move my computer. As the week passed I made a couple of journeys each day the mile or so up the road to move more bits and pieces. In between times I fell on the snow twice. It was an ill omen.

With everything complete I made calls to disconnect the phone and the Internet. I took a final look at the now gleaming flat with new carpets, bathroom, and freshly decorated walls. I would never see the use of it. With that I left the keys for Michael and headed off up the road.

For the first time in my life I was living in a flat on an estate. A far cry from the oak wood even if they were but a mile apart. My mood was low and my anxiety still heightened.

That evening I went over to the pub which the few friends I had had all warned me not to go in. Going through the door something very odd happened to me. People actually started talking to me. That was a first for Hertfordshire.

Chapter 38
The Headsman's Block

My late starting career had taken many twists and turns. Mostly these were on the upward spiral towards success. As each job passed into the past and a new one started it was another step up the ladder. The field remained constant but the people varied enormously. There was but one constant throughout that journey; every organisation I had worked for had had budget cuts every year. And that was during the good times when the arrogant chancellor had trumpeted his foolish claim that he had defeated boom and bust economics. He would later go on to inadvertently claim to have saved the world; I wonder what Freud might have made of that statement.

There was of course some distance between the claims and reality. New Labour claimed to have pumped lots of money into health. But I rarely saw it in my quiet and largely irrelevant role. Mental health funding was never ring fenced as it did not win many votes.

When I had arrived at the University the previous year, budgets there had been cut year on year as well. Fifteen months on from my arrival the financial world was in tatters, banks had been bailed out with billions of tax payers' money, and the word banker was only uttered with absolute contempt. If we had had to cut in the good times, what on earth would we do in the midst of a recession?

If there were plans afoot for change there was no word on the street as I returned to the University following my enforced absence. My mood remained low and volatile. The anxieties continued as I did battle with BT and my mobile phone provider as I tried to sort out communications. For reasons that were never explained to me there was no cable connection to the building despite it being only a few years old. Houses in the surrounding estate were able to get it okay but not our building. So I had little choice but to get Sky. That would take a few weeks so I had to content myself watching DVDs in the evenings when I got back from work until it was sorted out.

Teething problems aside I was just relieved to have moved without too much trouble. Slowly as my second week back progressed my mood started to lift.

The frenetic pace of referrals continued and there was no let up. The blog that I had set up the previous April was almost paying too many dividends. Almost all the self referrals were from people who had seen the blog. In fact during that first summer of going live the blog had become the second most widely read in the whole university after that of the Vice Chancellor. It did not take long to get back into the swing of things.

I had never met the Vice Chancellor although he usually said hello to me in the corridor and he did much to my surprise know who I was. Every September just before the start of the new academic year he addressed the University staff. The first one I went to was baffling. The second the previous September had made a little more sense but even this far in there was much I didn't understand about such a vast organisation.

I'm not sure whether it was a shock or not when an email came round calling an extraordinary address to the staff on the third Thursday of January. Sensing there were big things about to happen I went over early to get a seat. 4 o'clock in the afternoon seemed to a strange time to meet. Being at the end of the day I knew I would have the whole weekend to mull things over as none of my colleagues were in the following day.

The room was packed by the time he came on to speak. Others watched electronically via monitors and webcasts. What followed was so broad ranging and drastic that the audience was left stunned. I didn't take much in but the main thrust was that the University was to shrink from the existing six faculties to four. One faculty would be lost completely and two others merged. There were many other cuts envisaged. Few appeared to affect me except a rather oblique reference to "streamlining central administration". That would be me but there were no details other than that.

What was clear was that there would be many job losses and natural wastage. Volunteers were being sought for redundancy. It seemed the bulk of those going would be at the very top of faculties and the administrative staff.

I don't think anyone had been quite ready for the extent of the cuts. I heard later that it had been kept so secret that heads of faculties were only told of the plan half an hour before the Vice Chancellor spoke to the University. There was of course talk of consultation with the unions although I was told that some people got redundancy papers that afternoon. Whether either was true I was never able to ascertain. What followed were many rumours but very little substance. The timescale for the changes to be in place was by that summer.

I went home that afternoon wondering as so many others must have been what it meant for me. Who would climb the scaffold to kneel at the Headsman's Block? Uncertainty gripped the University for the next six months.

It was not until the following week that I was able to consult other colleagues on their views. They differed but all were bleak.

For all the uncertainty though I knew there was nothing I could go about it. I could merely work with the students and staff who came in my direction as best I could. And as the weeks passed after the judgement, by God did they come. It just didn't stop.

Away from the chaos and uncertainty I was slowly trying to rebuild yet another life. The pub that I'd been warned about proved very different to what I had expected. It had a strange set up which I eventually unravelled as a business split between a brother and sister and their respective spouses. Not all was as it seemed and there were fault lines. But on the whole I was slowly able to make friends. That helped a great deal.

Ali came to visit on the last weekend of January and Marie followed soon afterwards. I also had occasional day visits from my old PGCE friend Katherine.

Other aspects of my life remained frozen and set to one side. There was simply too much to do to sort myself out. The most important of these forgotten areas was the book. By February 2009 I had come to a complete standstill on that. I had written to and been rejected by every literary agent in the country. The offer I had had fallen through as I couldn't raise a single penny in sponsorship. I had tried everywhere from the once promising lead of Janssen Cilag, to local philanthropists, to the big mental health charities. No one wanted to support me. The final throw of the die had come to nought when the Arts Council had deemed me ineligible for a grant.

As far as I could see the mainstream publishers would not even look at a manuscript unless an agent had sent it.

Deep in the recesses of my mind there were but two options left. I had been told early on that the University had a Press and it might be an idea to send it there. The other option was a niche publisher that specialised in publishing the stories of the mentally ill. I had discovered them in the summer of 2003. This had always been very much a plan B as it would merely be preaching to the converted. The people I wanted to reach were the people not in the know. Jan one of my readers whilst I wrote it had once remarked that "it is too good for that". She may have believed that but no one in the literary world agreed with her. It was not until years later that I discovered that many top agents receive in the region of one thousand manuscripts for every one they take on.

As the weeks of February rolled on the book was not in the forefront of my mind. That was to change the day that an email came round about a forthcoming seminar for staff who wanted to get published run by the manager of the UH Press and another publisher. Quickly I signed up and mused with intrigue on where that might lead me.

On the last Wednesday in February I wandered along to the assigned room for the seminar. It filled up very quickly, clearly there were many would be authors in the University. I sat for the next hour listening to the way to do it. This included scoping an audience and presenting the idea to a publisher. There was much advice all of which was the complete opposite of what I had done. My book was complete. I knew from the plethora of mental health and sad life stories most of which were not very good that littered our bookshops that there was a market. I simply could not find a way to tap into that.

Afterwards I approached the women who had led the seminar. She was called Jane and was manager of UH Press. Much to my surprise she expressed a real interest in the subject matter. I didn't really expect the University to publish a book of that type but she did ask me to email the files to her.

Sensing a possible way forward I emailed the script that evening. Early the following week I received a short email from Jane explaining that although she found it interesting it was not something she would take on. She felt it was too long and needed to be completely rewritten. She did say she would give more detailed thoughts if I wanted them.

That was not the news that I had hoped to hear. How could I completely rewrite something I had taken three years to complete? It was not until a few weeks later that I asked for more detailed feedback. She gave it but I could not read it sending it instead first to Heather. My take was not quite right and Heather was able to bring a more positive ring to what seemed so bleak. I made a decision after that, I would send it to the niche publisher. The two mainstream publishers she suggested did not take manuscripts unsolicited unless they were from an agent.

On the Tuesday after the seminar I attended my first funeral since I had moved. John was one of my oldest friends with whom I had sung as a child in Cambridge and later in Sussex. His remarkable father Patrick had experienced a stroke some time before. He had died the previous week. Taking the day off I went to London for the event. Sadly work followed and the phone still kept ringing even on a day off.

March meandered along at the same pace as we headed towards Easter. There were a few things on the horizon. I was due to speak to a CMHT in Sussex on mental health recovery after Easter. I was by then deeply involved in a cross county initiative aimed at preventing suicide. I was in demand to teach some more as well as working on the mental health nursing curriculum. And there was another possible book lead via Ruth and Mark. I was only stopped by a bout of tonsillitis in the middle of the month. My mood dipped for that but soon bounced back.

For all the uncertainty, my life looked on the up; it did not appear that I was approaching the scaffold as so many other colleagues were. Slowly but surely I was finding a place so far away from home.

Mark Edgar

Chapter 39
Icarus Flies Again

Spring has always been a time of rebirth in the world. Emerging from the cold dark winter, the first sign of spring is often the emergence of the bulbs and the daffodils. The air heats up, theoretically there is more sun light. Spring lamb with mint sauce adorns the tables of the English on a Sunday. The clocks go forward and we have more daylight. For some it is a time of abstinence as this coincides with the Christian season of Lent. People give treats up for Lent and some, my parents included, will refrain from eating meat on a Friday.

But of course what comes up in the spring has by necessity been planted in seed form before then in the autumn and winter.

During the really dark times of my illness I had always found the darkness of the winter months comforting. I hated the sunlight and heat. In that though I was something of an exception. Most people in my world became deeply depressed over the winter, the term Seasonal Affective Disorder was sometimes used to describe that. My illness was almost reverse cyclical. My many bipolar friends began to emerge from their depressive phases in the winter into the upward swing of spring and summer. The key with them was trying to keep the upward swings manageable. That was not something I had to worry about until the advent of Risperidone. That had created my mini highs, the buzzy times that so annoyed others.

As I emerged from the winter of 2009 my mood was already on the rise. It was true then that following my exchange with Jane I was heading for the final day of reckoning on A Pillar of Impotence but several seeds sown earlier were beginning to germinate.

My partnership with Ruth and Mark had me writing again that March. The brief was very straight forward. Up to 10,000 words on psychosis and recovery, any way I wanted to do it. When I started the shortened version of my life emerged and was complete in barely three nights' work. It was amazing what could be achieved with the mood and energy coming back. The plan was that several of us would each write in our own way then we would bring it all together in a book that became known as Voicing Psychotic Experience, a Reconsideration Recovery and Diversity that would then be edited by Ruth and Mark. If all went to plan it was hoped the book might be published that summer.

With that rapidly done and accepted with little alteration it was on to two events that had come directly from my workshop at the Recovery Conference the previous October. Just in the last couple of weeks of the term I delivered two lectures to a group of trainee probation officer students on recovery, the basics of mental health awareness in the first session then a more targeted session on personality disorders. I was acutely aware that would be an area they would come across a great deal when they qualified. Once again I got to tell my story to a very willing audience.

The lecturer told me after that they had gained a great deal from the sessions and she would like to do it again the following year. Here was the second academic programme I was effectively teaching on. Later that year there would be others. Each little success fuelled the not yet raging inferno of my mood. It just kept rising.

With the second busy term of the academic year over I headed to Kent for Easter. The experience from the year before suggested that the day job would lessen off after Easter. But it would not just be a time to relax. Instead I had to attend to another of those seeds that had been sown at the conference.

On a gloriously sunny morning two days after the Easter Bank Holiday I caught an early train down to Sussex. I had an entire CMHT at my disposal for the afternoon including a consultant psychiatrist. They wanted to know my story and how to integrate recovery into their practice. What followed was an extraordinary debate on how to reach those who were unresponsive to treatment and what message they should give to their people.

I was asked what word encapsulated recovery. I had only one and that was hope. Perhaps the greatest power of my story was that recovery can happen and people can move on in their lives. To some my story provided that hope.

As I sat on the train on the way back I mused on how far I had come. After all I was the one they thought would commit suicide within six months of discharge in the summer of 1994. Now here I was preaching to a variety of audiences on what was possible. I had a voice that more and more people wanted to hear it. How different was that to the one that no one had wanted to listen to for all those years. The fires were stoked a little more that day.

I returned to work after Easter full of energy and wild ideas on what was possible. True the day job did slow down as I had expected. But there were more calls for my knowledge. The week I got back was Staff Wellbeing Week. I was in demand for that.

Then came a most unexpected call to teach again, this time to group of CBT trainees. I had never had time for CBT. When I was forced to do it I was too ill and I learned nothing. But now I had the chance to teach them what they needed to know; more coal to the flames.

April turned to May and still my mood soared higher. It was then that we encountered the first of two major crises that year. I was called in to a student who had been arrested and deemed unfit to be interviewed. When he got to me he was clearly psychotic and should have been in hospital. But he had not been admitted as the police let us down and let him go. Left to clear up the debris as best we could he did in the end go back to his home country and never returned to the University. Another example of the extreme pressures put on our international students. It was the first time I had felt useful in the post Easter and summer lull in the action. More fuel. Drip by drip it reinforced my energy and mood.

There were one or two let downs. A job I had applied for as a trainer in Kent fell through without an interview. When I enquired why this was so I was told that a teaching qualification was not relevant to such a role. Clearly madness did not exist just in the mad world. But I guess not all the world was ready to hear from me. The Trust in Kent seemed far less enlightened than the one in Hertfordshire. I was certain there would be other opportunities.

A physical illness halted the march upwards in late May but after that it was business as usual. I was leading up to what I saw as the big prize. Ever since my arrival at the University I had wanted to make a big statement on being mentally ill. This had been firmly discouraged yet I was expected to challenge stigma and discrimination. A rather difficult task if I was being advised to stay quiet about what had become such a huge part of my life. If I couldn't disclose who else would? But that summer I had the perfect plan to make that statement.

I was to deliver the July lecture as part of the Working in Social Professions series. I had been an avid attendee and it had been mooted before that I should deliver one myself. But I had thought my work too boring for most to want to listen to. Far more interesting in its stead would be a lecture on the challenges of being both a service user and service provider. The programme lead had been most intrigued by this idea although she was a bit worried if I was okay to do it. I was fine. So the scene was set to finally out myself to a wider audience than just specific groups of students. That was what I was really aiming at during that summer. And my mood was just right to do so.

In the run-up to the epic planned outing I had been invited back to speak to the Rethink Carers' Group. The evening I had done before I had moved had been a great triumph and the second time around it was equally good even if the number was somewhat down. These people saw me for what I was and marvelled at how I was doing. I may have been disillusioned the previous summer but I was still one of the few who had got out of the mad world. They would always praise me for what I had achieved.

Coinciding with my trip to Kent we encountered the second crisis of the holiday. I was called in just before 4 o'clock on a Friday afternoon. We finished then and I was anticipating a visit from Ali that June evening. What I was confronted with was a student well known to services who was so paranoid he was too frightened to remain in his room. Conducting an assessment with my friend Geraldine on the grass verge outside our new campus it was clear he needed to be admitted. But it was also clear to me that he would not been deemed ill enough in that state if I took him to the hospital. Geraldine was stunned that that was the case but in the end I was proven correct.

As a temporary measure we moved him to new accommodation and arranged support over the weekend including me coming in if necessary.

The following week I had a call at 8 o'clock in the morning from Geraldine asking me to go to the hospital straight away. The student had been taken there by ambulance that morning. When I got to A&E there was no sign of him. Knowing there was little else I could do I called the police. They set out to search for him.

By a strange quirk of his psychosis he later found his way back to the hospital and was assessed. Even then they didn't want to admit him but were forced to do so when he refused to go home. We lived in eternal fear of being let down by our partners outside the University.

The gravity of the situation did not become clear until I went to visit him and take him some clothes. We found a knife in his bag. Days later he was detained. We had been very lucky.

That scenario played out in my life throughout June but it did have happy ending. He was discharged without going to a six month section 3 treatment order and was able to graduate with his peers in the following November.

It was such a contrast to the previous year as the days ticked by to my lecture. When that day finally came I was faced with over forty people from across the county and London. This was a surprising number considering it was July.

As ever I spoke with confidence and no notes. I told the story as it was written in both books. But as an add on I had gathered testimony from three friends all of whom had mental illnesses and did or had worked in statutory services, Ruth, Emma, and Lynne. I finished with the wonderful note from Emma in which she "looked forward to the day in which it would be unremarkable to be both a service user and a service provider". There had to be hope for us.

After a short break for a cigarette I took any questions that were offered and ended with a huge round of applause. I was finally out there amongst my peers and proud to be who I was. It proved the pinnacle of that flying summer.

The following day I attended the launch party of Voicing Psychotic Experiences in London with Emma, Ruth, Mark, and many others. Finally I was known and in print.

It had been a memorable summer. The man who had flown too close to the sun barely three years before was once again flying. It felt great. The big question was would I once again flame out. That thought was not on my mind. I was counting down to my 40th birthday

Chapter 40
Does Life Begin at 40?

Looking back at my life it is strangely compartmentalised. Not all the milestones were good but it was very easy to define my life into specific periods of time. I lived in Surrey until I was 5. My memories of that, such as they are are mainly good. The first big change in my life came when we moved house on my 5th birthday to a shithole of a derelict house in the middle of nowhere a few miles from Bristol. I hated it there. The next big change in my life was when I went away to boarding-school in Cambridge at the age of 9. At 14 I moved to another boarding-school in Sussex. When I turned 19 I returned to Cambridge to have a relatively happy, if at times lonely journey through that academic establishment. It was there that the great explosion in life happened when I got ill. I was just short of my 21st birthday.

The next decade was more or less catastrophic as I fought against a misdiagnosed illness without the necessary tools to do so; oh how the psychiatrists fucked it up. But in the run-up to turning 30, life was looking better. Many of the friends who I had met during the latter years of the 1990s were somewhat younger than me and all took great pride in telling me I was old coming up to 30. That was the age I returned to Cambridge to do my PGCE.

I needed to fast forward to the next significant date. That amazing day just a week after I turned 32 when I discovered Risperidone. That was the day my life truly started again. 32, a life defining age for me.

As I reflected on my life during that second summer in Hertfordshire, I was approaching 40 and the term "life begins at 40" held no fears or particular credence for me. But I did plan to party and party hard.

It was another Ashes summer. England had been humiliated 5-0 in the winter tour to Australia in 2006/07. Now back at home they were seeking revenge. As I basked in my exhilarated mood post my lecture and the launch of Voicing Psychotic Experiences, across the river Severn in Cardiff, England and Australia were fighting out the first of a five test series. It had not gone well for England yet somehow they had managed to salvage a nerve-wracking draw on the fifth day. This was to be the backdrop to my life that summer as my emphasis shifted from the University to other things.

There were two pressing needs at that time. I was tentatively trying to repair my friendship with Jayne. She was the woman I had met during my illness whom I had most associated with in terms of experience. Yet we had not met in the System but in the pub at the bottom of the hill on a winter's night in 1994 in that small coastal Kent town. Having had no contact with her since 2006 I had earlier in the year held out a tentative olive branch.

We had had sporadic contact through email and then Facebook and I very much hoped that we would meet at some stage in the not too distant future. But it was still early days and I didn't want to push anything too hard. Our correspondence continued as the weeks of July hurried on.

The second important thing in my life that July was taking the final risk on getting A Pillar of Impotence published. There seemed but one hope left, the niche publisher. I feared another rejection. Given what they had published already I thought it inconceivable that they would not be interested but I had been disappointed so many times before thoughts of a final rejection still lurked in my mind.

I decided that it was time to take action so I emailed the files to the man whose name I had been given. There was a very swift response which I was too frightened to open for a few days. When I did it was not a rejection merely a request to try to put it all together in one file. For someone as technologically challenged as me that represented quite a task.

After much swearing and cursing I managed that feat over a weekend and sent it back in one email. Then it was down to waiting.

Back in what passed for the day job it was the silly season. It was a time when little happened and much of the University resembled the deck of the Marie Celeste. Although I had little to do, my buoyant mood remained at its high levels. I delivered my first staff training session with great success that month. I had been angling to do this since my arrival at Hertfordshire but had not been given the chance to do it before. I'm not sure why but I chose not to disclose my madness on that occasion. Perhaps I was still frightened of some people's reactions. Another thread in the web of truths and half truths that surround the lives of the mentally ill.

In the Ashes, England won an epic test at Lord's on the back of Freddie Flintoff's final devastating bowling spell that destroyed the Australians in the second innings. It proved to be the final hurrah of what could have been one of the great careers barring injury; he never played for England again. It was the first time England had beaten Australia at Lords in seventy five years. The question then was could they hold on?

This proved to be the backdrop to the anticipated email from the publisher. It arrived and once again lay unopened for several days. When I opened it it was the news that I had waited for for so long. They would publish. Finally A Pillar of Impotence would see the light of day. The terms of the contract were not particularly good for me but I had never written it to make money. What mattered was that I could get it out into the open in my way. They asked for various things to be sent including a photo for the cover of the ebook. I hastily arranged for Beth to take some pictures in the back courtyard of the pub in the middle of the High Street and sent them off.

I was slightly confused on timescale, format, and editing but it appeared that it would come out in ebook form first then some time later in paperback. Having signed the contract it was now just time to wait.

That provided more fuel to the fire of my mood which for the main part was still burning very hot. There were setbacks that summer as July turned to August. It meant the dreaded appraisal which I always hated. That was a bad day but my mood soon returned to its lofty peaks.

I wrote my annual report which once again was well received. I had seen seventy four people that year, up by thirty three from the year before. The prophecy of others in UMHAN was being fulfilled; once someone was in post, the students would all start coming out of the woodwork.

After that it was just counting down the days until my holiday. Sadly Australia fought back to 1-1 at Headingley with a thumping victory after a draw at Edgbaston. The scene was set for a mighty finale at the Oval. That would be in the week of my birthday.

On the Thursday before my holiday I was summoned to the Equality Unit office just after lunch. Having been told it was something to do with my appraisal I was somewhat surprised to see all of my colleagues from the Equality Unit with a bag of presents and card for my birthday. It was the last day we would see each other before I went off. Somewhat overwhelmed as I always am when people give me gifts I wasn't quite sure what to say. They urged me to open them before I went. This was rare for me to do so early but I acquiesced. So many gifts and all useful. I guess one only turns 40 once but they had really pushed the boat out. It was a wonderful end to what seemed to have been a great second year at the University.

Miriam took me to lunch at Moro in London the day before the final test started. I had always wanted to go there having been an avid user of the three cookbooks by the owners. It was the first of many celebrations that week.

England won the Ashes at the Oval on a glorious day for cricket just before I headed down to Kent to stay for a few days. That was another reason to celebrate.

Down there, the days ticked by very quickly to my birthday. In the end we partied for three days. But it was on the actual day I turned 40 that the greatest surprise and present was delivered. Sat on a low stool around a barrel table in the pub in the middle of the High Street with Marie I heard a voice above me.

"Hi Mark." I looked up and there was Jayne. I had no idea she was coming and wasn't quite sure what to say. The unhappy schism of three and a half years was mended and we were back together again. She seemed happier than I had ever known her, complete with new partner. It would not be long until we met again.

It was a mighty three days' celebration even by our standards. Maybe life did begin at 40? Who really knew? But so what? Life was good and my mood was still on fire. And it stayed that way in the main when I got back to Hertfordshire. I had no thoughts of burnout.

Elsewhere in the world British forces had finally withdrawn from Iraq that summer. It was a quiet exit. The arrogant one would subsequently launch an inquiry into the war; he wanted to keep it secret but public opinion would not allow that. He would soon be forced to relent.

Closer to home he had other problems. They were not his alone but rather a stain on him and all of his colleagues as the expenses scandal blew up in the press. It would not be long before the word politician would be spat out with the same contempt as the word banker.

Mark Edgar

Chapter 41
Sleepwalking

Two years on from my move to the University of Hertfordshire and many academics had told me that there had been a sea change in the attitudes of students after fees were increased to £3,000 per year. On top of that there were maintenance loans accumulating for future discomfort. It was a discomfort I knew well as I was still paying off a maintenance loan from my PGCE days. My timing had proved appalling as it transpired to be the only year ever in which prospective teachers got no financial assistance.

I had started to pay it off when I worked for Rethink in 2003. Contrary to the propaganda put out by government it was proving a crippling financial burden for me. I had not had to pay fees. I often mused that the students that I supported and saw around the campus were almost sleepwalking towards financial ruin. My payments had increased enormously since my move and after our unexpected pay rise of the RPI the previous April my repayments had risen to an alarming £110 per month. And it would be another year until it was paid off. All for a career that never happened. But the students were oblivious to this as they got so many positive messages about it not being expensive to repay. Their future looked potentially more ominous when New Labour commissioned the Browne report that autumn to look at student finance; there was a great chance things might get much worse.

Of course compared to the chaos of the wider world my financial struggles were positively minuscule. The world was deep in recession and the outlook was utterly gloomy despite the claims of the arrogant one. In response the government was desperately trying to stimulate growth. That in part came with the lowering of VAT from 17.5% to 15% until the New Year. They were also running a car scrappage scheme whereby people could trade in cars of a certain age and get £2,000 off the cost of a new one. I was particularly interested in this as I knew my car wouldn't last for ever. But by doing the numbers there was no way I could afford to do that and pay off the student loan.

One of the early moves of New Labour had been to grant independence to the Bank of England. That autumn they were following a sort of Keynesian model by printing money and pumping it into the system via the disgraced banks. Interest rates were also at a historic low which helped those with certain types of mortgage but did nothing for tenants like me. Yet very little of that money seemed to be going back into people's pockets. And it would do nothing for those who had lost their jobs. In my environment there were so many of those. I was one of the lucky ones still standing at the new slimmed down version of the University; and it seemed my job was secure for the time being.

Yet as that new academic year started my mood was still flying in the main. It had been going on for months. I set off at the same frenetic pace that had marked my second year. More and more students came my way even before the beginning of term in October. September brought me more teaching as I was asked to do a session for some trainee CBT therapists after the high profile Improving Access to Psychological Therapies programme was underway. I had always been sceptical about CBT after my own disastrous brush with it in the 1990s. The day I saw them as a non believer I had the teacher's worst nightmare, an audience that simply didn't respond. I had even been told beforehand that they were a good responsive group. Irritated I walked away hoping not to be invited back.

My faith and confidence was more than restored the following week as I spoke to the second year social work students. They were great and seemed inspired once again by my story and willingness to answer any question they chose to throw at me. The fires of my high kept burning after that.

It was at the same time as my latest teaching success that I had a call from my dad that would prompt me to move in an unusual direction. He suggested what folly it was to throw money away to the government in the repayment of the loan. Instead he proposed that I put that money towards a new car and he would lend me the money for a deposit and to pay off the loan. I went into the car dealership up the road from the University and made enquiries. For just £36 per month more than my loan was costing me I could pay off a new car in four years. Realising that that made sense I ordered a new car as quickly as I could. As it transpired uptake had been so great that the pot of money was almost gone. I got in just in time although in the end the scheme would be unexpectedly extended.

It all seemed a miracle to me. In the dark days of unemployment and unemployability I could never have dreamed of owning a new car. In fact I never believed I would live to 30 let alone have my own flat. Yet here I was now taking yet another step to normality. As it happened getting the finance approved would prove to be major stress; every step of the way it seemed someone kept trying to put a stop to it. But stress aside it was something to look forward to.

The days of October proved long and at times complex. There seemed to be an avalanche of students coming to see me along with some very tricky staff work that involved me going off campus. But with my mood still flying I moved serenely on and felt I could almost do it in my sleep.

Away from the daily chaos as the weeks of October flew by I attended another Recovery Conference although this time I was not running a workshop. My name was getting about though as everywhere I went and introduced myself I usually elicited the response of "oh so you are Mark". Hertfordshire was proving a much more fertile ground than Kent had been. More and more I realised that my part of Kent really was the back end of beyond in mental health circles.

My manager also came up with the idea of having a launch party for Voicing Psychotic Experiences at the University. After much deliberation and consultation with Ruth and Mark we had set a date for the party to be on the 9th December.

It did not stop there. The next huge break came in early November when I delivered my first lecture for the Post Graduate Medical School. I had an audience made up mainly of psychiatrists but with other senior professionals there I once again told my story with great aplomb. Some were stunned by the story and the ease with which I took questions. Finally I had got to the audience I really wanted to get to. It had been two years since I had left the System but the power of the psychiatrist had not diminished in either that time or indeed for the nineteen years that I had had my illness. My voice was getting louder and people finally wanted to hear it.

This was followed very rapidly by my first solo training venture in Hertfordshire. I had offered to run a couple of sessions on mood disorders for the Centre for Mental Health Recovery in conjunction with service users from Viewpoint. It proved an amazing day despite chaos on the trains. I had more converts on my hands. Unknown to me though there was a greater prize just waiting to appear.

At the end of November as the weather turned cold I got the dream break. It was Friday afternoon. No one else was in that day. An hour or so before I was going to head home an email arrived from UMHAN. Cambridge was finally going to recruit a Mental Health Advisor. I scanned through the job description and of course found they wanted a qualification that I didn't have. But I had one priceless qualification that few other candidates would have, a deep understanding of how Cambridge University worked.

I quickly fired an email to the contact given setting out my position. The response came early the next week. He was quite positive and encouraged me to apply. Contacting Jacek to act as a referee I rapidly penned what seemed a gilt-edged application. Jacek would later tell me that in my reference he had described me as "a one man CMHT". An amazing compliment from a psychiatrist. All I could do then was wait.

As I waited we launched Voicing Psychotic Experiences with great fanfare at the University on 9th December. Ruth and Mark both came and spoke. Dozens of colleagues and friends came to a sumptuous buffet lunch. Miriam came along with some friends from elsewhere. I was delighted that Jacek came along to hear me speak. For those who didn't know about my past there may have had a rude awakening as I conducted another public outing of myself. It was a huge success.

Exhausted after speaking in what was something of a blur I took the rest of day off and went to the Fu Hao. It had been a mighty triumph. If it felt like that for a book I had co-written, what on earth would it be like when A Pillar of Impotence came out? There was still no word from the publisher but I knew it was only a matter of time.

As another hectic term wound down we all set our sights on the next great event. For the first time ever the University despite the economic climate was to hold a big Christmas party for all staff. And it would be free. A chance to maybe see people in a more real light. Even two years on I still had few friends there.

It transpired that the call about the car finally came that week. With all the drama it had taken to get the financial approval it had arrived at last. I arranged to pick it up the day after the party. Knowing I might be struggling I arranged to collect it in the afternoon. But I could not have foreseen what happened next.

On 17th December as the University planned to party like there was no tomorrow I got a message through from my manager to say Cambridge had got in touch requesting references. Later that afternoon I too heard from them. They wanted to interview me in early January. My mood exploded as never before. Maybe I could finally go home.

Flying I went to the party and drank heavily. It was strange to see so many colleagues finally being normal. It was absolute carnage. As a blizzard raged outside we partied on long into the night. I didn't make it home that night. It simply wasn't safe to drive on the roads in those conditions; taxis and buses stopped running right across the area. Much to my surprise as I fretted on how to get home two colleagues offered me a sofa to sleep on. Finally the break from colleague to friend came; it had only taken two years.

I awoke somewhat hungover to a call from the dealership asking if I would be in that day. I told them I hadn't even made it home so we had to put it off until the following Monday.

After much paperwork on that Monday I finally took possession of my first new car in my life. Once again a blizzard came down as I drove home but I made it in one piece.

The very next day I came home to an email from the publisher. I'd heard almost nothing since they first offered to take it on. The content was short and supremely sweet, it simply said that the ebook version of A Pillar of impotence was finally available. I put the publisher's website link up for friends but almost all said they wanted to wait for the paperback. Yet it added more fuel, I was that much closer to my goal that I had held for so long. Many times it had seemed out of reach but I had taken the next step. They promised to contact me in a few months about the paperback

Just before Christmas I drove my new prize down to Kent for Christmas. I was still flying. It was good seeing so many people again. It felt as if I had moved into a new and better part of my life. Perhaps life had begun at 40.

I spent New Year back in Hertfordshire. The party in the pub over the road also went on long and hard. When I woke, I didn't care about the hangover I had. I thought I could be going home to Cambridge. My mood still soared; could it get any better than this?

Chapter 42
A Boiling Cauldron

During the many years of my illness I had spoken to literally hundreds of people with mental illness. They may have had different labels and have been treated differently depending on what the label said but they had many things in common. Those who made it past the gatekeepers and into the System were bound by that system. They were on the whole judged and condemned by many in society. They were misunderstood by professionals and public alike. Many did not work and were totally dependent on the random acts of giving or taking away based on the whims of the DWP. Most that I met were all in the same boat and it was on rocky seas.

Looking more closely at what went on in their minds they were even more closely bound together by what we vaguely call mental illness. The one trait almost all of them said to me was that when their minds became unstable for good or ill, the thinking process speeded up. We all think in our own voice, talking our way through the day and the situations we face. For the mentally ill that spinning of thought in one's voice was much faster. Thoughts would work themselves up into a frenzied whirlwind. That was often why so many of us were cursed with the fate of insomnia. I had not had a night's sleep unencumbered by chemicals for nearly twenty years.

What happened next after the whirlwind started revolving and accelerated differed depending on the incarnation present. For me as a voice hearer at its height the people of my thoughts literally fractured off from my mind and became entities themselves. There were two of them, Rachel, and the man. I had no control over them or the volume with which they talked to me. Fortunately Risperidone had killed most of that. What we didn't know was whether it was working as an antipsychotic or that it kept my mood sufficiently good to stop the psychosis. I guess we will never get an answer to that.

For me though the speeding thinking as long as it stayed on the plus side of my mood scale was not a bad thing. I loved it even if people found me more difficult to tolerate at those times. Nine years on from Risperidone I had rarely had to worry about burnout. It never crossed my mind.

As the cold grey days of the first week of January moved onwards, my mind had been aflame for many months. Yet my thinking was entirely focussed on the goal of the interview set to begin on the first Thursday of the first year of a new decade. The process would take two days. For some strange reason they wanted to do a group exercise on that Thursday allowing those to be interviewed to meet each other and size each other up. I was intrigued by that but could not see the purpose of a group exercise nor how it would work in the context of a competition for such a prize. The formal interviews were due to take place on the Friday. By an ironic twist of fate the Counselling Service where the chosen one would be based was now in the very same building in which ten years before I had done my PGCE.

My plan for the trip was to go up on the Wednesday afternoon and stay with Jayne for the duration of the process. I hoped I would be able to reduce the stress by not worrying if trains were working to get me to the most important event I had attended in some years.

Cambridge, the place I considered my home. I would have given anything to go back there. Financially if I got the job it would actually be a sideways step. But it did offer the opportunity to move further up the ladder than my current post did. In fact my position on the ladder at Hertfordshire was under review anyway.

Most people around me were convinced that I would get the job. I had never failed before if invited to a mental health interview. I had the best references it was possible to get. And of course I had the priceless asset of knowing Cambridge and its peculiarities inside out. I seriously doubted any of the others would know that.

It was not just that people thought I would get the job, they really wanted me to get it. An old school friend who now worked as a journalist in Cambridge planned to do a feature on me if I was successful. Yet despite what my ego and confidence said I knew there was always something that could go wrong; I still didn't believed anything until it actually happened.

The boiling cauldron of my heightened thinking process though was supremely confident. For those who believed in fate this was the time. But then something unexpected happened.

On the Monday the snow came down. And down it came for two days. Under eight inches of snow by the Wednesday morning it seemed an impossibility that I would make it. I couldn't even make it to the station regardless of whether the trains were running.

Anxiety filled my mind and my thinking switched from sensing victory to overwhelming disaster. How could this be? The best laid plans undone by a cold front from the east dumping the land in a white sheen of snow. Perhaps this was just sent to try me.

But my mind didn't slow down. Having failed to make it on the Wednesday and firing off a stream of emails to the contact in Cambridge I did what I always do in times of trouble; I adjourned to the pub. And it was there that my luck changed.

One of the company in the pub drove an old Volvo. It had a priceless gift, it was four-wheel drive. He had no qualms about going out in any weather and graciously agreed to drive me to the station the following morning.

On the cold fateful Thursday morning I met him by the shops and he drove me the two miles or so to the station. Much to my relief the trains were running and once aboard my mind reverted to the focussed whirlwind that it had been. As we ran by snow covered fields I thought of where my destiny might be taking me. I had no fears of any questions. I was intrigued by the other candidates though.

When I got to Cambridge I walked carefully through the snow and ice covered streets to what had once been the Spread Eagle. Not a place I had frequented much in my undergraduate days but I had seen more of it during the PGCE. I ate a quick calming lunch and walked across the road to try to shape my destiny.

There were three other candidates, two older than me and one about the same age as me. Apparently they had had something like seventy applicants, so I guess I must have impressed as an unqualified applicant. All of the others worked for the NHS either locally or elsewhere.

For the next three hours they shared information, introduced us to potential future colleagues, and then tested us with a scenario. It was of a medical student who had bipolar. True at Hertfordshire I didn't see medical students but I knew enough about the vagaries of health and the Fitness to Practise issues. It was a gentle afternoon with nothing too taxing.

The others seemed coy and unless they were holding things back as I was, none of them seemed to have an understanding about the particular needs of students in a mental health context.

I was perturbed by a few things. There would not be an ability to take time off during term time which might seriously curtail my occasionally lucrative freelance work. There appeared less scope to do other things that I enjoyed on both a national and local scale; my beloved teaching would go out of the window if I went there. It seemed a less interesting job with far fewer requirements than I had at Hertfordshire.

But I could handle that okay. What worried me most was the off the cuff comment of the prospective line manager that they didn't want "a loose cannon". Would they be able to handle my maverick style if they selected me? Or would it be held against me?

As the afternoon ended my mood was once again flying. I headed off through the snow flurries to the Prince Regent for a couple of beers before going to meet Jayne.

When I got to her in another pub I was speaking in my very fast and judgemental way that had developed for several months. Strangely enough I felt I would win either way. She could barely get a word in. When she did it was quite shocking.

"You're manic." Those were not words I heard often. I never really got too high but she had known me for a long time and had been irritated by that mood before. In fact that was partly why our ways had parted four years before.

I tried to slow down but my mind was aflame. After going back to the house for a bath I once again joined her and friends in another pub to eat and drink.

Still flaming when we got back my mind would not switch off. I slept for barely two hours that night but felt none the worse for wear.

My interview was at 11 o'clock, plenty of time to get my thoughts in order. With my mood directed in a concentrated way I faced a panel of four people. I was just myself as I always was at interview. There was little they asked that troubled me. The only unexpected questions they asked were about my lack of a professional qualification and my links with Cambridge. I thought I had been clear on my application but they had not seen it that way.

After an hour or so they politely dismissed me with the parting comment that any decision would take some time to be made. With that I made my way out to the cold Cambridge streets that I had known so well since I was 9 years old and headed off to my old haunt Sala Thong for lunch.

I spoke on the phone to Christine my old PGCE tutor, Marie, and Beka. All had gone well in my eyes.

That evening I partied hard with Jayne and crew. My mind was still aflame although I was trying hard not to speak as quickly as before. It was indeed a good night.

Christine and I had lunch on the Saturday in a restaurant close to where I had lived during my PGCE days. It was a fine restaurant that I could never have normally afforded to eat at. We talked of old things and new. And of course what might come to be.

On the train home I marvelled at the savage beauty of the snow covered flat landscape. Having lived so long in Cambridge I had long grown used to the flatness of the area. Maybe just maybe I would finally be going home.

That night in the pub across the road back in Hertfordshire my mind raced about what life might be in the coming months. It might be great success. It might be great failure. Each held good and bad; there would be anxieties either way. But for now all I could do was wait. My life in the hands of others as it had been so often in the past. Whatever the outcome my mind was still a boiling cauldron of thought. But when I felt up, that thought process was good.

Mark Edgar

Chapter 43
O Fatal Day, How Low the Mighty Lie

What did we all do before the advent of email and mobile phones? Was life more sedate? The world of communication in those days revolved around letters and phone calls to landlines. The flow of information was indeed slower. There was little one could do to put off potential bad news down the phone but one could always delay the opening of letters until one was ready to do so.

During my battles with the DWP to get the right benefits I dreaded the brown envelope that arrived cursing or helping me as I found it on the doormat. I often waited days to open those until the one I really wanted arrived in March 1999 to finally be paid five years back pay of DLA.

When I got better and was trying to start a belated career in teaching I wanted phone calls but dreaded the inevitable letters that followed failed interviews. It didn't really matter if I waited to open them as the mere act of receiving them denoted the end of yet another failed adventure. My old room at my parents' house is still littered with such rejection letters. At least I got letters sometimes; most of my applications were simply ignored. Teaching in schools of course never worked out for me.

Fast forwarding my life to my third year at the University I was perpetually bombarded by emails, texts, and phone calls. Everyone wanted an answer now and to prioritise what I was doing to suit their needs. Life had become almost instantaneous. It was still possible to delay opening emails and texts but they were staring me in the face every time I logged on.

As I waited for news from Cambridge I knew it was a phone call that I wanted rather than an email or letter. They had warned us it would take time to confirm a decision. They had also promised us feedback on our efforts. I didn't really care about that, I just desperately wanted to go back to Cambridge. Emotionally I was perhaps too far down the road of getting there than was good for me. But my mind was still ablaze from my elevated take on life that had lasted so many months. I thought I could handle any rejection that might be forthcoming.

My world changed exactly a week after I had sat in the former School of Education building meeting the other candidates for such a prize.

The email came in the afternoon. I knew it was bad news and was reluctant to open it. Much to my surprise I did venture into it before the end of the day. I had failed. There was the usual bullshit of very stiff competition but nothing of any use. All I knew was that my quest was over. Trying to delude myself that there were greater opportunities to be had at Hertfordshire and that my life was more interesting there I told my immediate colleagues in the Equality Unit the bad news. Then I emailed out the news to my circle of people who I regarded as friends; yes I did have them at last. All were stunned. Everyone had been utterly convinced that I would get it.

My mood just about held out that day. Then the freefall started. The raging torrent of positive thinking and belief switched completely and I went into meltdown. It was on the Friday night that I increased the Risperidone and Trimipramine. I slept for fourteen hours.

When I did finally wake up on that Saturday I was utterly perplexed. I knew the world was falling apart yet I slept for so long. My normal reaction when I went into freefall was for my mind to speed up even more than normal and sleep became so hard to attain. I would lie awake for hours with my tumultuous mood moving into overtime. But not this time. I couldn't stop sleeping.

Throughout that weekend I was overwhelmed by a sense of failure, despair, and emptiness. As ever I hoped and prayed that no one would notice. But who could not notice? No one in the town where I lived barring my immediate manager who had lived round the corner from my old flat and our ultimate manager the Dean of Students knew of my illness. What would I say to people?

In reality I didn't want to speak to anyone however much they knew of me. I just wanted to isolate myself. But I couldn't sit all weekend in my quiet lonely flat. I did venture out to the pub across the road but said almost nothing to anyone. No one asked any questions.

Emptiness and exhaustion aside my mind was active in a very strange way. There were no voices, I think the Risperidone blunted them. Neither did I feel suicidal. This was indeed a very strange relapse. And whatever thoughts I held against giving in, this was a relapse and a very serious one.

I was of course confronted by what to do on the Monday. I didn't want to admit defeat that I was ill but I certainly wasn't much good to my students in my mental state. Then there was the issue of telling others at the University of the turn of events. I hated taking time off work at any time but it always seemed so much worse when it was down to my madness. Too much of my life had been lost to mental illness for it ever to happen again. But like it or not and Risperidone aside I still had that illness and the chances were it would never go away.

As I lay down in bed on that Saturday night my thoughts were still going but sleep did come. And lots of it; another fourteen hours. Was it the pills or the illness? As ever it was hard to tell.

Somehow I mustered up the strength to get up from my long slumbers on the Monday morning and go to work. But I achieved little. I was still overwhelmed by emptiness and failure. I stared for two days at my computer screen, talked blankly to my students then drove the lonely road home to my empty flat.

On the Wednesday morning I gave in to the inevitable and called in sick. But that merely added to my feeling of failure. That old bugbear of the depressed also played heavily on my mind; I was a fraud. I had bullshitted my way to where I was and didn't deserve to be there. It felt as if I had gone back in time twenty years without the overwhelming desire to die. Emptiness, always emptiness.

The week after that I did go back feeling a little better. I didn't quite believe that it was a mere blip as Caroline would have described it. And I was determined to face my madness head on and tell it to fuck off.

As chance would have it, I had an appointment with my GP booked for the following Thursday. I was due a blood test for the Risperidone and he had also asked to meet me every three months as I was no longer being monitored by a psychiatrist. Yet theory and reality were not the same thing. I had tried in vain to get an appointment with him for nearly nine months.

When I got to my appointment I told him I had had a bit of setback but that I was getting better. He saw straight through me though. He signed me off for ten days with the warning that "if you don't stop now much worse will follow". He was right however much I didn't want to hear it. I called my manager when I got home and left instructions to clear my diary. I had had to give in to my madness. That was not what I wanted, I had only taken time off twice for that since I went on Risperidone. But I couldn't fight something of that magnitude without taking time to step back and letting the Risperidone weave its magic.

Those ten days were amongst the most desolate I had endured for twenty years. The hardest part was that the demons that haunted my troubled mind were not always the same as they had been before. I was deeply depressed but it did not come in its usual incarnation of Rachel and the time to die voice. Voices were noticeably conspicuous by their absence. Instead there was that terrible emptiness that was all pervading.

People kept calling but I didn't want to speak to anyone. The only real exception was Heather and she kept the other world abreast of where I was. She knew deep down this was the worst relapse I had had since salvation had arrived in the form of those little white pills.

And all the time I slept. I had to go back to bed each afternoon and slept between the nightmares. They were bad but were not a new phenomenon.

But the sleep had a purpose. My mind and body needed to recharge from the severe burnout I was experiencing. For that was what it was. I had been too up for too long. My mind could never go on forever at that rate. True Cambridge had been the disastrous catalyst but the crash would have happened anyway.

By the weekend before I was due to return to the Doctor or to work my mood was slowly lifting. On the Friday I had called work to say I planned to come back on the following Monday. But I needed Occupational Health clearance so we set up a meeting. They were okay as long I restricted my hours.

I returned that Monday to do but a few hours. My workload had not decreased but it was clear we couldn't manage all that. I just prayed that fate would not bestow on us a crisis. It must have been a good fate as we got lucky. I was just as busy but we had no catastrophes.

Each afternoon I returned to my flat exhausted. I had no timescale of returning full time but I knew my ego and fear of failure would drive me to come back too soon. I needed others to watch out for me.

As the weeks of February went by there was little change; I was managing but only just. My mood did not hit even on my scale until the beginning of March. Perhaps the warmer weather would help after such a harsh winter. But I needed a sign that I was getting better. That sign had to be a good day and there might be not one but two on the cards. Training had always brought the greatest lift to my mood. And I was due to deliver a whole day for the Centre for Mental Health Recovery in the second week of March.

On the Friday before the acid test I travelled down to Sussex on the train to meet with Ruth, Mark, and Emma. We were due to do some filming for resources for medical students. That day my mood lifted long enough to do the interview. But what was better was seeing old friends who knew my illness for what it was. I was amongst my own people for half a day. And that helped.

The day I delivered my training I was full of anxiety. Not that I felt I would not be good but more whether I had the energy to do it. It was time to put the mask on again.

We spent a pleasant day at a Catholic seminary as I held court with the able assistance of a bipolar friend. The audience were utterly captivated by the world of mood disorders and seemed to react favourably. I was back doing something important. And I was succeeding. I had not felt that since the first week of January.

My mood did not fly as it once did after training. It was lifted above the zero mark on my scale but only to plus one. But plus one was better than the minus four I had had at times during the previous two months. I had my breakthrough.

For the remainder of March I continued in a good place doing my part time hours. I was aiming for a full return after Easter. I had been stunned by how much support I had received from colleagues at the University. I simply didn't think I was that valued. But I had been wrong on that.

As Easter came I took time out and travelled to Kent as usual. I was not quite my usual self but I was getting there. The hours of sleep had done their job during those long and dark three months.

Whilst I was fighting to get well the wider world was moving on. In Britain we were in the run up to the long awaited election. The day of reckoning was coming for the arrogant one and New Labour. Yet what had seemed an unassailable lead for Cameron months before was now looking shaky.

On the world stage Britain was out of the disastrous venture in Iraq but further east the Taliban learned lessons from their Iraqi counterparts and were fighting back with Improvised Explosive Devices; they were taking an ever increasing toll on soldiers and civilians alike. As I had fought my very private battle the wider war went on.

I could not influence the wider world save through my one and only vote. I would cast that on 6th May. But it was not just an election day for me. In my small world I would once again be raising my voice, this time at an international conference. Time to speak out.

Chapter 44
The Changing of the Guard

The power of the media has never ceased to amaze me. There had been so much change in my lifetime. As a small child we didn't even have a television. The radio was all I heard as a young child. When we did get a television there were a mere three channels to watch. That would change in the 1980s and 1990s with the coming of Channel 4 and Channel 5. In my small area of Kent we were unable to get Channel 5 as it interfered with a French channel just across the water.

When I moved to Hertfordshire in 2007 I had expanded my television repertoire as I finally got cable television; that would change to satellite when I was forced to move in the cold winter of 2009.

We had also seen the rise of the Internet. I had feared it a great deal as I feared all technology but I got used to it. Obama had used it to great effect during his election campaign. Always some way ahead of us there had long been televised presidential debates in the US. But until the spring of 2010, this obvious and interesting channel had never been entertained in Britain.

Although it was to an extent tarnished by the expenses scandal an election was coming. The country was aching for change from New Labour but with the outcome of said election still uncertain, political debate came to our screens in the form of three televised debates with the leaders. The arrogant one would be there with his dour and dark delivery. Against him would be the old Etonian, Cameron. And then there would be another leader, a man hardly anyone had heard of. Nick Clegg was something of an unknown quantity.

As the country moved towards its day of reckoning at the polls the audience was given a shock. The consensus view after the first debate was that the unknown Clegg had blown the other two out of the water. After that the future was even more uncertain; we were going to change, it was just a question of who would come out on top of an election where the pollsters suggested for the first time in years that we were heading for a hung parliament.

In my small part of the world that spring I was coming to the end of what had been my most hectic year yet at the University. We were now nearly two years removed from the colossal restructuring of the place. I had heard no more about the oblique reference to "streamlining central administration" made by the Vice Chancellor.

All that changed in a hurry during the countdown to the election. I was called at very short notice to an unplanned Equality Unit meeting early one afternoon. The message was simple, we would be disbanded and separated from 1st May. My mood had recovered sufficiently from my winter meltdown for me to take it rationally. Yet there was uncertainty where I would go. The Equality Office as it would be now known would move into the sphere of the Office of the Vice Chancellor. Disability Services would become independent and undergo a review but would remain within the Office of the Dean of Students. That then left me and where I should go. I was told we would talk behind the scenes about that one. In the event I was given no choice and ultimately moved to the Counselling Centre on 1st May.

Whilst I could see the real advantage in managing risk better and ending my isolation, I knew too that many of my students would not want to go to Counselling. Historically I had seen many students who had gone to Counselling first and not found it very helpful. I was of course aware that that process had also worked in reverse on several occasions. Not everyone responded to my unorthodox methods and some could and did find greater help from the counsellors. In my eyes it didn't really matter where a student went as long as we could help them. It had never been clear how or why any given individual had come to see me, Counselling, the chaplain, or Occupational Health. I knew though that it was a done deal; there would be no choice.

For all the change I faced as an individual and we as a country faced, life still had to go on. In all the time I had been at the University my workload had slowed down around exams. After Easter life usually became easier. Yet there were still people to see and coax towards the goal of beating mental illness and graduating.

But my life was not just confined to the University that spring. I did another session for Psychosis Revisited and delivered training for staff and for external partners through my association with the Centre for Mental Health Recovery. With each of these my story became a little more know. I also delivered my first lecture to the mental health nursing students that spring.

This was, perhaps more importantly, leading up to the wider stage of an international conference on Self Identity and Mental Health. I was asked to talk about what was put to me as "living with hybrid identity". It was actually a very interesting way of looking at how my life had evolved since teaching gave up on me and I accidentally found myself working in mental health. From the lowest of the low I had risen a long way and would soon share a platform with speakers from across Europe. It was set for Election Day and I was determined to be at my best. As ever I planned to speak without notes. So much more powerful than just reading from a MS-PowerPoint presentation as so many did on such occasions.

As the weeks slipped by towards the twin great day my mood was most buoyant. There may have been change afoot for me but I still knew I could speak and speak well. The election campaign rolled on marked by the arrogant one's stunning allegation that an elector who had questioned him was a "bigot". The power of the media again. With that he had to be doomed. Yet what would the outcome be?

I awoke on Election Day to warm sunshine. I donned my favoured linen suit that I had bought two summers before for Kym's wedding. Full of confidence and my mind rehearsing every word of my presentation I drove to the conference in a bright mood. It had the feel of a good day, a day for change.

When I got to the conference I was faced with the usual mix of those known and unknown. I was warmly greeted by the organiser although I could see she was slightly anxious that I would be speaking without notes. The audience was a mixed group of professionals and service users. As the morning progressed it was clear that some of the service users there were from the group I call the ranters. They were always intent of harassing delegates for not knowing what they were talking about. One in particular challenged every speaker. But I was determined I would blow her away. If she felt only service users had anything useful to offer I had every intention of proving her right but at the same time dealing with her conceited arrogance.

When I got up to speak I had the whole room in the palm of my hand. Effortlessly I took them through who I had become as a service provider. I challenged the widely held lunacy of rigid boundaries practised by Trusts and proved that I could indeed have a foot in both camps and not be a failure. I talked of what it was like to have an identity beyond that of mere nutter. For too long I had let my illness define my life. By that spring my illness was a mere part of me, not the whole.

I finished by giving a comparison between my life and that of my Cambridge peers. It all sounded as if I was worse off than them. Of course in the areas that matter to society such as wealth, family, marital status, and mortgages I was not even in the same league as them. But I was doing a role that was hugely significant for my students as well as being in the eyes of some service users an inspiration. I never really felt comfortable with the weight of expectation put on me by my people but to some I was just that, a giver of hope.

The room erupted into applause when I finished speaking. There was no jeering from the ranter but more positive comments. I found out afterwards that she had asked one of my friends and colleagues who on earth I was and was I any good. His response was simple: "just listen to him". Somehow I had tamed the beast of self appointed expertise.

The rest of the conference was something of a blur after that. I was exhausted by my part. Yet my mood was once again flying. I had done what I set out to do and my story was a little more widely known. I did subsequently write a MS-PowerPoint presentation to cover my piece which would be used by others in the future. That was always easy to do afterwards; harder to make an impact like that as a speaker.

When I got home I went down the road to vote before the eating and drinking had started. It was a night to celebrate and I did that in style in the pub over the road. Having booked the following day off work, I stayed up long into the night watching the results come in. It was something I had always wanted to witness but had not done so before.

Somewhat tired and hungover I emerged to a new world order. Cameron had the most seats yet not enough to secure a majority government. So we were heading for coalition for the first time in decades. The unknown Clegg now had a position of power.

What emerged after a week of negotiations was the least likely option, a Conservative and Liberal Democrat coalition. No one had expected that. Many were glad to see the back of the arrogant one. I for one certainly was. He shuffled off into obscurity and was rarely heard from again.

Whilst for many including myself there was post election euphoria there was also much that was uncertain. The country was virtually bankrupt and still being buffeted by financial storms the like of which had not been seen since the Great Depression of the 1930s. I knew that what Cameron and Clegg had inherited was in a very real way a poisoned chalice. Whatever they did it was likely to be derided by others. Yet no one really knew how to get out of the financial mess. What I did know was that the age of austerity and cuts was now well on top of us. I had no idea what that meant for me although it did appear that unlike countless thousands of others I had a job and it seemed to be secure for the time being.

As May came to an end my workload did indeed as usual slow down. I had seen an entire academic cycle three years in my new life. Those undergraduate first year students that I had picked up at the start were now graduating. Although it was not at all down to me many of my students got the firsts they craved. Two students took time out to see me although in working with them they had been on the opposite ends of the scale, one almost impossible and the other a sheer delight. They had both got their firsts. Those were the moments when all the difficulties were worth it. Those behind the scenes did not always get much praise but when it did come it was most satisfying.

May turned to June and the quiet season was well underway. My physical move had not taken place yet. In fact the Counselling Centre did not even have a spare office for me to work from. As the weeks went by I had more and more meetings with my new manager. We were both going into the unknown on how it would pan out.

It may have been quiet in the main but we were also moving towards the end of the long running saga with my suspended member of staff. Finally we got together early that summer and struck a deal. That had been a long and hard road for all concerned.

At around the same time I went back to a world I had not visited for several years. On a glorious summer's day I returned to Lancing to sing in a service to mark the 100th anniversary of the birth of the tenor Sir Peter Pears. I did not know it as I travelled down but I was one of a small and exclusive group that had been invited. It had slipped my mind that back in those days I had won a prize for musical performance. Now only those winners were invited back.

It had been so long since I had sung I had almost forgotten how to read music. But I got through it and the sumptuous lunch that was served afterwards. The day was another triumph. Summer had finally arrived after the trials of the deep winter. My life was intact but once again I was going into the unknown of another year. My third year at the University had been the busiest to date. Who knew what would happen next? What I did know was that life as I knew it at the University would change with the physical move to Counselling. That was due to happen in August.

Chapter 45
The Final Mile

The decision to write a book about what happened to me was taken very early on. I was stunned by my appalling incarceration during the late summer of 1991. New Cambridge graduate locked behind bars and metal doors away from prying eyes purely because I was ill. I swore one day I would tell the world although I wasn't sure if that world would be able or willing to listening. As 1991 became a fading memory and there was still no sign of progress it was clear that treatment such as it was then was still in the dark ages. I was surrounded by voiceless dehumanised individuals whose plight the world did not hear.

As time progressed I knew I had a priceless gift, the ability to write. Yet I had to be able to do it. The start point was straight forward, that early summer's day in June, the day I got Rachel's letter. My mind replayed that with utter clarity for all the years in between. And my mind recalled all the shocking catalogue of errors that had been my treatment phase.

The ability to write returned in the late 1990s when I had met Ian and gone back to education. From there I had a clear goal and that was to go back to Cambridge. Only then would my story be complete. The solution sounded obvious, from and to Cambridge, a record of the 1990s.

Throughout that time though I was troubled by the judgement of others. The challenge of anyone writing, drawing, painting, playing, or doing anything creative would inevitably have to stand up to the scrutiny of others. Acutely aware of this I had to be ready psychologically for the "slings and arrows of outrageous fortune" as Shakespeare had put it very well. All creations have to be subject to interpretation.

Not until I was 33 did I ever get to a point where I could start writing and it would be just short of my 36th birthday that my work would finally be complete. It was only then that the hardest part of the venture would begin. I had to get someone to publish it; and that meant many rejections.

Five years later with my life transformed in the run up to my 41st birthday it seemed the end was in sight. But I couldn't yet see round the final bend of the marathon course. During the quiet summer of 2010 I still had heard nothing about the next phase of the project. A Pillar of Impotence had been out in ebook form for eight months. Yet no one I knew was interested in an ebook. Kindles were not widely available or known about so that market seemed extraordinarily quiet.

Despite the stir that had caused on my already heightened and manic mind I knew deep down that the journey would only end as and when I had the first paperback copy in my hand and we could set up an official launch. It had taken me by surprise when my previous manager had suggested we have a launch party for Voicing Psychotic Experiences. Now with a new manager and a different department I did not know whether that would be possible again. For now the world was quiet as I prepared to move office in a few weeks time.

Student wise it was just as quiet as the summers had always been since my move. In reality the University resembled a morgue during July and August; almost nothing happened during those months. It would be a lull before the coming storm of September. I was getting restless although my mood remained fairly good. After my experience of the previous winter I was acutely aware I could not let myself get too high again. But with so little going on that outcome seemed unlikely for the time being.

Into the quiet of summer came the shift I had craved for. An email arrived from the publisher saying that it was time to set up the paperback launch. They included an attachment with the ebook version that had been out already.

Quickly I read through it. I was shocked at how bad a job I had done in editing it; the work was littered with mistakes. This cast something of a shadow over my mind but I set about correcting what I could see.

I had decided some time earlier that before I approved it for publication I would first get it proof read by someone else. A friend had agreed to do that for me so when I had been through it on my own I sent it to her. My impatience grew along with my mood; I just wanted it out in the open as soon as possible. I had yet to decide on the book cover although it seemed likely that Beka would do one for me.

With the manuscript safely with my friend I finally moved offices early in August. I had always hated moving but that was accomplished fairly easily. It was very quiet in the Counselling Centre that August as so many were on holiday. The Dean of Students had made an interesting comment when it was decided that I would move there. As he put it "we can't expect the counsellors to have the skills to do your work when you are away". It seemed an odd and almost redundant thing to say; I had never expected anyone to cover my work when I was away. I'm not sure if that meant I was more skilled or just had different skills. Yet in those few weeks of August as I headed towards a well deserved break I did find myself doing their job amid the absence of summer. It didn't worry me too much as it gave me something to do during the silly season.

Just before I went on holiday I wrote my third annual report. It had been the busiest year yet with support given to a hundred students and staff. In reality that was an absurd workload for one person. A care co-ordinator in a CMHT would likely have twenty five to thirty people on his or her books. The year had been interrupted by my winter relapse. We had been very lucky though as there were no crises during that space of time. Yet it had been a very successful year with teaching and training expanding the demand for my services. Now I faced the unknown of new department and the uncertainty of a new academic year.

As I went down to Kent it mattered not. I was doing fine. I planned to do very little whilst I was away, just a time to recharge my depleted batteries. I knew too that the end was in sight on the book. Just before my birthday I had a message from my friend who was editing it for me. She hoped she would be finished by the Bank Holiday. With that done I just needed to sort the cover.

I celebrated my birthday by resurrecting the old Cambridge tradition of the Day of Decadence. As we partied with unusual vigour I thought the world was fine. What I didn't expect was the deafening silence that would come from my proof reader. Unknown to me she was experiencing a relapse in her bipolar.

On my return to work my mood still held. We had an immediate crisis to deal with but that went on okay. In the third week of September I attended a PD training session in my home town. As usually happened I was drawn into the conversation knowing what I knew from my own experience.

The student front was quiet as I headed into the fourth week of September. It would be an unusual week as I was attending the three day conference in London on Recovery. All the great and good would be there including Mark and Ruth. I was still an unknown who just mingled with the crowd. I stayed with my old school friend Ellie for the duration and had a somewhat decadent few days in which I'm sure I must have put on half a stone.

Whilst chatting to Ruth at the conference I told of my growing frustrations at the delay in editing; I had still heard nothing. Very graciously Ruth agreed to give it a go - she had after all spent many hours editing the other book.

Having made useful contacts I headed back to work and attended another PD session although this time I ended up teaching part of it myself. It proved the final death knell of the Centre for Mental Health Recovery. What had started as an innovative project had folded in chaos when they lost the contract to provide cross county training. It would be the end for the time being of my freelance role.

Buoyed by September's events and reinvigorated by my break I taught three times during Induction Week at the end of the month. My mood was up but not too up. I was full of confidence that the end of my long writing journey was within sight. But nothing could prepare for the storm that was about engulf me as the fourth year of my tenure started.

Once the rush started there was no going back. From day one of the new academic year they came and they kept coming. It was not so much the number of people who wanted to see me but more the sheer complexity and risk posed by those that did. I had long voiced my concerns at the risks we took by not sharing information. We had gone some way towards alleviating that by setting up an at risk forum earlier that year. But I was still not being told of students with known histories coming along. If they said they didn't want me to know about them I heard nothing. That was of course until the shit hit the fan. And by God did it hit the fan that autumn.

As the first few weeks of that year flew by I was deluged with risk and complication. Much of my time was spent trying the get the

CMHT to take some responsibility for students who were on their patch. As far they were concerned students should be treated by others not them. Yet funding wise when they registered with a GP at the University they became under the orbit of the local CMHT.

Of course I had known for years that CMHTs didn't want to touch people with PDs. In the main it was left to us and during that first term my students with PD trebled from the previous year. Several had been well known to Children and Adolescent Mental Health Services (CAMHS). Most came no better than they had been when they started. These were the people who inevitably would attract the label of PD when they outgrew CAMHS.

Some had eating disorders too. It was an area I knew little about and had rarely seen in the previous years. For the first time, I came into contact with the specialists. Yet they too were often reluctant to help as they felt CMHTs should lead. That left us, and perhaps more importantly the vulnerable students to cope with it ourselves.

It was not long before I was also on the phone to the Crisis, Assessment, and Treatment Team (CATT). I had a reasonable relationship with them but they were at times impulsive. They had a habit is discharging people if they didn't engage.

As October turned to November we seemed in a phase of perpetual crisis. It was in fact a series of overlapping crises. And that was exhausting. My overall number was down as I feared after my move but it did not stop.

Yet all the while doing crisis management my mood remained buoyant. Not too high but just about right. I could still hang onto the bigger picture of life beyond the University. Having heard nothing from Ruth by November, I finally took the decision to edit it myself. I went through it three more times. At the same time Beka was trying to construct a cover for it. She had not read the manuscript so didn't know where to start. Being non visual I found it hard to conceptualise a cover. In a moment of brilliance Beka suggested I send it to a friend of hers in Bristol to advise her.

The recipient of the manuscript was stunned by the work. Katie had experienced mental illness through her mother's travails. She knew well the flaws in the System. Yet nothing prepared her for the impact the book would have on her; she was simply overwhelmed. Beka set about designing the cover after Katie's comments.

My world was on fire that November, a maelstrom of thought, hope, and fear. I was thriving but in danger of another burnout. Whether I burned out or not, only time would tell. But what I did know, as the chaos continued was that sooner or later the storm of complexity and risk would overwhelm us. It was only a matter of time as the last few weeks of autumn sped by with no let up.

Chapter 46
The Suicide Storm

Six months after the historic election that had brought the coalition to power the country was only just beginning to see the depths of the economic chaos that we faced. Each day brought news of more cuts. VAT was at its highest level ever at 20%. People were losing their jobs, defence was looking at meltdown in a time of war via the Strategic Defence Review, and there was much talk of welfare reform. The latter did not really impact on me but was likely to affect so many of my friends from my former life. Whilst I applauded the idea that people would in theory one day have a system that would make them better off by working I had doubts about how that would be achieved. There were many fearful people out there.

Back in the summer I had met the chief medical officer for the DWP at a conference in London. During the lunch break I had sought her out and told her a little bit of my story. Whilst my journey into the working world had been worth it, financially it had taken me ten years to be better off. She admitted to me that the instruments they had to test people's disability were a blunt weapon aimed more at seeking out fraudsters rather than really helping people. Furthermore, she also admitted it was not fit for purpose when it came to mental health. But it would go on.

Yet that was part of my old life. In my new life as we headed towards the winter the Browne report on university finances had recommended a huge increase in student fees. One of my friends had suggested that to attack such a plan all students should quit their courses and sign on on the dole queue. It didn't seem to have crossed her mind that such an eventuality would also bring me to the dole queue. The plan to possibly treble fees would undoubtedly anger many existing students as well as future ones. That November they marched in London. Hundreds of thousands took to the streets and some of them turned it into a riot in places.

It had become a very angry country. What struck me was that if the outcome of the election had been different we would still be facing the same chaos and austerity would have come in another form. Of more interest to me was that Tories had done a very good job in those first six months of blaming their coalition partners and potentially damning the Liberals Democrats to the obscurity of history when we would next go to the polls in 2015.

On the other side of the world England's Ashes Tour of Australia was about to get underway. I eagerly awaited the tour in the hope that we could finally beat them over there. As luck would have it the final test would be scheduled for the first week of 2011. Hopefully I anticipated being away from work so I would see the finale.

In my small and insignificant part of the larger world that was the University of Hertfordshire I had been working flat out for two months. It was certainly the riskiest group that I had ever met during my time there. I had known from early on that sooner or later the suicide attempts and admissions would start.

A week after the student march I was preparing to go and teach some CBT trainees when my office phone rang.

"The shit is hitting the fan" were the only words that came from a quiet detached voice that I recognised instantly as one of my most vulnerable students.
"I'll get there as soon as I have finished teaching."

My greatest fear in my job was being let down by statutory services. It had happened too often before. Now I was faced with a student who had only just been discharged from CATT.

I rushed over as soon as I could and was confronted by a slight, curled up, and exhausted young woman talking about jumping off the nearby multi-story car park. And I knew she meant it. Whilst it was very scary I was able to ascertain that she had too much to do before she would jump. The ritual of suicide that I had known so well from my own experience. I decided to take the chance and put in visits overnight rather than take her straight to the hospital. That could wait as I knew it was highly unlikely she would be admitted if CATT had just discharged her.

Just after 5 o'clock as I was in the accommodation office setting up the overnight visits my phone rang again. I knew straight away that we needed an ambulance. One of my other students had taken an overdose and was in deep trouble.

We went straight over to her room and saw another young woman struggling for life and refusing offers of help. When the ambulance arrived I tried in vain to explain to the paramedics just how risky this young woman was. It was only sometime later I was able to explain how complex her situation was.

By 7 o'clock there was no more that I could do. I had one student on her way to hospital and I intended to take the other one there in the morning. It was a day on which I had certainly earned my money.

The following day I travelled by taxi to A&E to get my first student assessed. Much of the day was spent shuttling between there and the inpatient ward where my second student was recovering from the night before. Finally she acknowledged that she needed help and that another psychiatric inpatient stay was inevitable.

Having apparently conveyed both of them to safety the morning after the night before I was stunned when psychiatric liaison did not admit the first student. They did not seem to be taking her seriously. They patched up her cuts and sent her home with me in the afternoon. I knew differently though, she meant it and would come to try again. But what could I do? Technically I suppose my arse was covered and so much of my business was about covering one's own arse. Yet that of course would not make me feel any better emotionally if she did end up killing herself. I had done my job though.

As things turned out she would be admitted a few days later and I breathed a huge sigh of relief. Both were now safe. Unknown to me though this was just the beginning; the suicide season was well underway.

It must have been early December when another of my most vulnerable students took an overdose and was admitted. Winter had come early and not just with the coming of the cold in what turned out to be another bitter winter.

Against the backdrop of permanent crisis management we were in the final stages of getting the book out. Emails came in a three way conversation with attached cover designs between Beka, the publisher, and me. My patience was still tried but each day took me closer to the finale of my epic journey.

With all the carnage of suicide attempts and hospital admissions came the everyday meetings to provide support to the less risky students. As had happened the previous year the constant work and exhilaration of doing the hard parts lifted my mood. But I was very careful to not let it get out of hand as I had the previous winter. I was flying once again but had a constant eye on my mental altimeter.

As the snows fell in mid December the University was preparing to wind down for Christmas. For the second year in a row there was a University wide Christmas party planned. I had had mixed memories of the year before when I had been flying and stranded in the snow in the run up to my epic crash. I ordered a ticket and fully intended to go along again. Although my mood was high I knew that I needed the break and a slowdown. In the event though I never made it to the party. I spent that day in Cambridge attending a ward round at the Eating Disorders Unit at Addenbrookes Hospital. As the snow flurries continued in the place I had long regarded as home I met Miriam for dinner in the Backstreet Bistro.

A week later as the snows came tumbling down again in that bitter winter I travelled down to Kent by train for Christmas. It was not as I had planned but the weather forced me off the roads. I went down a day before I had originally planned. The train never managed to make it beyond Ashford but the weather held just long enough for my dad to pick me up. It came down again just as we arrived back at the small insignificant town on the Kent coast.

I stayed a few days to recuperate and catch up with friends. The Boxing Day run was an epic one with a background of England thumping Australia in the third test in Melbourne. I drank away the days as was my wont and wondered what the New Year would bring. It might be more chaos but I didn't know that. What I did know was that I was but days away from approving the final version of A Pillar of Impotence.

As I travelled back to Hertfordshire by train in the bitter cold I knew not that I had had my final Christmas together with my mum.

I returned to work having witnessed England's final victory to secure the Ashes in Sydney; it had taken twenty four years for them to achieve victory away from home. I had had a full three weeks off to try to regain my energy. I had succeeded as far as I could see. But my hope for a slightly less crisis ridden second term of my fourth year at the University was sadly mistaken. I was visiting the ward once again in that first week back. I went to visit one student and found two there at once. I did not know it at the time but would find out later that there was a third member of the University of Hertfordshire there too. I was in for another long term.

At the end of that first week back I sat at my computer composing one of the most important emails of my life. Having been through the manuscript one more time looking for errors and with the cover art work now done, I sent the final version of the book to the publisher. It was just then a matter of waiting.

When I got back to work after the weekend once again the phone rang with news of another suicide attempt and admission. With a precedent set in November news came almost every week of January of more admissions. It would not slow down. But I coped having had a break and still my mood was good.

I came home from work on the third Friday of the new term to find a small padded envelope on my doormat. I knew straight away what it was. There were no distinguishing marks on the cover but as I wasn't expecting anything it had to be the book. I was too anxious to open it straight away but did so two hours later. There in my hand I finally had a physical incarnation of my nine year project. My quest to get my book published ended on 25th January 2011. A Pillar of Impotence at last had a real existence. Over the coming days I read through it. All I could see was mistakes that I had missed during the editing.

My sagging mood was quickly restored when news started to come through that in response to my mass email some people at least had bought it. And they all raved about it. I took it into work and was most delighted that my manager and department felt we should have a launch party.

The next few weeks were just as busy but tarnished by a concussion I sustained in a freak accident at work. I realised then that I was truly middle aged - recovering at 41 was much harder than it had been when I had had two sporting concussions in my twenties. Of course the work didn't slow down though; the admissions kept coming as the last days of that cold winter played out in February. It took three weeks before I felt okay after my accident. By that time it was decided that we should have official launch during Staff Wellbeing Week in April. Each day invites went out but I had no idea who would come or indeed if anyone would come.

February turned to March and life was in still in full swing on many fronts. As we got to mid March there had been fourteen suicide attempts made by students who came into my orbit and eleven psychiatric admissions. These figures were close to three times what we had experienced the year before. It was only as we went towards the end of term that they stopped. Somehow, all had survived. We had been extremely lucky. It was not down to any agency of mine, it was pure luck.

As I reflected on my life being aflame in those early days of spring the wider world moved on apace. But what happened next had been predicted by few people. Almost ten years into the war the unexpected happened as across North Africa and the Middle East the Arab people rose up in revolt against their leaders. The so called "Arab Spring" was underway and the world was once again rocked by major life changing events. It showed me just how small and insignificant I was in my life and times.

Chapter 47
The Trumpet Shall Sound

Have you ever wondered about those curious events in life that take you in a different direction? Events take place that impact on our lives. These are often beyond our control. Invariably it is people who change our lives and sometimes it is just chance that we meet such people. I am lucky enough to have met so many remarkable people who have impacted on my life and changed its direction.

For years during my illness I kept asking myself why me? What would have happened if I had done something different or if others who found their way into my story had altered their behaviour? Of course I never did get an answer to the why me question. Recovery only began when I stopped asking myself such a question.

Throughout history people have sought explanations on why their lives proceeded as they did. Some say it is down to God. Others to fate, and still more to destiny. In more recent times some have believed in chaos. Is life just chance or is it planned? I don't know the answer to that but I do know that my life was taken down different paths by people I met along the way. Some were for good and some for ill.

I have no idea how or why I was born with the gift of music. There were certainly no obvious precedents in my family history. Miriam too was born with such a gift. Music for good or bad had taken me to many places. I had sung in some of the great buildings of the world as well. There were many memories of those times. Yet the place of greatest impact on my life was not one I went to as a professional in my childhood but rather in the pompous arrogance of my early twenties when Cambridge seemed to lay the world at our feet. Granada is a place I hope everyone sees one day. It was the most significant place of my travels for it was there that I had met Rachel at Easter 1990.

Whatever we had together, and we both have different versions of that, it was but short lived. Barely two months later she chose to walk away from my life. I don't know why but as I look back in middle age I do recognise that we were both desperately young. Meeting her changed my life and threw me down the path of madness. That madness had nearly destroyed my life for years.

Yet as I faced the final few weeks before the official launch of my account of that madness I had few regrets. I had lived with mental illness for half of my life that spring. Now there were just a few short weeks until that journey would be over and another one begin.

During the last two weeks of March the chaos of the previous months had stopped but I was no less busy. Some days I had six or seven students or staff to see. They kept coming just as that term started to wind down to its finale. I hoped as had been the case during the previous three years it would get significantly easier after Easter. I was operating on autopilot and my mood was buoyant but not too high. Life was good as those days ticked by.

On the last weekend of March I travelled to London to spend time with Beka, Katie, and Mike. I had suggested that perhaps we could all go along to the Boat Race that Saturday. I had not been since the first year I was ill. But fate, if that was what it was, intervened as hundreds of thousands marched through the streets that day to protest against austerity and cuts. The transport system was shut down and we wisely stayed at home. It was a cold and bleak March day as we sat all day in a pub in Greenwich. We lost the race but there would always be the following year for Cambridge.

As I got back to work on the Monday my mind was mulling over what I would say on the day of the book launch. I seemed to have been effective speaking without notes and I had no desire to use them on that special day. It had to be high impact as I hoped the book was.

Whilst in many respects I was loving the run-up, deep down I still feared that no one would come. My manager whose budget would pay for the lunch was somewhat alarmed at the number who said they would come but I knew it was likely fewer than half those who had promised to come.

But before then I had another speaking engagement. I had been involved in a project about the link between staff wellbeing and health and their performance across the university sector for some time. As the only advisor who worked with staff as well as students I had been asked to speak at an event in Birmingham about my work. That was set for April Fool's Day, precisely six years after we had had the book party in the bar on the beach.

I was not overly happy to have to get up so early on a Friday to catch my train but it was a nice day and would be a good diversion from everything else. For once I spoke using a MS-PowerPoint presentation at the event after a request from the organisers. Ready to stand up for who I had become I disclosed about my illness during my presentation; how could I not? It seemed to work as I was subsequently told by the organisers that almost everyone had regarded it as the highlight of the day. One person I would meet again later at a conference described it as inspirational. My mood was grand but not overly grand as I got the train back to Hertfordshire for another weekend in another busy term. I had eleven days left until the final triumph regardless of who came along.

History will not recall much about the next ten days. I know from my diary that I was still very busy right up to the end of term. I know too that my mood was elevated to heights I never thought I would reach during the darkness of my despair. For me though I recall very little of that short period of my life; a few days in a journey that had taken nearly twenty one years since it began.

The morning of Tuesday 12th April 2011 dawned bright but cold in my little corner of Hertfordshire. I knew it would be a long day. I dressed in my linen suit, a blue shirt, and a fine yellow tie. I drove to work contemplating what would be. In my office, I had a large box of books to sell on that day. The incomparable Karen who kept our lives together at work as our administrator helped right up to the end. Late in the morning I went to pick up Miriam and Nigel from the train station. Together we went to the allotted room to set it up for the launch. My friends from the Trust who worked so hard on recovery arrived with a huge Time to Change banner. That ambitious programme to tackle the stigma that had riddled my life had been in operation for nearly four years.

As the minutes ticked by and the food arrived, my mind was still concerned that no one would come. I was after all not very important and in the grander scheme of the literary world a nobody. But it would be my day one way or another.

It was only as the doors kept opening and we crept towards the start that I began to believe. They came and they came in their droves. From across Hertfordshire, from London, and Cambridge, friends and colleagues they all seemed to come. Just before I was due to speak I surveyed the throng that was now seventy strong. I had never believed so many would come.

My manager spoke briefly having raced through the book over the weekend. She struck the right note when she mentioned that we all needed to get better at listening. Then it was my turn.

To a hushed room I attempted to go through what was planned in my mind. But I was so stunned by the sheer number who had come out to support me that those words failed me. I was almost struck dumb by it all. But words did come even if those words were not the ones I expected. I regretted that I forgot to thank some people but made it into a passionate free flowing speech of utter conviction.

It had taken so long but finally my voice was heard; I had screamed for years in the wilderness of my madness and no one listened. Today there would be no arrogant dismissal by those in power. In that room at that time I was the power. The trumpet shall sound. And by God it sounded that day.

As I finished the room erupted in applause. It was a room aflame with emotion. I'm told that my speech was utterly emotionally moving. People would recall that day for many months to come.

For me I was flying but exhausted. For the next hour I worked my way round that room seeing so many people. I slipped out late for a cigarette to calm me down. But I was spent.

As people left to go back to their lives we packed up and headed for a local pub. Some who had seen me in my mad days came along, Miriam, Nigel, Beka, Mike, and Katherine from my PGCE days. One of my close allies came along too; he knew as much as I did about living with madness and getting better.

I only had one drink as I had to drive afterwards. I could barely speak in there such was the level of exhaustion.

Miriam and Nigel came back to my flat afterwards. We spent the evening in the Fu Hao, my second home in Hertfordshire. I had gone there on the day I arrived and now found myself in there once again as my journey ended.

What a journey it had been. It began on a warm and sunny Saturday morning at Selwyn College Cambridge in June 1990, the day I got Rachel's letter. It now ended in another place and another time. I had my voice back and it was a voice that people wanted to hear. The book had started out as a piece of vengeance against those who had wronged me. But now that it was done it was more than that. For it marked the day that my recovery was achieved. No one believed that I would recover back in the old days. I had found my way out of the world of madness and was now firmly back in that other world, the one that too many take for granted. I certainly would never do that again. As I reflect I hope that in some small way my painful journey has helped others. Only they can decide that but I know that something good has now come out of the wreckage of my life.

For years I wanted to die. Now I am glad to be alive. And maybe, just maybe it was all worth it.

Mark Edgar

Epilogue
Charon's Ferry

Nineteen days after we launched A Pillar of Impotence US Special Forces found and killed Osama Bin Laden. He was not found in a cave somewhere in the badlands of the Northwest frontier as expected but rather in compound in an affluent Pakistani town alarmingly close to the Pakistani Military Academy.

By the coming of the following winter Gaddafi too was dead, killed by his own people following the Arab Spring. It had taken many years but Gaddafi, Bin Laden, and Saddam, the great scourges of the West were dead. But did the war end there? Sadly not.

Only history will record whether it was World War III. Even the start is disputed depending on the angle one comes from. It has been an extraordinarily dirty war, a war of bombs and beheadings on the one hand and rendition and waterboarding on the other. I have long since ceased to know what it is all about.

What I do know though is that the greatest number of victims has been innocent civilians and the majority of those have been Muslims. Neighbours have turned on neighbours across Asia, the Middle East, and Africa. It is as much sectarian as it is political.

Western powers are out of Iraq but the killings still go on. The plan is for NATO to withdraw from Afghanistan by 2014. But I have no doubt the war will continue after that.

Al Qaeda is no longer based in Afghanistan but instead has moved to Pakistan, Yemen, Somalia, Iraq, and North Africa. East Africa is bearing its brunt and so it seems is West Africa. No one knows a solution.

I have no doubt that there will be more young people trying to bomb my country as they did in 2005. There were no more successful major terrorist attacks in the West between the 7/7 bombing and the end of my journey in the spring of 2011.

Yet the world is not just defined by what happens on a battlefield close to home or far away. The year in which my journey came to an end the world had more than its usual share of natural disasters. It also stands still mired in economic turmoil following the banking crisis of 2008. When it returns to prosperity is anyone's guess. Whatever is being tried now does not seem to be working and we stand as we did in the 1930s deep in crisis.

Closer to home the political world has changed. New Labour is no longer and the age of coalitions seems set for a while. I can have a very small influence on that stage through my right to vote. Not all across the world have that right. Maybe that is a Western invention that does not work elsewhere, I do not know. What I do know though is that trying to impose that model elsewhere has led to endless crises. My influence on that is negligible; I am but a small person amongst billions.

And what of me and my small world? Twenty one years on from when I got ill I have come a long way. For too long I let my illness define who I was. That was a big mistake. Time may not heal but it does change us. I am no longer the little boy with wild crazy hair, smiling eyes, and the voice that everyone wanted to hear. Neither am I that angry, damaged youth with wild crazy hair, and sometimes smiling eyes who still had a voice. Nor am I the destroyed young man with wild crazy hair, sad and forlorn eyes which never connected with those of others, and a voice that had been silenced by circumstance and judgement. I am now middle aged. I still have wild crazy hair although there is less of it now, it is shorter, and it is greying. I smile again now which I didn't do for a long time. Once again though I have a voice, a voice that many seek the wisdom of through my writings, my speaking, and my mental health practice. That is perhaps the greatest step forward after the darkness of my madness.

I have gone back to being a son, a brother, a friend, a colleague, and an acquaintance. I am not just judged by my madness although it does feature prominently in my life. That was not perhaps what I would have chosen but more what life has brought me. Once upon a time I wanted to be a teacher and now I am a mental health practitioner. A strange change but one that I had no control over. Our lives take many paths most of which we don't control; some are good and some are bad. What I do know is that I'm infinitely better at working with the mentally ill than I was at teaching history to Year 9 on a Friday afternoon.

Yet I do still teach if only sparingly. For right or wrong I now influence the very people whose failures colluded to destroy my life when I was in my twenties. Nurses, social workers, psychiatrists, therapists, and others now hear my voice. And if I believe the feedback that can be life changing for them although I don't see myself as being that important. The word I keep hearing over and over again is inspirational. Do I really have the power to inspire? I guess that is for others to decide.

I am not the only one of my kind who has influence on the mental health world. Since the advent of the philosophy that is recovery, the powers that be now recognise that we the mentally ill do have something to offer. Increasingly Trusts are seeking these people out. There are always mental health nursing and social work students among my charges at the University. Perhaps those who have been wronged feel they can right the wrongs of an utterly flawed System.

When I stumbled into that world I thought I could change it. What better place to change the System than on the inside? I was of course wrong. But I can influence those that now man it through my story. It is always the people who make a System go well or ill. But the System tried to change me and get me to change sides.

Sadly the us and them still exists on many levels. I pride myself on making up the rules as I go along. I did not change sides; I merely looked both ways. I no longer care if professionals don't approve of my friendships and relationships, I am who I am. But the position I now find myself in allows me to do that. It is not a luxury afforded to all service users. We treat them in different ways depending on the context in which we meet them.

I have not been in touch with secondary services since 2008. But my standing in the mental health community in Hertfordshire is sufficient that I can just pick up the phone if I am in trouble. Maybe one day I will need to do that but not so far. What of the others? Well their fate is mixed. The world still fears and judges us despite the efforts of campaigners such as Time to Change.

My world has changed but is it for the better? I take great pleasure that the old asylums in the main no longer exist. Less helpful though is the decline of other facilities. The resources that were always limited are even more so now.

Teams too have changed and I greatly applaud the introduction of Early Intervention in Psychosis teams. How different might my life have been in the 1990s had they been in existence? It is hard to tell as I was misdiagnosed so I would never have met their criteria. All around me those criteria are being tightened and fewer and fewer needy people can get through the door.

In this age of cuts the move towards short termism and the other sectors troubles me greatly. I have worked in both. They are different but are becoming closer. The reality is that it is funders who drive my world not people like me.

Few of the charities can any longer be called independent; it is central pots of money that influence their direction. If we allow the agenda to be defined by funding we will miss the reality of what we need to do to help people.

For all the systemic problems there is also a need for service users to make changes themselves. I languished on benefits for too long. Looking back now I could have worked far earlier than I did. This is also true of many of those I knew then and who have changed little. In part the System maintains them in their stuckness though.

Redefining my life to align it to the expectation of the wider world was a long and costly journey. For ten years I had less money than when I was on those benefits. Most service users will say they are in poverty and they can't afford to change. In truth when I was an STR worker almost all of my clients, if they were on the right benefits, had at least 25% more money in their pockets than I did. A full time job did not make me richer but it made me more careful with what little I had.

The option to opt out of the wider society of work is no longer there. Whether it is right or wrong the economic crisis has forced the government to make changes that have been long overdue. However, I fear the casualties along the way. Official suicide rates that had been on the decline saw a sharp change with the coming of the economic crisis. I fear that trend will continue.

Someone once told me that only one in a hundred people ever get off long term benefits. Whether that is the exact figure or not I don't know, I certainly couldn't source that statement. Yet whatever the figure is, it is widely acknowledged that people are more likely to die or retire than to achieve what I did. Others too made it. But I could only do that whilst I was in recovery. I stress that it is in recovery rather than being recovered. I will always have a mood disorder and will almost certainly be on Risperidone for the rest of my life. I know there is lots of evidence that long term use of atypical antipsychotics can dramatically shorten life. But so be it, I have a life now and it is far greater than it was in the darkness of my despair. I am one of the lucky ones; few others have made that journey as successfully as I have amongst my friends and peers.

The ancient Greeks believed the underworld of Hades existed beyond the river Styx. The souls of the dead were ferried across the Styx by Charon. As payment for Charon the dead were buried with a coin in their mouths. It was a one way journey. There was one man who made it back across the Styx. He was Orpheus and he like me was a musician.

When I first entered the mental health System in the hot summer of 1991 that too was a one way journey into the underworld. People simply did not get better. They just lumbered around in the living death of mental illness kept separate by the flaws of that System. Somehow I was guided back over the Styx by a quiet softly spoken Scottish Doctor who finally got it right in the autumn of 2001. A week later 9/11 happened and the wider world changed.

I am no longer who I was. Now I traverse the treacherous waters of the Styx. I go into that underworld many times a day and try very hard to bring people back from that nether world. Isn't that what practitioners should be doing? Isn't that also the essence of recovery? Sometimes, just sometimes I can bring people back to the land of reality. I have finally found my greatest skill, one that is more important than all else I have achieved. I ride on Charon's Ferry, and now I am at the tiller.

Postscript

On Thursday 3rd November 2011 A Pillar of Impotence was launched in Kent at an art exhibition organised and featuring work by my friend Beka Smith. The event was on the eve of the annual Folkestone Book Festival. Amongst the vast throng of people who came were my mum and dad as well as my sister Miriam and my brother-in-law Nigel. I had always feared my mum and dad reading it and was concerned it would forever destroy my already challenging relationship with them. It is true that they were stunned by the brutality and pain in the book. But I had to write it as it was and none of us come out all the time as we would have hoped. Yet the book provoked a change that I did not foresee. It allowed me to forge a new and infinitely better relationship with my parents. They after all had their son back.

My greatest memory of that memorable night was the look on my mum's face. She knew now that I was in recovery and her many prayers had been answered.

I would only see my mum twice more, on the occasion of her 80th birthday in January 2012 and when I once again retreated to Kent after another relapse struck me in early March. She died on Wednesday 28th March 2012 after being taken ill in the sea the day before. The sea that she both loved and feared finally took her.

She was cremated on a filthy day of wind and rain on Wednesday 18th April. She would not have swum on that day. Scores of people came along. It was a sad day but I had achieved something I feared I would never do. I had finally made peace with her.

Mark Edgar

Printed by BoD™in Norderstedt, Germany